T0320080

The Economics of Ethics and the Ethics of
Economics

The Economics of Ethics and the Ethics of Economics

Values, Markets and the State

Edited by

Geoffrey Brennan

Professor of Economics, Research School of Social Sciences, The Australian National University, Canberra, Australia, Professor of Philosophy, UNC-Chapel Hill, USA, Professor of Political Science, Duke University, USA

Giuseppe Eusepi

Professor of Public Finance, Faculty of Economics, Sapienza University of Rome, Rome, Italy

Edward Elgar
Cheltenham, UK • Northampton, MA, USA

Published by
Edward Elgar Publishing Limited
The Lypiatts
15 Lansdown Road
Cheltenham
Glos GL50 2JA
UK

Edward Elgar Publishing, Inc.
William Pratt House
9 Dewey Court
Northampton
Massachusetts 01060
USA

A catalogue record for this book is available from the British Library

Library of Congress Control Number: 2009933412

Mixed Sources
Product group from well-managed forests and other controlled sources
www.fsc.org Cert no. SA-COC-1565
© 1996 Forest Stewardship Council

ISBN 978 1 84844 654 0

Typeset by Manton Typesetters, Louth, Lincolnshire, UK
Printed and bound by MPG Books Group, UK

Contents

Figures and tables

FIGURES

TABLES

Contributors

Marcello Basili, University of Siena, Siena, Italy.

Geoffrey Brennan, The Australian National University, Canberra, Australia and Duke University/UNC-Chapel Hill, USA.

James M. Buchanan, George Mason University, Fairfax, VA, USA.

Reiner Eichenberger, University of Fribourg, Fribourg, Switzerland.

Giuseppe Eusepi, Sapienza University of Rome, Rome, Italy.

Lars P. Feld, University of Heidelberg, Heidelberg, Germany.

Maurizio Franzini, Sapienza University of Rome, Rome, Italy.

Bruno S. Frey, University of Zurich, Zurich, Switzerland.

Michael Funk, University of Fribourg, Fribourg, Switzerland.

Luisa Giuriato, Sapienza University of Rome, Rome, Italy.

Stefano Gorini, University of Tor Vergata, Rome, Italy.

Alan Hamlin, University of Manchester, Manchester, UK.

Philip Jones, University of Bath, Bath, UK.

Hartmut Kliemt, Frankfurt School of Finance and Management, Frankfurt, Germany.

Susanne Neckermann, University of Zurich, Zurich, Switzerland.

Acknowledgements

This book owes its genesis to the conference 'Objective Values, No Values and Subjective Values: The Ethical Bases of Market and State', held in December 2006 at the Faculty of Economics of Sapienza University of Rome, Italy, organized by the European Center for the Study of Public Choice (ECSPC) as a key part of the centennial celebrations of the Faculty of Economics.

The conference served as the impetus for part of this volume. In fact, the selection of chapters has been enriched with five chapters by scholars who did not attend the conference, but shared an interest in the topic. To our friends and colleagues who have helped make this a more comprehensive book, we are deeply grateful.

The conference and this book would not have been possible without the financial support that the ECSPC received from Open House Investment Service, BancApulia, the Faculty of Economics and the Department of Public Economics of Sapienza University of Rome.

We have been very fortunate having the services of Maria Delle Grotti, permanent secretary to the ECSPC, who has managed to do the donkey work during the publication of this book. We are deeply grateful to her.

These acknowledgements would not be complete without recording our grateful thanks to the Edward Elgar editorial staff. Specifically we would like to mention Elizabeth Clack, Matthew Pitman and Laura Seward.

Geoffrey Brennan
Research School of Social Sciences, Australian National University and
Duke University/UNC-Chapel Hill, USA

Giuseppe Eusepi
Faculty of Economics, Sapienza University of Rome, Rome, Italy

Introduction: ethics vs economics – in praise of the 'disciplined' life?

Geoffrey Brennan and Giuseppe Eusepi

ON THE DIVISION OF INTELLECTUAL LABOUR

When Adam Smith first conceived the intellectual enterprise of which *The Wealth of Nations* is perhaps the most famous part, he was Professor of Moral Philosophy at the University of Glasgow. In this sense, taking *The Wealth of Nations* as the point of departure for the study of economics as a separate academic discipline, economics could reasonably be said to have been born 'out of ethics'.

If so, however, we economists have moved some distance from the family home over the intervening 230 years. The traffic between economics and ethics at the academic level these days is, if not negligible, rather thin and cordially regarded on both sides of the divide as an eccentric occupation, even when practised by respected professionals.

Imagine for example that you are a young economist seeking employment at one of the better US universities. In the preliminary interview at the Annual Meetings (a standard part of the job market process), you are likely to be asked about your 'fields'. And suppose, having listed your relevant mainstream areas of interest – say, public economics, and applied microeconomics with perhaps a subsidiary competence in labour (economics) – you confess to a serious interest in moral philosophy. Suppose that, in an even more reckless burst of candour, you say that would like to do some of your work at the intersection between moral philosophy and economics. Predict, on this basis, your chances of being asked to visit the hiring institution and 'give a talk' – the next step in the hiring process. More than likely, you will be met with a wan smile and thanked, and your file quietly consigned to the waste-paper bin as you leave the hotel room. If you have such a philosophic interest, better to keep it entirely to yourself.

The analogous picture from the philosophy side is probably not quite as inhospitable. Conceivably, if you can show an economist's facility with some of the higher reaches of mathematical decision theory, or a familiarity with game theory and its applications in political philosophy, the interview process will not immediately be terminated. Perhaps you will even be eyed favourably as a possibility for the Business Ethics course – something that no self-respecting philosopher really wants to teach. But at the end of the day, you are likely to be overlooked in favour of someone whose interests fall squarely within the traditional fields. Specifically, if 'philosophy and economics' is itself your main game, you had better not be too optimistic about your job prospects. If you want to maximize your professional chances (and who does not) then you would be better advised to stick to the high-prestige, core areas – philosophy of mind, philosophy of language, metaphysics, epistemology and the like – and leave the interdisciplinary work to others.

Actually, there are sound reasons why 'interdisciplinary' work is regarded suspiciously – reasons we shall explore below. Even if philosophers do not utter the term with quite the same splendid contempt as the economists use, the suspicion is present – and especially so at the assistant professor level, where the scholar is still to develop his or her professional persona. Better to turn to interdisciplinary interests when you are tenured and your credentials as a serious philosopher are better established.

Or at least these are our impressions based on our observations and conversations with our disciplinary peers. The record needs to be moderated here by reference to our own personal experiences. In fact, both of us have enjoyed a great deal of interdisciplinary hospitality. Brennan, coming as an economist to philosophical subjects in mid-career, has always been received extremely cordially by the philosophers – almost without exception. And Eusepi, having been imprudent enough to start his intellectual career with a PhD in Philosophy, has nevertheless been able to make his way in the Italian system as an economics professor without serious obstacles. Furthermore, it needs to be conceded that, at the level of university administrators and outside funding bodies, interdisciplinary endeavours of all kinds seem to exercise a curious attraction – somewhat, it must be said, to the alarm of many of the academic professionals in discipline-based departments.

All that conceded, it remains true that interdisciplinary endeavour is regarded with some suspicion by more mainstream members of the participant disciplines. But is such suspicion mere disciplinary prejudice? More particularly, is that suspicion well grounded intellectually, or does it reflect, rather, intellectually incidental features of the way in which academic life is structured?

It is tempting to think that disciplines are a natural expression of the division of labour in the intellectual enterprise. In exemplifying the division of labour in the first chapter of *The Wealth of Nations*, Adam Smith explicitly refers to the academic case. And Smith's own arguments about the role of market size would lead to the prediction that the division of labour in intellectual matters would have become much more finely grained in the two centuries or so since Adam Smith wrote. And so it is tempting to identify the gradual separation of ethics from economics as academic disciplines – the separation, that is, of moral philosophy from economics – as just a necessary feature of an increasing division of intellectual labour.

We think there is more at stake. Disciplines are institutional artefacts. They not only form the basis on which communities of common intellectual interest emerge; they are, as well, the monitors of quality and the providers of credentials. They are reproduced in the departmental structure of universities; and they determine who gets a job and who is granted tenure. Professional societies are constructed around them, and those professional societies run the journals on the basis of which professional standing is calculated.

Consider the following institutional fact. You are applying for a job in the economics department at a good university. You happen to have considerable expertise in some neighbouring discipline – let it be philosophy. And you would be quite useful to the Philosophy Department in teaching a variety of their courses. But of course that fact is relevant to the head of the Economics Department only if there is someone in the Philosophy Department who can teach in the Economics Department and for whose time yours can be traded. But the arranging of such trades is difficult, even if your opposite number exists. And there is an issue with divided loyalties as to whether you will be answerable to the Economics head or the Philosophy head or both or neither. Given the structure of the university, it would not be surprising if either of these heads considered any such arrangement all too complicated.

Being a person with broad interests and competence to teach across a wide range of fields is an asset if and only if those interests and competencies fall within departmental boundaries. Any interests and competencies that lie outside those boundaries will be severely discounted, if indeed they count at all. And this fact is common knowledge across the system. So it establishes a set of incentives: breadth within disciplinary boundaries, great; breadth across, hopeless.

The point is not just an administrative one. Disciplines are characterized not just by subject-matter but also by method. It is, for example, perfectly respectable these days for someone in an Economics department to work on the analysis of political processes, provided the analysis in question is 'economic' in character. Economics is, after all, at least as much defined by its 'way of thinking' as by its subject-matter. Political science, by contrast, is a field defined almost entirely by subject-matter. So it is not unusual to discover a professor in a Political Science department with a PhD in Economics. But it is almost inconceivable that a person with a PhD in Political Science would get a job in a self-respecting Economics department. So as far as the economists are concerned, someone who has interests in another discipline (as distinct from other subject-matter perhaps) is cordially regarded with suspicion. Does this person really think like an economist if he or she is seriously interested in philosophy? Can this individual be 'one of us' if he or she spends much of his or her time talking to political scientists? Or, worse, to sociologists?

Perhaps these questions are reasonable. One certainly needs to be able to 'talk a different language' to be able to engage in cross-disciplinary conversation. But it is not entirely obvious that being intellectually multilingual corrupts one's capacities to speak one's own disciplinary language (whatever it happens to be). Our guess is that the underlying anxiety about interdisciplinarity derives from the fact that the home discipline no longer exercises a monopoly in the provision of professional esteem. If you as a philosopher look to earn esteem from the economists, you will be less under the thrall of those forces that support compliance with professional norms and to that extent are less reliable.

But there is an entirely proper role as well as a dubious one that disciplines play here. Suppose you are an economist attempting, as one does more or less automatically, to assess how good your interdisciplinary colleague, X, is. You may have reservations about X's competence in economics, but have a perception that the philosophers think well of him or her. That perception though is not one that you are well placed to verify. You do not know many philosophers and you do not know enough to know whose opinion within philosophy is really worth having. The situation from the philosophy side may be perfectly reversed. The philosophers do not think much of X as a philosopher, but understand that X is a gifted economist.

The situation might be worse: X may be gifted at presenting economics to philosophers and philosophy to economists, but not have serious gifts as a practitioner in either field. So X develops a reputation as an economist among the philosophers and as a philosopher among the economists. X is like a translator whose translations of English verse into German are thought by the Germans to be original.

And these possibilities are known – and have their own implications for academic incentives. If I am mediocre as an economist, I might well enhance my reputation by drifting over the border into philosophy. The 'jack of all trades and master of none' prospect looms. And this is indeed the reputation that interdisciplinary academics tend to suffer. Not without some justification. We all can recognize that there is a kind of interdisciplinary activity that is the lowest common denominator across the participating disciplines. There must be some presumption that interdisciplinary activity does not attract the best minds: if they were really good they would be making their mark within a disciplinary home.

It is important to recognize the force of these arguments. As the etymology suggests, disciplines operate to discipline performance. In a complex division of intellectual labour, every 'user' of the 'knowledge' generated needs some assurance that the knowledge is indeed valid and/or the insights genuine. Public evaluation by recognized experts is the only means we have to make this validation. Short of becoming expert ourselves (an expedient which if generalized would simply negate the division of intellectual labour), we have to rely on the authority of those recognized by the profession as competent to judge. That this procedure can lead to a kind of self-referential circularity is a possibility almost too obvious to mention. But there clearly are rewards on offer to those who can persuasively demonstrate that certain propositions widely held in the profession are false, and the presence of that self-checking process gives us some confidence that disciplinary judgements are tolerably accurate.

But for this very reason, disciplines exercise a strong centripetal pull. If the discipline is where practitioners get their credentials, then there are strong incentives to be obedient to disciplinary dictates. The forces for convergence are considerable, and as we have already noted, these forces operate not just in relation to having one's work taken seriously (something most of us value for its own sake) but also in the allocation of jobs. One piece of evidence as to how strong these centripetal forces are lies in the observed similarity of departmental and disciplinary structures across different universities – and, for that matter, the observed similarity of course structures and specific course content. It is, when considered in abstraction, a rather peculiar fact that pretty much all of the universities in the English-speaking world have a very similar structure of faculties and departments. It is perhaps an even more striking fact that economics course programmes, both what is required for an undergraduate major or the structure of graduate programmes, and the precise content of the courses at the various levels, are also very similar. With only a handful of exceptions, what passes for a course in Economic Principles or Intermediate Microeconomics is essentially the same across the vast array of universities worldwide. This is, one might suppose, just what it means to be a single discipline.

All the same, one might have thought that some departments would experiment with something rather different, would search out a niche in terms of the material taught or the style of its teaching. But rarely so: most departments are virtual clones of each other. Economics is a conspicuous case in these respects. There is nothing like the same homogeneity across Political Science departments – and indeed, political science exhibits little in the way of consensus as to what an undergraduate must know, or what the 'basic principles' of political science are, or indeed whether any such exist.

Philosophy seems to lie somewhere between economics and political science in this respect. There would, for example, be pretty wide consensus within Anglo-American philosophy as to the 'pecking order' in terms of academic quality of different university departments. And there would be wide consensus, at least within the analytic tradition, as to what the core of the discipline consists in. Course structures would be broadly similar. But with philosophy there is a major rift along the so-called analytic–Continental divide. This divide involves differing views as to the importance of philosophers like Heidegger, Foucault, Derrida and so on, and as to the centrality of certain kinds of 'analytic' methods. Although the analytic tradition is dominant in the Anglo-American scene, there are some small number of departments who boast a Continental predominance and whose views of the appropriate rankings of departments reflect that orientation.

This bird's-eye picture of the state of the three disciplines with which we are most familiar invites several conclusions:

- Disciplines are an important quality-control mechanism in the (necessary) division of labour in intellectual enquiry.
- In that sense, disciplines are a feature of that division of labour, but they are not merely a manifestation of it.
- Disciplines exercise very strong centripetal forces, creating incentives for certain kinds of conformity around the methods and topics regarded within the discipline as mainstream and/or high prestige.
- Interdisciplinary work is therefore subject to certain systematic hazards – namely, the lack of clear institutional mechanisms for monitoring and quality control, and the associated attraction of that lack to those scholars who have most to fear from quality review. Simply put, much interdisciplinary work is of a predictably 'mediocre' kind. And having that reputation, interdisciplinary work may fail to attract the best minds. At the same time, it is notable how many of the Nobel Prize winners in Economics have had significant interdisciplinary inclinations: Arrow (philosophy[1] and economics), Becker (law, sociology and economics), Buchanan (politics and economics), Harsanyi (philosophy and economics), Sen (philosophy and economics). Perhaps precisely because the areas that lie along (and across) the borders of the disciplines attend to be avoided by most scholars, there are interesting 'pickings' there. That at least is our belief. The centripetal forces within disciplines draw research away from the 'borders'. It is in this way that disciplines, while a crucial piece of the landscape of enquiry, can distort the intellectual agenda.

CROSSING THE DISCIPLINARY BORDER

In the particular instance of border crossing that this book represents, the main concern is with the relation between ethics and economics. There are three kinds of issues that emerge.

First, there is a strong tradition within economics of maintaining a rigid separation between positive and normative aspects of analysis. That separation – as expressed perhaps most notably in the work of Lionel Robbins (1932) – connects with a distinction between motivation and justification at the level of the individual agent. In particular, economists have been inclined to model agents as entirely self-interested, leaving justificatory matters to be imposed 'outside the model' by some idealized ethical observer. The brute fact that no such ethical observer exists – or better put, that all agents act simultaneously as participants and observers in the social processes of which they are part – means that any normative element must, as a matter of logic, be introduced via the views and judgements of the economic actors themselves. In other words, a serious confrontation between ethics and economics invites economists to adopt a broader set of motivational assumptions within their models. In the first instance, agents have to be modelled as evaluative individuals and their values have to be understood in terms that cannot be reduced to mere 'preferences' (in obedience to a distinction that those agents themselves make). But once economic agents are modelled as 'somewhat moral', then other extensions to the standard psychology are invited. So, for example, agents might be modelled as concerned with esteem (as in the Frey and Neckermann chapter in this volume, Chapter 5) or self-esteem (Basili and Franzini, Chapter 11) or emotional bonding, even between such implausible partners as tax collection agencies and the taxpayer (Feld, Chapter 9) or expressive concerns (Jones, Chapter 6) as well as with moral requirements more directly (Brennan and Hamlin, Chapter 7).

Of course, attentiveness to a richer motivational structure also reminds us of the role that moral motivations can play in securing acceptable outcomes even within market processes. An example may be found in the current (2009) global financial crisis. It is notorious that corruption has preceded those events; and the endless scandals that have been constantly on the rise on both sides of the Atlantic are testimony to an increased distance between economic and ethical behaviour. Thus much of the energy of an ever-increasing number of scholars has gone into understanding the phenomenon of widespread illegal conduct, especially in public economy, and in procurement foremost of all.

Of course, we do not mean to imply by this observation that exclusive attention should be devoted to moral exhortation. We think that the institutions that govern and coordinate behaviour should remain a primary focus in normative reasoning. But the structure of motivations (whether people are morally responsible or not) is of course not irrelevant, and whether institutions promote or undermine moral responsibility is one aspect of how institutions ought to be evaluated.

Second, and relatedly, there is a range of questions that arise when moral pluralism is taken seriously. Much moral philosophy is concerned with identifying the true moral theory – but when moral beliefs are held by individual agents, there is an issue of how the views held by those agents might appropriately be aggregated and what the status of any emergent moral quasi-consensus might be. This is the issue that is addressed in the Brennan and Eusepi chapter (Chapter 2) and to some extent in the Brennan and Hamlin chapter (Chapter 7) as well – and in quite a different way in the Gorini chapter (Chapter 3).

Third, there are chapters that maintain the traditional 'positive–normative' divide – but point up distinctive features of the world that bear on normative assessments (such as increasing returns as in the Buchanan chapter, Chapter 1) or distinctive domains in which normative criteria can be applied (say, to a wider range of political institutions as in the Eichenberger and Funk chapter, Chapter 8) or taxation design (Giuriato, Chapter 10).

All of these chapters exemplify the fusing of ethics with economics in one way or the other, and all exhibit what we see as the strengths of interdisciplinary work: the preparedness to think 'outside the box' and to allow one's disciplinary tools to be resources rather than slave-drivers.

Interestingly enough, it was just when economic science began to outgrow the epistemological classification made by Lionel Robbins (1932) that economics needed to fashion a new approach for understanding its relationship with other disciplines, namely politics and ethics. This is well brought out in the works of neo-Ricardian economists of whom Piero Sraffa was the intellectual godfather (see Sraffa, 1960). When Sraffa tried to set criteria for the distribution of the surplus, he found that he had to distance himself from neoclassical economics and its objectivity and think in terms of political or, perhaps, ethical choices.[2] Sraffa held that capital cannot be objectively measured, nor can the contribution of capital to production, thus inducing him to distinguish between production theory and distribution theory, which is hardly ever necessary in neoclassical analysis. When one shifts from a theoretical setting to the real-world setting, discipline independence becomes short-winded. This explains why an ever-growing attention has been given to cross-border work than the disciplines themselves entirely approve of. The exclusive focus on intra-disciplinary discourse produces some misallocation of intellectual effort.

In sum, when it comes to be applied to real-world phenomena, disciplinary independence, treated as a value, is a much less safe or trustworthy ground to work with than the theory of the division of labour would have us to believe. When transplanted into the ethical domain, in fact, the division of labour seems to lead towards the division of responsibility – something analogous to risk-sharing. In its extreme form, the division of responsibility may simply amount to lack of responsibility.

BOOK OVERVIEW

Prices and values are the focus of this volume. The first part, 'Pathways through prices and values' opens with a chapter by James M. Buchanan, concerned with 'Ethics and the extent of the market'. Buchanan takes as his point of departure the notion of generalized increasing returns that plays such a central role in Adam Smith's account of the operation of the market. Unlike Smith, Buchanan draws a sharp distinction between the notion of increasing returns to scale within a specific firm (a pin factory, for example), and the generalized increasing returns that operate across the entire market system. He is concerned to underline the ethical value that is embodied in a market governed by constitutional rules.

In Chapter 2, 'Value and values, preferences and price: an economic perspective on ethical questions', Brennan and Eusepi attempt to clarify the relation between economic and ethical accounts of social phenomena by appeal to a distinction between 'economic value' and 'ethical values'. Beginning with Ricardo's concerns about the concept of value, and specifically Ricardo's ambition to secure the 'objectification' of value, the authors highlight the ambiguities inherent in the Ricardian treatment of the value–price nexus. The authors emphasize the double duty that the term 'value' does in the analysis of price determination: first, as an element in the agent's motivational structure (the agent's 'values' as distinct from the agent's 'preferences'); and second, as the outcome of social processes, in which the 'value' of different goods and services emerges from the process itself.

In Chapter 3, Stefano Gorini presents 'An economist's *plaidoyer* for a secular ethics: the moral foundation and social role of critical rationalism'. He inquires into the theoretical, ethical and social implications of the adoption of critical rationalism as a method to understand the world. His reasoning revolves around four connected claims. The first claim equates the distinction between morality and economics with the distinction between values and interests. The second claim relates the theoretical foundations of critical rationalism – a secular worldview – to the ethical foundations of that method. The third claim highlights the crucial civic role of the associated secular ethics, as compared with the non-secular moral positions of religion and ideology, and underlines the secular ethic of well-being, social success and power. This kind of analysis gives rise to a distinctive individual sentiment of social solidarity and a liberal social order free of any form of fundamentalism. The fourth claim distinguishes morals from social justice.

In Chapter 4, 'Conceptual confusions, ethics and economics', Hartmut Kliemt argues that economists who intend to make non-relativistic claims for their value judgements may legitimately propose a concept of welfare economics that allows them to do so. For Kliemt any claim that this may happen within the constraints that Lionel Robbins imposed on the normative economic argument is illegitimate. The author offers a convincing argument that a conceptual confusion arises in the treatment and justification of value judgements by using the Robbins framework.

The second part, 'Money and medals: the role of motivations in collective choices', opens with a chapter entitled 'Awards: a view from economics' by Bruno S. Frey and Susanne Neckermann. The authors develop an argument about the dynamics of awards in terms of orders, decorations, prizes and titles. They argue that this kind of non-material extrinsic incentive is not much studied in social sciences. In their view, the demand for awards has to be interpreted as an individual's desire for distinction, and the supply of awards as a mechanism for enhancing motivation. They concentrate on the differences between awards and monetary compensations, and offer a comparative analysis of the usage of awards around the world.

In Chapter 6, 'Assessing collective decision-making processes: the relevance of motivation', Philip Jones argues that while collective decision-making processes appear to 'fail' if policies differ from policies prescribed for instrumentally motivated citizens, this assessment is sensitive to analysis of motivation. Revisiting Downs (1957), Jones shows that instrumental citizens have no incentive to vote when the probability that a single vote will change an electoral outcome is minuscule. If citizens participate, they do so in order to derive intrinsic value from expressing identity. He notes, however, that if intrinsic value depends on how individuals act, 'choice' at the ballot box is likely to differ from 'choice' revealed instrumentally. Policies that 'interfere' with consumer preferences may simply reflect deference to voters' choices rather than dismissal of consumers' preferences. Jones questions how collective decision-making processes are to be assessed in the face of the fact that individuals derive intrinsic value from expressive voting.

In Chapter 7, 'Positive constraints on normative political theory', Geoffrey Brennan and Alan Hamlin consider the relationship between positive and normative political theory, emphasizing both the role of normative ideas in motivating political behaviour and, particularly, the constraints on normative theory imposed by positive theory. Taking as their point of departure Tom Christiano's recent claim that the rational choice approach to normative political theory is self-defeating, Brennan and Hamlin outline a revisionist rational choice approach, which they claim serves to build a bridge between positive and normative political theories and to broaden the scope of positive constraints on normative theory.

The third part, 'Political market processes and liberal ethics: tax fairness vs tax morale', is made up of four chapters. In Chapter 8, 'The deregulation of the political process: towards an international market for good politics', Reiner Eichenberger and Michael Funk focus on certain restrictions that routinely apply to the political process. They argue that three such restrictions in particular weaken politicians' incentives to produce outcomes in accord with citizens' preferences. First, in most countries, only nationals and residents are allowed to run for political office. Second, firms are excluded from running for office. Third, the compensation of politicians is fixed by law, and often the salary is lower than that received for a comparable job in the private sector. The authors suggest that these regulations should be abolished and that an open market for politicians should be conceived. The authors' recommendations are based on the suggestion that increasing prices for political services can crowd out bureaucratic rents and resources from special interests.

In Chapter 9, 'Do we really know much about tax non-compliance?' Lars P. Feld directs attention to non-compliance behaviour – especially tax evasion, black market activities and the shadow economy. Economists are inclined to think that these activities can be explained in terms of low punishments or low probability of detection. However, empirical evidence indicates that social norms, like tax morale, play an important role in compliance behaviour. Feld provides recent evidence on the shadow economy and tax morale in Germany showing that deterrence, though not totally unimportant, has a less robust and less quantitatively important impact than social norms do. He explains that these social norms, based on a psychological tax contract between taxpayers and tax authorities, go well beyond pure exchanges and involve loyalties and ties between the contract partners. Tax morale is therefore a function of: (1) a fiscal exchange wherein taxpayers get public services for the tax prices they pay; (2) political procedures that lead to this exchange; and (3) personal relationships between taxpayers and tax administrators.

In Chapter 10, 'Searching for fairness in taxation: lessons from the Italian school of public finance', Luisa Giuriato investigates the issue of justice in taxation. Revisiting the mid-century scholars Vanoni and Berliri, she gives an account of the debate on just taxation in Italy during the period of constitution-making (1945–48) leading up to the 1951 tax reform. The essence of these two scholars' work can be found in their adherence to the principle of interest. Vanoni used it to lay down his principles of ethical taxation and Berliri to solve the problem of sharing the benefits of indivisible public expenditure among taxpayers. Berliri and Vanoni's theories are confronted with some of the controversial issues in the debate on just taxation. Their contributions are essentially normative and are of little help in dealing with operational questions. However, those contributions deserve attention for their usefulness in rethinking the fiscal relationship between citizens and the state.

The third part ends with Chapter 11 by Marcello Basili and Maurizio Franzini, entitled 'Cooperation, reciprocity and self-esteem: a theoretical approach'. The authors suggest that cooperation often occurs, even though it is not predicted by economic theory, owing to what is widely recognized as too narrow a conception of self-interest. They introduce and evaluate the reciprocity hypothesis and present a model of interaction between utility maximization and moral values based upon the notion of self-esteem. Moving from a principal–agent setting they test how the notion of reciprocity relates to self-esteem. They also relate self-esteem to fairness and analyse self-esteem in a setting where there is moral hazard and adverse selection, in order to estimate the influence of self-esteem on securing the best contract.

NOTES

1. If one is prepared to treat social choice theory as moral philosophy, as we would resolutely insist one should.
2. There is not the slightest question that distributive problems cannot emerge if the system does not produce surplus (Sraffa, 1960, Chapter 1).

REFERENCES

Robbins, Lionel (1932), *An Essay on the Nature and Significance of Economic Science*, London: Macmillan.
Sraffa, Piero (1960), *Production of Commodities by Means of Commodities: Prelude to a Critique of Economic Theory*, Cambridge: Cambridge University Press.

PART I

Pathways through prices and values

1. Ethics and the extent of the market

James M. Buchanan

As a young public finance economist, I was early on dismayed at the absence of any model of politics, either positively or normatively used, in familiar treatment of the basic fiscal variables: taxes, expenditure, budgets and public debts. In part influenced by De Viti de Marco (1936), whose treatise was the only book from a whole tradition of Italian scholarship that was translated into English, my own first paper (1949), was little more than a simple admonition to my fellow economists – a call for them to signify what model of politics, or collective action, they presupposed in their analyses.

This initial effort was followed by my negative reactions to the whole mid-century discussion centered around the Arrow–Black rediscovery of the majoritarian cycle – a discussion that seemed to reflect a generalized disappointment that majority voting could not generate a social welfare function. Although I voiced my concerns in two 1954 papers, it was only my more extended exposure to the Italian scholarship with a year spent largely in Rome that brought me to a full realization of how the Hegelian and the utilitarian mindsets had permeated English-language social science.

Without the Italian year, I could never have quite faced up to the analysis of politics without some vestige of the romantic delusion of the benevolent state. Both public choice, as a research umbrella, and constitutional economics, as a subsidiary program, can be classified to fall within a tradition of political realism that was and is standard fare in Italy, as familiar here as its opposite was at mid-century in America.

I make these comments specifically to underline that for about two decades, my interests and emphases have shifted toward the economics of ethics rather than the economics of politics.

> Products have to circulate. It's the law of the market, of life. Not selling should be banned. It's almost a crime. (Pérez-Reverte, 1996, p. 172)

INTRODUCTION

If I were constrained both by my title and by my parent discipline, I should concentrate immediate attention on Adam Smith's central argument to the effect that specialization (division of labor in his terminology) is the source of economic progress, and that, in turn, specialization is limited by the extent of the market. The theorem directly implies that there is an ethical component in behavior, whether private (individual) or public (collective) that results in a change in the effective size of the market exchange nexus. This relationship will indeed be a central organizing theme for this chapter. But I note here, and at the outset, that my own interest in this research program, which has dominated my work for almost two decades, arose not from any roots in economics, as such, but instead from my ethical intuition. Clearly, for me, the ethics trumped the economics, rather than the other way around. I was never directly motivated by any scientific desire to discover either the patterns of international trade or the ultimate sources of economic growth. I was, instead, simply puzzled by the apparent conflict between the implications of the economic theory that I had incorporated in my thinking, and the strongly felt ethical impulse that determined my own behavior patterns as well as my evaluative attitudes toward the behavior of others.

Specifically, and as I have noted in several autobiographical essays, I was locked into the dominating ethical intuition that several of the so-called Puritan or Victorian virtues, and especially that of work, must involve measurable economic value. But how can this value be integrated into the corpus of the received neoclassical construction? Something seemed amiss.

My first step was a call for assistance from younger colleagues, who are more competent than I am in modern tools. To no avail, because I could not persuade them to think outside the neoclassical box, even to the extent of recognizing why the puzzle mattered.

At this stage in my odyssey, I came to a begrudging realization that the whole neoclassical edifice that is based on a constant-returns postulate must be scrapped and replaced by that of increasing returns. More or less by default, it was necessary to re-examine a dissident line of inquiry that I had, personally, neglected. Returning to Adam Smith's theorem that relates specialization to the extent of the market, I soon identified one source of major confusion in Smith's own famous pin factory example. This example conceals the differences between the purely engineering or physical relationship between inputs and outputs, and the value relationship that must be the focus of any meaningful economic inquiry. From Smith forward, increasing returns came to be associated with economies of scale, from which the presumption was drawn that such economies, if they exist, describe the input–output relationship within the production processes faced by separate firms, as framed by the post-Marshallian separation between consumer-demanders and organized firms.

THE ORIGINS OF EXCHANGE

It is useful to strip Adam Smith's insight down to the minimal essentials in a model that is far removed from descriptive reality, but which retains elements of the logical structure. To take this step, it is necessary to go back to the logic of exchange itself. Why do persons trade, one with another?

The stock answer would invoke differences in preferences or in endowments, or both. Ricardian comparative advantage would be introduced in almost any economist's response. This seemingly innocuous step, in itself, obscures Smith's more general and more basic argument. It is helpful to model a setting in which all participants are identical both in preferences and in endowments (capacities). Confronted with such a highly stylized model, for many economists exchange would lose its *raison d'être*.

This model, however, allows the foundational Smithean principle to emerge as a stand-alone explanation. Trade takes place because specialization, as such, is productive. Persons would recognize that specialized production, followed by mutual exchange, generates results that are valued more highly than those in autarky, and by all parties.

In this stylization, specialization is chosen, as opposed to the Ricardian setting in which specialization is exogenous. Differences become endogenous in the pure Smithean model; participants become different as they choose to specialize. They do so in order to secure the benefits of potential exchange.

There are ethical components in the implied behavioral content that are beyond those present in the Ricardian model. Persons who choose to enter the exchange nexus through specialization of the resources under their control generate potential benefits to others with whom exchanges are consummated.

The simplified two-person example demonstrates this result clearly. By choosing to commit resources to activities that extend beyond internal consumption-usage limits, with a view toward exchange with another, an individual makes mutual gain possible. Clearly, another person is affected by the reference person's behavior.

The great discovery by Adam Smith and his eighteenth-century peers was the recognition that the effect on others need not be the behaviorally motivating force and, indeed, may not be sensed at all by participants in the market. The individual who enters the nexus as a specialized producer with the objective of ultimate trade may be exclusively motivated by his or her own interest, even to the absence of any directly felt interests of others. Hence, the way was prepared for economics and economists, the science and the scientists, directed at elaborating the first principles of a self-organizing system of human interaction.

THE NEGLECTED CHOICE MARGIN

In the process through which ideas develop in scientific and public consciousness, the foundational ethical implications of market behavior were neglected. Economists proceeded within the generalized understanding that persons must, willy-nilly, participate in the emerging and complex nexus of market exchange, and that specialization is a necessary requirement in such participation. Implicitly at least, persons, or resource owners generally, were not modeled as facing genuine choices involving participation or non-participation in market interaction. It is not surprising, therefore, that as the market order came to be more and more complex, some of the fundamental prerequisites were often overlooked, including the ethical structure.

More or less by default, little or no consideration was given to Adam Smith's theorem relating the extent of the market to economic development through exploitation of the advantages of specialization. Neoclassical analysis was constructed in application to a setting in which the extent of the market was presumed to be exogenously settled, at least in its potential. The thrust of analysis was aimed at examining processes through which resources are allocated to their most highly valued uses; a meaningful exercise only in the Ricardian framework.

It is not mysterious as to why my simple inquiry concerning the economic value of the work ethic left orthodox neoclassical economists nonplussed. There is no way in which the choice of a person, or of many persons, in the exchange nexus to work either more or less can be handled in models that are descriptive of the ongoing theoretical discourse of the late nineteenth century.

LACUNA IN THE RETURN TO INCREASING RETURNS

As noted above, I found myself forced to abandon the neoclassical postulate of constant returns and to trace out contributions in a dissident strand of analysis, summarized under increasing returns. Interest in this strand had resurfaced in the 1980s, as a series of challenges. Descriptively there was, indeed, a 'return to increasing returns', which Yong Yoon and I used as the title for a volume that collected the separately developed arguments, from Adam Smith through Alfred Marshall and Allyn Young, along with the modern contributions (Buchanan and Yoon, 1994). These modern contributions were not, however, directly aimed at elaborating Smith's theorem relating specialization to the extent of the market. A partial, but significant and surprisingly neglected exception to this emphasis was the work of Xiaokai Yang (2001), whose basic model comes closest to that which seemed to me to be Adam Smith's understanding.

A serious oversight characterized almost all of the modern contributions; an oversight that explains, in part, the continuing neglect of the ethical implications. With the exception of Yang, attention was concentrated on prospects for increasing returns to scale in production processes, attention influenced by Smith's misleading pin factory example and, differently, by Marshall's introduction of external economics among producing firms in inclusive industrial groupings. The puzzle to be resolved was that of reconciling increasing returns to scales of production with the observed competitive organization of industry. The choice margin that was indirectly relevant was the rate of output of the producing firm. And the external economies construction introduced by Marshall offered the analytical means through which increasing returns to scale and viable competitive structures are rendered compatible.

The ethical component was considered irrelevant, or at least secondary, in explanations of the behavior patterns of profit-seeking firms. Firms are established in the expectation of being able to make profits, and competitive pressures prevent firms from departing from maximizing behavior, which is indirectly tested by survival criteria. How could a firm internalize external benefits that its actions might generate, even should it desire to do so?

Economists, generally, may have inadvertently extended the Alchian evolutionary-like explanation for profit-maximizing behavior on the part of firms to utility-maximizing behavior of persons in their roles as input suppliers and output demanders, with the implicit presupposition that some criteria akin to competitive survival indirectly constrain departures from narrowly defined and interpersonally comparable norms (Alchian, 1950). In other parts of their analyses, however, economists fully recognize that personal utility functions are open-ended, and even if net wealth must be accorded pride of place for any predictive science to emerge, there must exist a much wider range of behavioral prospect than that which is relevant for firms. In other words, individuals may, if they choose, internalize the subjectively assessed external benefits that their actions generate (Buchanan, 1969).

FIXED SPECIALIZATION PARAMETERS

Note that the presence or absence of external economies in the production processes of firms in particular industries or sectors does not directly bear on any examination of Adam Smith's general theorem. How can an expansion in output by a firm increase the extent of the market, even in the assumed presence of external economies?

Return to Adam Smith's conjectural model of the simple deer–beaver economy. Suppose that deer are produced under external economies. A generalized increase in production by all deer hunters would be cost-reducing. Given patterns of demand, more resources would be shifted into deer production with a subsequent increase in aggregate value in the whole economy. The allocative shift improves efficiency, as measured by the ratio between valued output and valued input. In this construction, however, there is no increase in specialization; there are no new goods, whether outputs or inputs. The extent of the market nexus, as such, has not been changed. The potential value of the given resource base has been fully exploited by the internalization of the externalities, but further expansion in the size of this base offers no promise of aggregate growth in value.

Marshallian external economies, and particularly the modern contributions in this genre that call attention to the knowledge–information-producing industries, call attention to allocative distortions and to potential efficiency-enhancing corrections rather than to any relationship between market size and economic growth.[1]

ETHICS AND THE USES OF RESOURCES

As instanced earlier, the framework of modern analysis shifts attention away from the more general choice margin at which ethical elements in behavior come directly into play. The relevant margins that emerge directly from the Smith theorem are the dual supply–demand choices that involve increasing the supply or offer of inputs to the market, and the return of the income secured from such supply as demand for outputs on the market. The first half of this dual choice is between offering a unit of potentially productive input to the market and withholding such a unit from the market, in either idleness or other non-market uses. The second half of the choice is between returning the income resultant from sale of the input offered to the market to the spending stream as additional demand, and withholding or hoarding such income.

The focus here is necessarily on decisions made by persons (families) rather than those made by organized firms (in this respect, the Marshallian dichotomy is misleading). And, as noted earlier, there is no competitive pressure that directly forces persons separately to act so as to sublimate the ethical aspects. David Gauthier's reference to the market as a 'morals free zone' reflects a serious misunderstanding (Gauthier, 1986). In making the basic market versus non-market usage of resources, individuals may be, and are, influenced critically by the ethos of the culture in which they find themselves to be participants. This culture may or may not place emphasis on the Puritan virtues of work, thrift, productive investment and fairness.

BACK TO SMITH'S THEOREM

Two points remain to be further examined. First, it seems useful to discuss in more depth the foundational economic theory that establishes the Smith relationship. Second, the value premise upon which the whole treatment rests must be exposed for possible criticism.

How does an increase in the extent of the market yield value to all participants in the inclusive interaction? This basic question tends to be neglected or papered over in the external economies constructions, both in Marshall and in the derivative modern variants. What are the necessary conditions that must be met to validate the Smithean proposition?

Recall that Smith's theorem relates the degree of specialization (division of labor) to the extent of the market. The productivity of specialization itself becomes the engine that generates the enhancement of aggregate value. But what does specialization mean in this context? As discussed above in the simple deer–beaver setting, there is no new specialization that takes place as mere allocative adjustments are made. Adam Smith had something other than such adjustments in mind in this respect, as opposed to the predominant emphasis in neoclassical analyses. As the extent of the market increases, an extent defined by the two-step process involving an increase in the offer of productive inputs and a return of the proceeds of this transaction to the market, prospects for new goods, whether classified as outputs or inputs, must increase. Goods that remain non-viable, the production and sale of which does not cover opportunity cost in the smaller nexus, become marginally profitable as the size of the network expands. And this fact of profitability itself guarantees that aggregate value in the economy is increased.

Orthodox neoclassical analysis commences with the implicit postulate that the number of goods produced and traded is fixed exogenously. As noted, if restricted by this postulate, the Smith relationship no longer holds.

Consider a fully competitive setting in which there are no Marshallian externalities present in any industry and in which the number of goods produced and exchanged is fixed. An increase in the supply of inputs along with the return of income to the market cannot generate a shift in the ratio between valued output and valued input. In the context of the discussion here, there is then no ethical implication of the location of the choice margin between smaller and larger exchange networks. The basic validity of Smith's theorem depends on some prior existence of goods that are valued by participants but which remain beyond the range of economic viability. Whatever the size or extent of the nexus, there must always remain a 'sea of goods' potentially available for exploitation through further specialization, each one of which remains of positive value.

Precisely how does a shift of a potentially productive input unit from non-market to market usage generate increased aggregate value, unless an external economy of some sort is present before such shift occurs? This question is not directly addressed by exclusive concentration on the production or supply-side choice margins that has described most of the contributions, again with the exceptions of Allyn Young (1928) and Xiaokai Yang (2001). It is necessary to adopt the more inclusive perspective which incorporates both the supply of inputs to the market, and the return of income earned from such supply to the market as demand for outputs. If a unit of productive input is offered on the market and earns a market return, this allows the owner of that unit to return to the market and demand goods, a demand that is not present prior to the change in market-offered input. Through this process, aggregate demand is increased and this, in turn, allows some new specialization to become viable. The increase in input supply does indeed create its own demand, albeit indirectly.

Note that the increasing returns present are those for the whole market, rather than any producing unit, sector or industry. These may be called generalized increasing returns to distinguish this effect from the conventional derivation from economies of scale of the standard variety. The external economy here, if that term is insisted on, extends over any and all margins where the offer of inputs to the market and the return demand of output from the market are within the behavioral determination of separate agents, in either their private or public capacities.

Note, also, that the potential for enhancement of value does not involve any necessary allocative shift of inputs among separate existing uses. The effect here emerges whether the initial impetus stems from suppliers of deer, beaver, ships, sealing wax or cabbages. The impetus can arise from any supplier of input to the market for any good. The person or persons who add to input supply need not, and would not normally, be themselves coincident with those who might shift to the new specialization as the network expands.

The problem of reconciling the presence of generalized increasing returns with observed competitive organization of production does not seem to carry either scientific or normative weight here. A zero-profit equilibrium remains conceptually possible, and no firm need sense an opportunity to secure rents from expanding its own rate of production beyond that dictated by price–cost relationships. The firm that decides to exploit an emergent opportunity to introduce the new good through a previously unused specialization will, of course, hope to earn differential rents by so doing. At the same time, however, freedom of potential entry will ensure that any such differential rents, should they be captured, will be dissipated. The persistence of genuine market power, such as would be required for monopolization, cannot be characteristic of the dynamic economy in which potential rents are continually being dissipated. There is no first-mover threshold advantage since, by assumption, anyone can produce the new good which an increase in aggregate demand might make viable.

In the conceptualized equilibrium of such an economy, no person in the employment of any firm need feel frustrated in an unfulfilled desire to offer more or less inputs. (In the model implicitly used here, it seems best to presume that the individual input supplier effectively controls the choice margin rather than being locked into involuntary subjection to institutionalized rigidities.)

The conceptualized zero-profit equilibrium will not satisfy the condition for Pareto optimality, as normally defined. The presence of generalized increasing returns to the size of the market along with normal preference relationships ensures that there must exist some range over which an increase in input supply and the consequent increase in aggregate demand that calls forth some positively valued new good could be utility-enhancing for all participants, or at least for some participants without utility loss offsets for others. The potential 'correction' here cannot, of course, be measured, and any attempt at politically coerced behavioral departure from voluntary adjustments might well overshoot any stylized Pareto target.

The analytical structure traced out above explains my early suggestion that the instillation and maintenance of a work ethic does embody positive economic value. The presence of an ethic of work, as opposed to its absence along relevant choice margins, can be interpreted to be descriptive of an element in basic preference patterns. If the utility functions of participants in the economy are such as to give relatively more weight to goods produced for and available from the market or exchange nexus, the conceptualized equilibrium will embody a relatively higher aggregate value, as determined by the choices of participants.

ETHICAL PRESUPPOSITIONS

As the analyses in preceding sections have made clear, the choices made by any and all participants in the market, as potential input suppliers and output demanders, embody ethical content in the straightforward sense that the set of choice options available is changed. From this result, there is no implication that an increase in the size of this set is always to be valued positively. The set of choices available to market participants may indeed be larger but the change may be evaluated negatively. An increase in aggregate market value, as emergent from the separate and decentralized patterns of individual behavior, may be adjudged to be value-reducing in some contexts and by some persons, and especially in some ethical systems. That is to say that an increase in the extent of the market, whether internally or externally generated, may evoke normative condemnation rather than approval, as evidenced by anti-globalization demonstrations in Seattle and elsewhere.

Even among persons who follow Adam Smith and consider value, in some measurable market-determined sense, to be an appropriate policy objective (perhaps only one among others), there may be relatively few who would place positive weights on all particular extensions of the exchange nexus. There will remain some goods and services that persons would produce and exchange if markets were totally unfettered – goods and services that are deemed to be 'out of bounds' on basic moral and ethical principles. And through the institutions of collective or political control, persons may prevent or regulate the liberties of others in specifically designated market dealings. The failed Eighteenth Amendment to the US Constitution early in the twentieth century offers an example. Supporters sought to enforce constraints on market production and exchange of alcoholic spirits. The effort represented a deliberate objective to restrict the aggregate size of the economy and to eliminate specialization in the production and ultimate use of specifically designated goods.

As this example also suggests, however, collective restrictions on the liberties of persons to engage in markets emerge from moral and ethical norms as applied to particular goods and services, with little or no regard to effects on potential specialization. These specifically directed efforts to constrain market behavior, even if they are exclusively motivated by ethical concerns, need not be introduced into the discussion here. The presence of generalized increasing returns, as analyzed in this chapter and elsewhere, necessarily introduces a quite different ethical consideration, one that directs attention to the aggregate extent of the market nexus. And the evaluation of changes in this dimension is not universally shared. To Adam Smith and most economists who have succeeded him, the aggregate value placed on goods and services by the voluntaristic behavior of persons interacting in markets is a reasonable measure of progress, and increases in this value are evaluated positively. Such judgment, whether or not expressly stated, implies acceptance of the ultimate location of the origins of value in the individuals who specialize and engage in trade.

This stance is rejected by persons who find origins of value outside of and beyond those which emerge from market dealings. The whole counterculture, at least counter to the market, may seek to 'correct' results, both as to the allocation processes within markets and as to the extent of the market itself; in either or both cases based on some external criteria, as presumably revealed by God or right reason.

The continuing debate with those who espouse the counterculture to market-based interaction need not be directly discussed here. It is sufficient to emphasize that the whole treatment of the relationship between ethics and the extent of the market is best interpreted as taking place within the inclusive framework that does place positive value on aggregate economic growth, as normally measured. And, in this setting, there is a straightforward relationship between the extent of the market and the total value generated through the market.

NOTE

1. For a good summary treatment of one strand of modern development, see David Warsh (2006).

REFERENCES

Alchian, Armen (1950), 'Uncertainty, evolution, and economic theory', *Journal of Political Economy*, **58**, 211–21.

Buchanan, James M. (1949), 'The pure theory of government finance: a suggested approach', *Journal of Political Economy*, **57**, 496–505.

Buchanan, James M. (1969), *Cost and Choice: An Inquiry in Economic Theory*, Chicago, IL: Markham.

Buchanan, James M. and Yong J. Yoon (eds) (1994), *The Return to Increasing Returns*, Ann Arbor, MI: University of Michigan Press.

De Viti de Marco, Antonio (1936), *First Principles of Public Finance*, translated from the Italian by Edith Pavlo Marget, New York: Harcourt Brace and Co., Inc.

Gauthier, David (1986), *Morals by Agreement*, Oxford: Oxford University Press.

Pérez-Reverte, Arturo (1996), *The Club Dumas*, New York: Harcourt Brace.

Warsh, David (2006), *Knowledge and the Wealth of Nations: A Story of Economic Discovery*, New York: Norton.

Yang, Xiaokai (2001), *Economics: New Classical versus Neoclassical Frameworks*, Malden, MA: Blackwell.

Young, Allyn (1928), 'Increasing returns and economic progress', *Economic Journal*, **38**, 527–40.

2. Value and values, preferences and price: an economic perspective on ethical questions

Geoffrey Brennan and Giuseppe Eusepi

> One might reserve the term 'values' for a specially elevated or noble set of choices. Perhaps choices in general might be referred to as 'tastes'. We do not ordinarily think of the preference for additional bread over additional beer as being a value worthy of philosophic enquiry. I believe, though, that the distinction cannot be made logically, and certainly not in dealing with the single isolated individual. If there is any distinction between values and tastes it must lie in the realm of inter-personal relations.
>
> (Arrow, 1963)

INTRODUCTION

It is said that America and Britain are nations divided by a common language. What presumably is meant by this remark is that words that mean one thing in the US mean something rather different in the UK – and this for enough words and expressions to make talking at cross-purposes frequent and occasionally comical,[1] and yet more occasionally, seriously problematic.

The conversation between moral philosophers and economists, after years of lying dormant, has somewhat revived in the recent past. And the scope for miscommunication in this conversation seems no less than in the US–UK analogue. The situation in this case is exacerbated by the fact that economists, unlike philosophers, have little taste for extended conceptual analysis over the use of terms: we economists tend to save our rigour for the equations. In this chapter, we are going to attempt a little clarification about words, in the interests, we hope, of improved communication.

Often of course what look like mere terminological disputes turn out to involve something of substance. If economists use 'values' and 'tastes' and 'preferences' interchangeably (as the quotation from Arrow nicely illustrates), and if at the same time they refer to 'value' and 'price' as if these two terms meant the same thing (as, for example, in the traditional reference to 'price theory' as the 'theory of value'[2]) then confusion immediately beckons. Just what is the connection between 'values' in the first sense and the 'value' in the second? That is one relatively simple issue that we hope to clarify in the ensuing discussion.

Of course, that exercise in clarification could be regarded as entirely internal to economics. However, we want to broaden the discussion to include the issue of the relationship between corresponding uses of the term 'values' in ethics as well as in economics. Our conjecture is that moral philosophers may have something to learn from the ambiguities in the economics case. In part, this conjecture arises from the fact that when we economists talk of values or value, we often import ethical freight into our discussions. But there is a further consideration. Economics is often described as the 'theory of choice' or as having its subject-matter defined by choice. And although that description is neither entirely clear[3] nor uncontested,[4] it is clear that there is a close connection between economics under that choice-based description, and ethics. For ethics too is concerned with choice – with the evaluation of alternative actions. In what ways, we might ask, do the economic account and the ethical account of choice diverge – if indeed they do diverge? And what exactly is the relation between choice (whether economic or ethical) and value or values?

We will begin with the issue of the relation between 'values' and 'value' in economics. In the following section we turn to the issue of the relation between 'values', a term that has a significant life in both economics and ethics, and 'preferences' a term mainly restricted to economics. Next we shall consider the question of whether the simple clarification of meanings we have drawn from economics might have any useful application in the ethical setting. The final section brings together our conclusions in summary form.

VALUES AND VALUE IN ECONOMICS

The issue of 'value' has a long and complicated life in economics. In a letter to Malthus, Ricardo confessed his belief that, sooner or later, he would have to confront the term 'value' and that he saw no escape from the problems that this concept invoked. It seems clear that Ricardo, like all classicists before and after him, conceived value as closely connected to price. And this usage is hardly eccentric. In contemporary ordinary language, we often refer to the 'value' of a bundle of shares or a house or a painting, meaning the price it could obtain in prevailing markets.

Economists, perhaps with Smith's diamond–water 'paradox' in mind, might well want to register a distinction between marginal and average value, and to emphasize the problems that failure to make that distinction can give rise to. But in fact, the problems Ricardo seems to have had in mind appear to have been of quite a different kind. His quest appears to have been for a unit (a numeraire commodity perhaps) whose value would remain stable in the face of varying prices. Ricardo thought that the real task for the economist was that of finding a truly objective value theory able to overcome the difficulties arising from what he took to be the dual theory of value in Smith. Smithian theories are described in most political economy textbooks (at least the classical ones) in terms of a distinction between a 'labour-embodied account' of value and a 'labour-commanded account'.[5] Ricardo believed that the labour-commanded conception of value violated some of the characteristic requirements of an acceptable metric. As Ricardo saw it, the exchange between labour and capital, on which the labour-commanded conception depended, took place among unequals and hence any such conception of value was intrinsically flawed on both economic and ethical grounds. Accordingly, Ricardo eliminated the labour-commanded variant in the Smithian theory of value. But he retained the labour-embodied theory and used it exclusively – among other things, as a basis for (re)assessing the exchange between labour and capital.

This brief historical excursion is not of central concern here except for two lessons that we can draw from it. The first is that to Ricardo[6] 'value' was a central concern and getting the right conception of it was, for him, an absolutely critical piece of what he saw as proper economic analysis. The second is that an important ambition in the Ricardian programme revolved around the 'objectification' of value. In fact, Ricardo's distinction between values and prices – although he made such a distinction – was rather restricted in scope. One interpretation of the Ricardian enterprise is that he was trying to find an objective theory of opportunity cost able to eliminate at its roots the critical distinction between values (an intrinsically subjective concept) and objective, observable market prices. In the spirit of the Ricardian discourse, we might say that objective values are revealed as prices emergent from market exchange, and values are only the subjective evaluations that are merely preliminary elements in the processes of price determination. In that sense, the process of price determination effectively transforms and renders obsolete the underlying subjective values that the individual participants bring to the marketplace. In this spirit, we might say that real values originate only in a process of reciprocal exchange between individuals and do not emerge if there is no exchange.

But there is something very strange in all this. Since values are subjective evaluations, they would be present even within a single-individual context like that of Robinson Crusoe on his solitary island (that is, before Friday arrives). In whatever sense we understand 'values', we must say that they precede prices and are ever present, even in a one-individual setting where market prices *lato sensu* can hardly be conceived. In the Ricardo treatment of the value–price nexus, something very important is hidden. The assumption that values precede prices does not imply that values are fully absorbed in prices. Nor does it necessarily follow that values have no connection with prices. What we have to recognize here is that the term 'values' does double duty in the price determination story. In terms of contemporary price theory 'values' refer both to the relative prices of goods in terms of some numeraire (usually money) and also to the underlying preferences on the basis of which those relative prices emerge.

In the interests of underlining the obvious, it may be useful to consider a simple two-person exchange of two goods in the context of the Edgeworth–Bowley box formulation. Figure 2.1 illustrates. There are two goods, X and Y, which for the purposes of the exercise are in fixed supply, X and Y. There are two individuals, A and B, who have preferences over the two goods which exhibit the standard convexity and transitivity properties. We denote A's consumption of X and Y by X_a and Y_a (X_b and Y_b are to be understood analogously). So $X_b = X - X_a$; and $Y_b = Y - Y_a$. B's preferences are indicated by the indifference curves drawn with O_b as the origin, while A's preferences are drawn with O_a as origin (in the conventional way). Let the initial 'endowment point' be S. Exchange from S up to saturation yields say the point E. Where exactly E

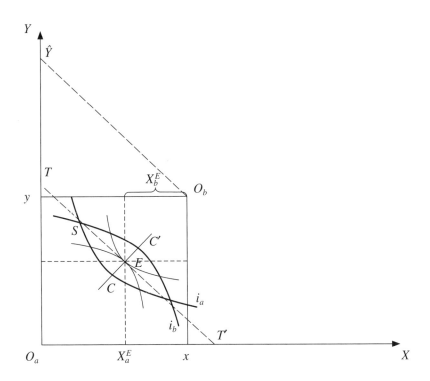

Figure 2.1   Value(s) in exchange

is along the segment of the contract curve $C'C$, will depend on the relative bargaining strengths of A and B – but at any such point on $C'C$, prospects for mutually beneficial exchange will be exhausted. At E there will be a common value of X in terms of Y, represented by the slope of the two players' indifference curves at E – the slope, that is, of the line $T'T$. The location of E and hence the emergent value of X in terms of Y (the slope of $T'T$) is clearly a function of the location of S, the relative bargaining strengths and the underlying preferences of the two players. The (minor?) terminological complications arise here because those preferences are also referred to as the agents' 'values'. So 'values' in this representation might be understood variously as:

- the complete indifference maps of A and B;
- the relative price of X and Y in equilibrium (the slope of $T'T$);
- or the total value of X in terms of Y (based on the slope of $T'T$) which is the amount of Y from Y to $\hat{Y}$.

What we might say of the process of exchange (the move from S to E) is that 'values change, though there is no change in values'. This rather extraordinary sounding remark involves two of the senses of values – the value of X measured in terms of numeraire Y (or vice versa) certainly changes; but the preferences (underlying values) of the participants (of A and B) do not. Economists do not of course have much difficulty negotiating remarks of this kind. But it is hardly surprising if disciplinary outsiders like philosophers have some problem in understanding what is going on. And when sociologists, for example, say: 'The introduction of markets changes values', economists might respond with: 'Of course' (thinking of the values of goods as determined by market prices) or 'No way!' (thinking of the basic preferences).

Much of the conversation that occurs between disciplines involves less in the way of genuine disagreement and much more in the way of talking at cross-purposes. Economists are somewhat to blame for this confusion because the term 'value' which is so central to economic discussions has just too many different meanings to be a helpful term outside the set of fellow professionals who are entirely accustomed (we hope) to the nuances. And of course, all this is to abstract from the important extra distinction, when talking about the 'value' of goods (X and Y), between marginal and total value (see Buchanan, 1962) (or more to the point, between total value including infra-marginal surplus and total value measured as price times quantity).

Terminological confusions aside, we should not lose sight of the fact that economists have used 'value/s' for a variety of distinct concepts because the term is ambiguous in common parlance. One modest but important role for economists is just to point that fact out. And in the process, to emphasize that processes of exchange do work a strange kind of alchemy in transforming the variety of 'values' (preferences) into a common market 'value' for each good (the price of that good in terms of some conventional numeraire). This transformation, we shall want to argue, is in its extreme form a distinctive feature of markets in private goods. When we enter the world that philosophers inhabit, where 'values' are described in terms of collective abstractions like 'justice' or 'freedom' or even 'aggregate well-being', the possibilities of such transformation are highly limited – which is not to say that some elements of the market exchange analogy do not survive. But that topic is for a later section. At this point, we want to take up the question as to the relation between preferences and values.

VALUES AND PREFERENCES

For the purposes of argument in the foregoing section, it was reasonable to draw no distinction between agents' values and agents' preferences. It is now appropriate to withdraw that forbearance. Here we want to explore the relation between values as the moral philosopher might understand them on the one hand, and preferences in the economist's lexicon on the other. And we shall pursue this exploration from the economist's end, as it were, by asking what, if any, distinction between values and preferences the economist might recognize.

Three possible connections between preference and values seem worth distinguishing:

- the 'preferences as values' possibility;
- the 'values as preferences' possibility; and
- the 'values vs preferences' possibility.

We take these in turn.

Preferences as Values

The idea that the satisfaction of agent's preferences is a normative objective that ought to be pursued, at least *pro tanto*, is one that has a long history in economics, part of the heritage left from the traditional association of economics with utilitarianism (from Hume and Smith, through Mill and Edgeworth, to Marshall and Pigou). Amartya Sen, in his decomposition of utilitarianism (Sen and Williams, 1982), distinguishes three separable aspects:

- the consequentialist aspect, according to which actions (or policies or whatever is to be evaluated) are assessed by reference to the way the world lies as a result of the action (or whatever) chosen;

- the 'welfarist' aspect according to which states of the world are assessed in terms of the well-offness of the individuals who compose the ethically relevant community; and
- the 'aggregationist' aspect according to which the measure of overall desirability is the simple aggregate of the welfares of the relevant individuals.

The emerging professional consensus in the 1930s surrounding the 'impossibility of interpersonal utility comparisons' put paid to the third of these elements. But the other two remain essentially intact. In particular, the Pareto criterion (vector dominance) that came to replace the aggregate-utility rule fully absorbed the welfarist commitment: 'better-off' and 'worse-off' for each individual remained the central concepts in all normative comparisons.

But how was individual 'welfare' or 'utility' to be conceptualized? Given the increasingly subjectivist turn in economics, the natural candidate seemed to be 'preference satisfaction' – rather than simple 'objective' measures like income or wealth or life expectancy (or some index of these). A similar kind of epistemic modesty that fuelled anxieties about interpersonal comparisons of utility also raised doubts about the capacity of external observers to know what individuals' well-being consisted in. If one person had a preference for a more adventurous but possibly shorter life, while another cared little about material things but placed a high value on the quality of her relationships, these were differences that acceptable measures of individual well-being ought to recognize. Individual 'preference-satisfaction' seemed, to economists at least, the conceptually appropriate notion. Moreover, the deep professional commitment to the assumption of agent rationality in the explanation of individual behaviour meant that agents could be relied on to act in accord with their preferences in a wide variety of contexts. Prisoner's dilemma and public goods problems might mean that decentralized individual action could not deliver what individuals really preferred. But at least for private goods and in tolerably well-working markets, the most authoritative guide to preference satisfaction was thought to be the free choices of the individuals concerned. In this way, a general presumption in favour of 'consumer sovereignty' became a characteristic feature of the economic approach to normative questions. It came to be seen as just self-evident that 'individuals are the best judges of their own well-being'. And though that presumption might be suspended in cases of minors and the mentally disadvantaged, and perhaps (though perhaps not) in relation to certain addictive substances and activities, such cases were seen by economists to be exceptions and to be resisted in all except extreme circumstances.

It is not our object here to examine this general commitment in any great detail, but it might be useful to make a few points about it. One relates to the status of 'preferences' as a category. In the Humean picture of rational action that underlies the economist's conception, the primary categories are belief and desire: it is a distinctive move of the economist to suppose that separate desires and the beliefs that relate to them can be satisfactorily aggregated into a 'utility function' or ordering, with the relevant completeness, transitivity and convexity properties. There are, after all, many different ways in which competing desires might be reconciled. The process by which this is done remains totally unanalysed in economics: preferences are just taken somehow to emerge and maximal preference satisfaction is taken to have the same normative status as maximal overall desire satisfaction would have (whatever that normative status exactly would be). This move from desire and belief to preference seems to us to be a remarkably under-remarked issue – at least given the normative weight that preference satisfaction is assigned in economics. Of course, beliefs in themselves are not beyond the reach of rationality requirements, but it seems clear that philosophers worry much more about the status of agent beliefs than economists typically do. Somehow, agents either manage to get complete information; or if information is costly, at least optimal information; or at least optimal information about where information is to be found; or if information is a relevant economic asset (as in the asymmetric information literature) agents will at least optimally use the information to which they have access. Agent rationality seems to erode all prospects of general normative improvement within the information 'economy'. And the conclusion that economists have drawn seems to be that even ill-informed preferences ought to be satisfied.

However, the real point here is not to critique the claims of individual rationality, or of the epistemic authority of the self in identifying individual preferences, or the status of the preferences themselves in terms of underlying desire-satisfaction. It is rather just to emphasize that the welfarist claim is itself a value – a normative commitment without which preference-satisfaction can have no normative authority. The foregoing discussion is designed to make that designation clear by suggesting several senses in which, as a value, maximal preference satisfaction might not be self-evidently desirable. One cannot move from the observation that maximizing preference satisfaction is what agents do (even rational agents), to the claim that maximal preference satisfaction is normatively desirable, without some value commitment to overall preference satisfaction. And this is true, quite apart from the additional point that value premises are required to decide on what the proper measure of 'overallness' is – that is, exactly how we should weight the different individuals in forming a workable measure of preference satisfaction overall. Our point is that 'preferences' become an object of 'value' to the extent that preference satisfaction is taken to be normatively desirable.[7] Economists do so take, in general. But what they take thereby is a value – not a fact!

Values as Preferences

The idea of preference satisfaction as an object of value presupposes a distinction between values and preferences that some economists might feel requires explanation. What are these 'values' that are taken to exist independently of individuals' preferences? After all, values exist, if at all, in human minds – and they purport to be addressed to questions of human action. If they are to have any traction there, they must be addressed to human actors. How then can values exist independent of preferences? (This question seems to be Arrow's anxiety, as expressed in the epigraph.)

Or think of the challenge in purely behavioural terms. Given the assumption of rationality, actions are to be explained in terms of preferences. If values play any role at all in influencing behaviour – indeed if they are to be conceptually capable of doing so within the rationality framework – they must fit into the category of preferences somehow. So how would we distinguish between actions driven by values and actions driven by preferences of other kinds? And if we cannot distinguish values from other preferences behaviourally, what is the point of the distinction? How might we distinguish a mere taste for, say, giving some of your money away from a value judgement that this is something you ought to do? It all comes down to utility maximization in the end. Or so the economist might say.

Here are several suggestions about what might be at stake in the distinction. One suggestion is that when you act on the basis of values you feel guilt (if the act is bad) or a special kind of moral satisfaction (if the act is good). A Smithian might say that you get a special pleasure from the esteem of the impartial spectator – the man within the breast – and endure a special pain from his disesteem. For the tastes of some moral philosophers this description might seem to psychologize morality excessively, and from the economic viewpoint one might query whether this difference has any real behavioural bite. But still, it is a possibility.

A second suggestion might be that when you act according to values, there is a necessary reference to the behaviour of others. This reference might take the form that right action is how you think others ought to behave – and wrong action is how they ought not behave. When you choose apples over oranges, you don't think others should do likewise. Indeed, it may be better for you if they don't do like you do – in the case where the supply curve for apples is upward-sloping, say. In these cases of market choice, you may not have much scope for influencing what others do, except via the market mechanism itself. And the market might not exercise incentives of the right kind. (More on this anon.) Sometimes, though, you do get the chance to determine not only how you will act but also how others will. This is the case in collective decisions, for example, and you might think that values have distinctive purchase in the arena of collective action for precisely that reason. This is an interesting thought. It suggests that values are connected to what has come to be known in coordination game settings (and elsewhere in small-number interactive settings) as 'we-thinking'.

The reference to others might, though, be of a different kind. Values might be the product of conventions (Hume famously thought this) in which behaviours of the relevant kind derive their compelling qualities partly because other people do them. Part of the reason why you behave according to moral values is because others do. Values are, on this reading, analytically connected (though perhaps in a complex way) to the same forces that encourage you to obey certain traffic rules. You have reason to obey those rules by virtue of the fact that others obey them. Or perhaps you have reason to endorse the values because others do. In the endorsement case, even if others do not act in accordance with prevailing values much of the time, they (as well as you) nevertheless think you (and they) ought to. Perhaps they will disesteem you if you do not behave according to those values, and perhaps you care about their esteem. Perhaps they will disesteem you if you do not endorse those values and pay those values due respect, even if you cannot manage to keep up to the standard the values propound.

If any of these things are true, they seem to lend values a different character from other kinds of preferences. Values are somewhat like language. Although created by and embodied in human agents, they do quite genuinely exist 'out there', independent of any individual. Radical subjectivists make a mistake, on this reading, by denying the relatively objective quality of values – though preferences (understood as distinct from values in this sense) remain entirely subjective.

A third thought, attractive to moral realists, is that values play a role in behaviour much more like beliefs than like desires. This conception captures three significant features of values. First, as a simple empirical matter, people do routinely argue about ethical issues as if there were a truth to be obtained. Second, like beliefs, values are impervious to certain sorts of considerations. This point is obvious enough but may need some elaboration for those who are inclined to think that everything is just a matter of prices or incentives. Suppose you are giving a paper at a conference. And you seem to be having some difficulty in convincing your audience. You hit on a brilliant idea. Quickly you whip out your wallet and offer to pay the audience if they will accept your arguments. Your audience might well accept any cash that is on offer, but it is unlikely to influence their beliefs about your arguments one way or another. How could it? Belief is quite route-specific. It is a psychological state brought about by coming to accept something as true. It is susceptible to argument and evidence, but it cannot simply be bought. Take another example, which the authors first heard from John Broome. Suppose you are sick. Suppose your speed of recovery is positively related to your state of mind and that the more optimistic you are, the more quickly you will recover. Specifically, if you believe that you will get better in n days, you will actually get better in $(n + 1)$ days. So if n must be no less than 1, it is best for you to think that you will get better tomorrow (belief Z) , because in that case you will get better the day after tomorrow – the earliest feasible date! So it is best for you to have belief Z, but the fact that having that belief is better for you cannot give you a reason to believe Z, because the reason for belief involves Z's negation. In the same way, my promising to give you $20 if you will believe my wild theories may give you a kind of reason to believe them – but it is not a belief-inducing reason: it simply cannot do the required work. If values are like beliefs, there are certain things you can do to modify behaviour in the case of (non-value) preferences that do not apply in the case of values.

The third point relating to beliefs is that the norms governing belief have an independent force. Consider some abstract belief about the nature of things that has no behavioural relevance for you at all – say, the distance of the planet Jupiter from the sun; or the gross domestic product (GDP) of Iceland in 1740. Suppose you have a belief about what the magnitude in question is. It will by the nature of that belief matter to you that it is true – otherwise you cannot retain the belief. And this matters in itself. You may well be prepared to spend scarce time and energy verifying it (a behavioural consequence) even though it has no other implication for your preference satisfaction. What we might say here is that attitudes are objects of utility no less than actions are. Various actions may be undertaken for their own sake. Various attitudes are entertained for their own sake. And the attitudes we hold for their own sake include the ones we take to be fitting to their object, in much the way that truth is to propositions.

At least some moral philosophers think this about values. They think it matters to get evaluations 'right' for their own sake. It matters in particular to get our attitudes to match imagined circumstances – even though those circumstances do not apply and might never do so. Aesthetic judgements might be like this for some people: it matters that we give a piece of music or a painting its due for its own sake (we mean here for the sake of getting the attitude right, rather than for the sake of the painting).

One final thought. If values are like beliefs, then they ought to respond to arguments of the right kind – arguments of the kind that such and such a value is misguided or depends in some way on reasoning that is flawed. Preferences of other kinds are presumably not responsive to such arguments: they are primary. Behaviourists (and economists as a subset) ought to respect the additional explanatory power that comes from observations of behavioural response to certain kinds of stimuli – in this case arguments of a particular character. But of course, this only bears if values (as distinct from other kinds of preferences) do indeed influence behaviour; and at least some devotees of *Homo economicus* might be sceptical on that front.

All this may well strike the moral philosopher as rather naive and elementary. But the economistic challenge is not to be taken too lightly. It is not unreasonable to ask how the distinction between values and preferences of other kinds cashes out, and in what terms. If that distinction had no behavioural consequences at all, then that in itself is instructive. We would then have to rethink the relevance of all moral reasoning, including reasoning about the consequences of various actions and policies which would only have relevance if people cared about values. In other words, we should not rule out on a priori grounds that normative economics (and positive economics rationalized by appeal to its normative relevance) is an exercise that goes on exclusively in economists' minds and actually has no influence on anything (else). But in fact we do not think that is so. We think values can be distinguished from pure tastes – where 'pure tastes' are characterized by a kind of *de gustibus non est disputandum* rule (on this point see Stigler and Becker, 1977) – and that the distinction does have behavioural consequences of various kinds and at various levels. The object of this small section has just been to sketch what some of these behavioural consequences might be.

Values vs Preferences

The picture laid out in the previous subsection was of values being special kinds of preferences. So, to use 'preferences' as the encompassing term, the distinction is between two types of preference, 'values' and 'tastes' – with values having certain distinctive properties (for example, that they respond to arguments of a normatively relevant kind). This 'partitioning of preferences' strategy has some specific implications: most particularly, that values have the same structure as preferences (and so have properties like completeness and transitivity and convexity). But the partition view seems to overlook the special claims of values, and especially their claims to a kind of motivational primacy.

Suppose for example (plausibly enough) that A's 'values' were thought to indicate what A believed A should do, all things considered. They might also include A's views about what B should do all things considered as well, but we want to focus on the personal case here. Then it looks as if 'values' will trump 'tastes', whenever the two come into conflict. Of course, tastes will bear to the extent that 'taste-satisfaction' is itself a value – but only to that extent. And this gives values a kind of trumping quality – the quality of public defensibility that 'tastes' as such cannot have (more or less by definition).

This thought – that 'values' take primacy – has been considered by some philosophers to enrol 'true rationality' in the service of values. How could you be fully rational, one might ask, and fail to do that which you believe you ought to do, all things considered? This seems a fair question. But of course, economists have long answered it by insisting on a clear distinction between 'rational behaviour' and 'moral behaviour'. The whole idea of the 'invisible hand' (IH) – and the economists' enthusiasm for IH mechanisms – depends on the idea that (fully rational) agents can recognize patterns of behaviour as desirable or valuable (hence the idea of a 'hand') and yet not be motivated to bring those patterns about (hence the virtue of 'invisibility').

On quite a different front, some economists (Amartya Sen most notably, perhaps) have worried about treating values as preferences for a rather different reason – namely, that value-based behaviour is seen to yield 'utility' just like bread and beer consumption. Consider two widows, both with three children. One gives virtually all her meagre income to support her children, and ekes out a miserable material existence, but has at least the satisfaction of behaving in a manner she regards as morally defensible. The other consumes most of her income herself – and hence has to endure the spectacle of her children's distress: she feels guilty about this, but her 'revealed preference' is for her own consumption. Compare these two with a third woman, with the same aggregate income but no children. Sen is anxious to resist the claim that all these women are equally well off in any sense. But a simple preference satisfaction story would suggest that the first-mentioned must be better off than if she had opted for the consumption pattern of the second – that this is what rationality assumes. Ergo, in making any assessments of relative well-offness, response to moral values is just like response to 'tastes' (other preferences) and has no different status for, say, relative deservingness in redistributive exercises. Sen attempts to finesse this issue by appeal to a distinction between sympathy and commitment. Action in fulfilment of some values, Sen thinks, is rather like consumption: this is the sympathy case in which the giver actually 'enjoys' the consumption of the recipient. But not all cases are like this, he thinks: in the case of 'commitment' one obeys the value-based requirement 'in explicit violation of one's preferences' (Sen, 1977). We are not convinced that this distinction captures what it is that would be needed for calculating ethically defensible judgements about redistribution – but at least in some cases, agents who act on the basis of values do seem to be doing something different from those who are (merely?) satisfying their tastes. Whether one can draw this distinction satisfactorily without endorsing the values in question or appealing to other value premises,[8] we rather doubt. But Sen's anxieties do speak to one aspect of the possible distinction between values and tastes (or preferences of other kinds).

Some scholars have wanted to admit 'values' by appeal to meta-preferences – preferences about the substantive preferences that agents actually have. This is a means for discussing cases like addiction where the addict would prefer to lose the addiction,[9] and doubtless some values may take this form. But it seems bizarre and wrong-headed to conceive of all values in this way. When A cheats on his wife, it is the cheating that he disvalues, not necessarily the desire to

cheat. In any event, when meta-preferences do not endorse substantive preferences, it is simply not self-evident that the meta-preferences ought to prevail.
One cannot, in any event, make that claim without endorsing the meta-preferences normatively: the mere fact that they might be construed to represent A's
values does not do that work because A's values might be mistaken.[10]

The bottom line here is that the conception of values as just another set of
preferences does not seem to take adequate cognizance of the fact that values
and tastes frequently conflict, and that where they do, values seem to take a kind
of natural primacy: they show you what you ought to do. So the picture of values
as preferences is not faithful to the psychological reality: values stand against
many preferences. If that were not so, then everyone would simply be operating
according to their values all the time and no appeals to values – of the kind that
moral philosophers (or practical ethicists) are inclined to make – could ever
have any purchase: such appeals would simply endorse what agents are already
doing.

Once we recognize the likelihood of a tension between values and tastes,
however, it is difficult to see how one might endorse the idea of consumer sovereignty – itself a normative idea – without committing to pretty strong
violations of other values: ones that agents themselves possess. The view of
'preferences vs values' is, it seems, at odds with the idea of 'preferences as
values'. This is not itself perhaps a surprising conclusion when stated in the
abstract, but it reveals that the idea of 'consumer sovereignty', as standardly
endorsed by economists, is in a decidedly precarious position. Consumer sovereignty appears not as an expression of agents' values but an explicit violation
of them – which is not, we think, a comfortable place[11] for a normative principle,
widely held among economists, to lie.

VALUE DIFFERENCES AND EXCHANGE

Earlier, we made the observation that trade in private goods allows an interesting
transformation of different values or preferences into a set of relative values of
goods, common across agents. Is there anything analogous to this transformation
about the kind of value conflicts with which philosophers deal?

One block to such exchange might seem to rest in the fact that philosophers
often specify ethical values in terms of ideals – or otherwise as conditions that
have to be met. In short, they specify values 'deontically' – in terms, say, of
what is 'permissible' and 'impermissible'.[12] Such a formulation is inimical to
trade-offs between objects of value. So 'justice' and 'liberty' are specified in
terms quite different from X and Y, which can be traded off against one another
at terms given by the overall 'feasibility frontier'. But even if justice and liberty
(and whatever) were specified in terms of more and less (as we believe they

should be), no exchange possibilities analogous to the marketable goods case would be on offer. This is because the values philosophers are generally interested in operate as 'public goods' – they must be accepted as states of the world by everyone equally. There will be some limited scope for trade-offs to be made. Not all combinations of liberty and justice will be viewed as equally appropriate by the valuing community. But full consensus around the relative marginal value of justice in terms of liberty forgone cannot in general be achieved. The 'values' environment is one analogous to a world of several purely public goods – with no private good at all.[13]

What is required to achieve anything like the private goods trading case is an individuation of the 'values' in the sense that A's and B's liberty (or justice) are distinct objects, which can be traded off individually. Perhaps there is some scope for this. It is not self-evident that liberty for A is the same as liberty for B (and analogously with justice for A and justice for B). But in any case where what is at stake is 'the basic institutions of society', these basic institutions do indeed seem to be characterizable as public goods – arrangements that have to be more or less the same for all.

We do not take issue with the philosophers in this matter. We think that many values do have this public good character – and that there is no currency of compensation that could plausibly be used to simulate anything remotely like full market exchange. The idealized market in private goods operates as a special case in relation to its transformation of disparate values into common (marginal) value; and that is a fundamental fact that economists ought to recognize.

SUMMARY AND CONCLUSION

This chapter is an attempt at semantic clarification. Our aim has been to take terms with a variety of meanings – words like 'values', 'value', 'tastes' and even 'preferences' and 'price' – and examine those meanings first in the exchange setting characteristic of markets, and then in the context of moral philosophy.

Ethics, like economics, involves choice between alternatives. In the economics case, the options are usually thought of as actions. In ethics, they are sometimes actions, sometimes beliefs, sometimes attitudes. The apparatus that guides such choices in economics is that of 'preference'. The apparatus that guides such choices in moral philosophy is 'values'. For economists, typically, 'values' just are preferences. There is a distinct and special meaning reserved for the term 'value' – often the quantity of an object times its marginal value. In that latter sense, the classical economists thought there was a puzzle in the joint facts that 'values' pre-exist exchange and that 'value' is made 'objective' via the exercise of exchange. But this kind of puzzle just reveals the use of the term in two different senses.

Most of our discussion has been concerned with the relation between the term 'preference' as used by economists and the term 'value' as used by moral philosophers. Moral philosophers can learn something from economists here, in that the 'value' of an element of ethical desirability (liberty say) will in general depend on how much liberty is already enjoyed and how much of other elements of overall desirability is enjoyed also. However, the forces of exchange that produce common marginal evaluations of goods across participants in the marketplace do not in general apply in the case of ethical values.

In recognizing that ethical value and preference are different, we have isolated three cases:

- that where preferences are an object of value (that is, preference satisfaction is held to be ethically valuable);
- that where values just are preferences (perhaps with some special properties); and
- that where values have a somewhat different conceptual status from preferences. In this latter case, values and preferences may well struggle for influence in the arena of action – but there is no reason to think that 'preferences' will always trump 'values'.

A final remark. In this chapter we have intentionally avoided using the term 'cost'. This strategy has allowed us to pass over: (1) the ambiguities surrounding the term 'cost' as has been used by economists (Buchanan 1969); and (2) the sense in which cost might apply in ethics.

One conclusion to which our discussion gives rise is worth emphasis. Most economists adhere broadly to a principle of 'consumer sovereignty': this is itself an ethical principle and one which seems to be extremely vulnerable. To say this is not to suggest that satisfying individual preferences may have something to be said in its favour in some cases. But it seems implausible that it should occupy the kind of status that economics has broadly afforded it.

NOTES

1.   One of us recalls an occasion when he innocently gave rise to much amusement among the local mechanics at a gas station (garage) in rural Virginia, by referring to various parts of his car. There is perhaps nothing especially surprising about the transliteration of 'bonnet' for 'hood' or 'mudguard' for 'fender' or 'boot' for 'trunk' – but that terminology was certainly the source of considerable incredulous hilarity in Floyd County.
2.   A usage that is admittedly now somewhat old-fashioned, though still by no means unknown.
3.   Buchanan (1969) for example makes a nice (and useful) distinction between the 'science of choice' and the 'logic of choice'.
4.   Our own preference is for a definition that foregrounds exchange rather than choice per se – again a move in the Buchanan spirit. The chief protagonist for this view historically was

Richard Whateley (1831): sadly, his recommendation that 'economics' should be termed 'catallaxy' never caught on, though it was taken up by Mises and later Hayek as an important element in so-called Austrian economics.

5. See J.A. Schumpeter (1951).
6. And to the long tradition of writing in the Ricardian tradition, of which Piero Sraffa's (1952) is among the most notable.
7. There are interesting questions as to how to deal with 'preferences' that include the agent's value commitments. This has been a life-long concern of Amartya Sen's, beginning with the 'sympathy'–'commitment' distinction in his famous 'Rational fools' paper (1977). We shall refer to this issue in greater detail in the next section.
8. In Sen's case, it looks as if the issue is one that arises for a range of broad quasi-utilitarian calculations.
9. Not all cases of addiction are like this: people can become addicted to education and not wish to relinquish the addiction. In that case they have 'acculturated' themselves to a taste that they deliberately sought to acquire and thoroughly endorse.
10. One can of course construct examples of the following kind: A finds himself afflicted with a moral desire to give half his income to the world's poor. He would rather not have this moral desire: he thinks he would be happier and generally better off if he were indifferent to their plight. But his values are, well, what they are.
11. Not a comfortable place for us economists, we think.
12. Economists are also prone to do this in certain settings – and most notably in the social choice literature. We think that such formulations are generally ill-conceived, but the argument is not suitable for development here. See, however, Baurmann and Brennan (2006) for a more extended discussion.
13. This case is analysed in Buchanan (1976).

REFERENCES

Arrow, Kenneth J. (1963), *Social Choice and Individual Values*, New York, London, Sydney: John Wiley & Sons, Inc.

Baurmann, Michael and Geoffrey Brennan (2006), 'Majoritarian inconsistency, Arrow impossibility and the continuous interpretation: a context-based view', in L. Daston and C. Engel (eds), *Is There Value in Inconsistency?* Baden-Baden: Nomos, 93–118.

Buchanan, James M. (1962), Appendix 1, 'Marginal notes on reading political philosophy', in James M. Buchanan and Gordon Tullock, *The Calculus of Consent: Logical Foundations of Constitutional Democracy*, Ann Arbor, MI: University of Michigan Press, pp. 245–7.

Buchanan, James M. (1969), *Cost and Choice: An Inquiry in Economic Theory*, Chicago, IL: Markham Publishing Company.

Buchanan, James M. (1976), 'Methods and morals in economics', in W. Breit and W.P. Culbertson Jr. (eds), *Science and Ceremony: The Institutional Economics of C.E. Ayres*, Austin, TX: University of Texas Press, pp. 163–74.

Schumpeter, Joseph A. (1951), *Ten Great Economists: From Marx to Keynes*, New York: Oxford University Press.

Sen, Amartya K. (1977), 'Rational fools: a critique of the behavioral foundations of economic theory', *Philosophy and Public Affairs*, **6** (4), 317–44.

Sen, Amartya K. and Bernard Williams (1982) (eds), *Utilitarianism and Beyond*, Cambridge: Cambridge University Press.

Sraffa, Piero (1952), *The Works and Correspondence of David Ricardo* edited by Piero Sraffa with the collaboration of M.H. Dobb, Cambridge and New York: Cambridge University Press.

Stigler, George J. and Gary S. Becker (1977), 'De gustibus non est disputandum', *American Economic Review*, **67** (2), 76–90.

Whateley, Richard (1831), *Introductory Lectures on Political Economy*, London: B. Fellowes.

3. An economist's *plaidoyer* for a secular ethics: the moral foundation and social role of critical rationalism[1]

Stefano Gorini

INTRODUCTION

The adoption of the rationalist attitude to the understanding of the world, also known as critical rationalism, is a vital matter not only for philosophers, scientists and intellectuals, but for people from all walks of life. It has theoretical, moral and social implications placing it on a collision course against the demands of religions and ideologies. This chapter is structured around four tightly related theses. The first thesis equates the distinction between morality and economics to the distinction between values and interests. The second thesis is that the theoretical foundation of critical rationalism – the secular world-view, and its moral foundation – the secular ethics of individual freedom-independence embedded in the 'belief' in reason alone, are inseparable components of a single existential conception, and logically incompatible with the non-secular world-views and morals of religions and ideologies. The third thesis credits such secular ethics with a unique social role, embodied in the special ethical nature of its imperative for social solidarity and a liberal social order. It is the special nature of this imperative that makes it into the only force capable of withstanding rent-exploitation as the dominant economic incentive encoded in the secular non-morality of personal well-being and social success, and social fundamentalism as the non-liberal substance encoded in a formally liberal social order which allows non-secular moral principles to enter its ethical foundation. The fourth thesis separates moral from social justice. The former belongs to the domain of the protection of values – the secular value of individual freedom-independence, or individual sentiment of self-respect, and has nothing to do with the interpersonal distribution of the satisfaction of interests (well-being). The latter is instead precisely about the equality/inequality of such interpersonal distribution, and has nothing to do with morality.

VALUES AND INTERESTS

In distinguishing values and morality from interests and economics I rely – with some freedom – on Benedetto Croce and Robert Spaemann. In Croce's moral philosophy (1908 [1950]; *filosofia della pratica* in his own words) morality and economics are distinct moments of the life of the mind: I act morally when I want the 'good', whereas I act economically when I want the 'useful'. In Spaemann, theoretical and moral philosophy are essentially one and the same thing, their common core consisting in the 'quest for the truth and meaning' of existence (2007, 1976; *Wahrheits- und Sinnfrage* in his own words). Combining the two perspectives into one I shall say that morality (or ethics, using the two words to mean the same) is concerned with values or ultimate ends, while economics is concerned with interests or instrumental needs or preferences. Moral values – or values *tout court* – are universal principles representing the ultimate end of human life. They lift human life out of its conditional-contingent status by giving it absolute truth and meaning. On the contrary, interests are conditional-contingent facts, things and conditions of the world, regarded as instrumentally useful in relation to the pursuit of some further end. (To say that facts and things of the world have a conditional-contingent status means that they have no intrinsic necessity: their existence depends on the existence of other facts and things of the world, whose existence depends in turn on other facts and things of the world, and so on and so forth. In other words, it means that they are in themselves pointless. In a later section I shall further clarify this concept using Steven Weinberg's characterization of modern science.) In strictly philosophical terms, moral values are a question of belief. In order for a person to have moral values he or she must believe in certain such universal principles, from which he or she derives guidance about what actions are morally good and what morally bad. Instead, interests do not require belief in the absolute meaning of something. A person has interests insofar as he or she regards certain facts of the world as instrumentally useful in relation to some further end that he or she pursues, as means for the satisfaction of needs or preferences. The concept of interest just outlined is a very general one. With philosophical consistency Croce regards the world of economics as complementary to that of morality, encompassing by definition the whole domain of human interests. But most economists regard their research programme as restricted to those interests whose physical nature is such that they can in principle be satisfied by facts, things and states of the world tradable among people, that is, capable of becoming the object of market transactions (Olson, 2000). In view of a later point I need to qualify this restriction by distinguishing between the interests that are rival, that is, conflicting with those of others, and those that are non-rival, that is, not conflicting but shared with others. The former can become the object of trading precisely because of their rivalry. The latter, though they are interests just the same, cannot become the object of trading only and precisely because of their physical non-rivalry.

VALUES AND WORLD-VIEWS: THE SECULAR VIEW OF CRITICAL RATIONALISM VS NON-SECULAR VIEWS

Following conventional practice I use the word 'world-view' for the primary theoretical concept, encompassing statements about facts, or truth-reality, and the word 'ethics' for the primary moral concept, encompassing statements about values, or meaning-goodness. In philosophical terms, in order for true moral values to exist they must by definition be embedded in a corresponding world-view, the theoretical and moral counterparts being strictly inseparable components of a single perception and conception of the world (whatever rational awareness one may actually possess of such intrinsic connection). The most effective way to identify the respective cores of the secular and non-secular views is to put them face to face.

The secular world-view (we may also call it 'scientific', but only on condition that the adjective be stripped of the vaguely dogmatic content attached to it by popular ignorance) is that which underlies the adoption of the so-called rationalist attitude towards the understanding of the world, also known as critical rationalism, whose clearest definition so far is due to Karl Popper (1945 [1966], Chapter 24). It is the particular attitude towards the understanding of the world, including ourselves, according to which such understanding can only be based upon, and expanded by, argument (logic) and experience (facts) – that is, by critical reason. In theoretical terms, the reality of the secular view is the natural world, in the broad sense of both the physical world of the nature investigated by modern hard sciences, as well as the psychological, social and cultural world of human life and history, because it is only this natural reality that allows its understanding to be supported, criticized, corrected and extended, by argument and experience. A consubstantial feature of the rationalist attitude is that it has no room for certainties, or absolute truths. The understanding of the only reality accessible to critical reason can never be certain or absolute, but only and always conjectural or hypothetical, precisely because any piece of it is always, by its very definition, open to the possibility of being invalidated, changed or extended through further arguments or experiences.

By exclusion, non-secular views are those that do not satisfy the requirements of the secular one. They are basically of either the religious or the ideological type. Religious views stand on the claim that the world has some 'ultimate', absolute truth and meaning, reaching out beyond its appearance. They postulate the existence of some ultimately true, absolute, reality encompassing the conditional-contingent natural reality accessible to critical reason. Relative to such superior, transcendent reality the world of critical reason, and critical reason itself, play at most a subordinate role. The 'understanding' of such ultimate reality is non-hypothetical, because it rests on mental processes (faith, beliefs) surpassing critical reason.

As for ideologies, what they do, often only implicitly and in ways that are neither fully apparent nor fully self-aware, is to confuse principles with social facts by assigning some ultimate, absolute truth and meaning to certain facts or conditions of the social (economic and political) order, or to entire social systems or theories. But social facts are conditional-contingent facts of the world which cannot possess as such any absolute meaning. Ideologies fail to comply with the insuperable distinction between conditional-contingent facts of the world and absolute meanings. They are closely related to, though not coincident with, social utopias. Religions give absolute meaning to the natural world by subsuming it into a transcendent, non-contingent reality. Ideologies and social utopias perform a similar type of transposition, but with no claims to transcendence. The former by assigning absolute meaning, and thus also the status of moral values, to conditional-contingent facts and states of the social world, the latter by conceiving an ideal, though non-transcendent, perfect social order with no more obstacles to the complete self-fulfilment of everybody.

NON-SECULAR VALUES

I have already explained my proposition that moral values are universal principles representing the ultimate end of human life, that this is equivalent to giving human life itself absolute truth and meaning, and that if moral values exist they must be embedded in a corresponding world-view. Non-secular values are those that are embedded in non-secular views – religious or ideological. Religions endow the natural world, and human life within it, with absolute truth and meaning by subsuming it into a transcendent reality. By their very nature they also postulate *ab initio* certain values, because a person who believes in an absolute, transcendent reality must also believe in principles representing the ultimate end of his or her own individual life as part of that same reality, that is, in values from which to derive guidance about what actions are morally good and what morally bad. The same is true for ideologies. If a person believes in some absolute meaning of conditional-contingent social facts, then he or she must also believe in principles representing the ultimate end of his or her own individual actions in society, that is, in moral values guiding social behaviour. Ideologies are philosophically untenable, yet psychologically and emotionally powerful answers to the human need for principles capable of giving meaning to one's life and moral guidance to one's behaviour.

THE SECULAR VALUE OF INDIVIDUAL FREEDOM-INDEPENDENCE

A Secular, Meaningless World

Adopting the rationalist attitude has an inescapable implication. The fact that the understanding of the world can only be based on argument and experience implies that such understanding can only be conjectural, because it remains always open to invalidation, change and extension. This implies in turn that by remaining inside the boundaries of the rationalist attitude no absolute truth and meaning can be given to the world. The world of critical reason is meaningless, in the precise sense that all its facts and things have the same, exclusively conditional-contingent status. To clarify what I mean by 'conditional-contingent status' I shall first consider the world investigated by ordinary hard science – the physical and biological sciences – under the universally accepted perspective (accepted in practice by all practicing scientists, and also in theory by almost all of them) described with remarkable clarity by Steven Weinberg (2001, pp. 42ff., 146ff.; 1993, pp. 204ff.). In his words such perspective rests on two lasting scientific discoveries. One, going back to the work of Newton, is that nature is strictly governed by impersonal mathematical laws. The other, going back to the work of Charles Darwin and Alfred Russel Wallace, is the demystification of life engendered by the biology of undesigned evolution. It is a perspective under which the universe is pointless, and life in general and human life in particular have no special place in it. The alternative perspective, which assumes a non-conditional, non-contingent status of the facts of nature, and is being constantly reproposed by Christian believers, is the doctrine of intelligent design: the facts and things of nature are there because there is someone who wants them to be. As a belief this one is, like all others, legitimate, but since it does not rest on any combination of argument and experience it has no relation to the secular view of critical reason. I have referred to the world investigated by ordinary hard science in order to make my point as clear as possible, but it is an essential feature of the secular view that the conditionality-contingency of that world extends *in toto* to the psychological, social and cultural world of human life and history, even if the latter's knowledge and understanding is still widely regarded as lying outside the province of ordinary hard science. Indeed such 'territorial' separation has long since been under challenge in the scientific community by the research programmes of sociobiology and the neurosciences, trained on bringing back the whole world of animal (human and non-human) behaviour into the domain of ordinary hard science. Psychological states like emotions and sentiments, as well as the mental processes forming the very acts of thinking and choosing – in short the life of what is known as the 'mind' of humans and other highly developed species – are to be understood as the product of undesigned biological evolution, in the same way as we understand, for instance, the specialization of Brazilian leaf-cutter ants into foragers, workers of different sizes and giant soldiers. At a deeper level the animal brain is to be treated as a 'machine', albeit enormously complex, whose mechanical working is investigated by the neurosciences.[2]

A Secular, Valueless World

By my logic so far, the meaningless world of critical reason has no room for true moral values, because these require a belief in the absolute meaning of something. A meaningless world is by definition a valueless world, and those who embrace – more or less consciously – the secular view are, by logical necessity, people without truly moral beliefs. By this I do not mean that they cannot be honest, tolerant, generous and altruistic. They can, of course. My point is different. It is that reducing morality to a person's altruistic sentiments and behavioural code is a mistake stemming from a deficient understanding of morality's place in spiritual life. Therefore we must conclude that their 'moral sentiments' – genuine and deep as they may be – simply cannot ultimately rest on any belief in true moral values.

A Unique Secular Ethics

It is one of the central contentions of this chapter that the preceding assertion would be true only if the adoption of the rationalist attitude underlying the secular view were not brought to its ultimate logical consequences. If it is, then the assertion is doubly false for the following reasons: (1) there exists a unique moral value which is logically compatible with the adoption of the rationalist attitude, and which I shall call the secular value of individual freedom-independence; and (2) this unique secular value is actually also logically implied by that adoption. In other words, what is true for the non-secular views and morals of religions and ideologies is also true for the rationalist attitude. Like religions and ideologies, the rationalist attitude has not only a theoretical foundation – the secular world-view; but also a moral foundation – the secular value of individual freedom-independence, and the two are bound together as inseparable components of a single perception and conception of existence, based on the non-rational yet secular belief in reason alone.

   The assertion that the adoption of the rationalist attitude cannot in turn be itself supported by argument and experience, that it depends instead on the 'irrational' option to believe in reason alone, and that it has a moral dimension, has been argued with powerful simplicity by Popper on the ground that the opposite claim is logically untenable because it is a form of the paradox of the liar (1945 [1966], Chapter 24). Other philosophers of the critical rationalist school, notably Hans Albert, claim that also all moral beliefs should be regarded in principle as subjectable to rational criticism (1980, pp. 55–79). But this would somehow strip them of their non-conditional, non-contingent nature, and I hold Popper's characterization of the critical rationalist option as irrational to be precisely what gives it its truly moral nature.

Connecting the logical necessity of a non-rational belief in reason alone with Croce's concept of the identity between consciousness, freedom and morality (1943 [1988]) yields the logical basis for identifying the essential moral counterpart of the secular view in the unique secular value of individual freedom-independence. Reason is not only an abstract concept. It is also a fact of the natural world: the personal experience of consciousness and self-consciousness, or capacity to have thought and volition, which coincides with the individual's awareness of his own identity as a free and independent being relative to the rest of the world, with nothing above and nothing below himself. The individual moral freedom-independence I am talking about here is not to be confused with the completely different non-moral concept of freedom of action, which consists in the absence of physical or social obstacles to doing something or other. It coincides instead precisely and exclusively, in itself and without qualifications, with individual consciousness and self-consciousness.

Believing in reason alone is the same thing as believing in individual freedom-independence. But reason is the hallmark of mankind, and the belief in reason is also the belief in the unity of mankind, because it cannot concern this or that individual, depending on circumstances, but necessarily and always everybody everywhere. It necessarily becomes the recognition of the freedom-independence not only of oneself but also of everyone else. Popper says that 'rationalism is closely connected with the belief in the unity of mankind', but I carry his point one step further: the two are more than connected, they are inseparable components of the same belief. It follows that this special concept of individual freedom-independence is in itself the absolute, yet secular meaning of human life.

Independence and Responsibility

But the idea of independence is inseparable from that of (moral) responsibility. In fact the two ideas taken separately are meaningless, and acquire meaning only by being related to one another: there exists no independence without responsibility nor responsibility without independence. The belief in reason alone forces upon whoever understands and accepts its full existential implications a responsibility towards himself, his fellow men, and the living world in general of which he is a part (Wilson, 2006, 1984), and confers on him a dignity and honour, of a very special kind. It is the unique responsibility, dignity and honour intrinsically associated with the universal secular principle of individual freedom-independence. Thus this concept of individual freedom-independence is also the secular value embedded in the secular view of critical reason. It is the essence of the unique secular ethics encoded in the acceptance of a world with no god (Weinberg, 2008, 1993), no hopes in an afterlife, no promises of a final justice. It is logically compatible with the adoption of critical rationalism because the personal experience of consciousness and self-consciousness is a fact of the natural world. It is also logically implied by it because critical rationalism does not stand on itself. It stands on a 'belief' in reason alone which goes beyond reason itself, conferring on reason and individual consciousness and self-consciousness an absolute meaning:

> Since freedom is the essence of man, and man owns it in his quality as man, we can't take literally and materially the proposition that we must 'give freedom' to man, it being something that cannot be given to him because he already has it. So much so that it also cannot be taken away from him ... That proposition, properly understood, means simply that there is a moral obligation to always favour and promote freedom, which is the very life of man, and while in its negative content that proposition prohibits every action aimed at diminishing it, in its positive content it commands to only act for its increase ... It is sometimes foolishly asked what should one do with the freedom he owns or has regained or revived, as if it were some idle force waiting for somebody to use it or to suggest or order what it should do. But idle forces do not exist in reality ... because a force exists only when it works ... and freedom doesn't search or ask others for a content which it is lacking, because it is itself this very content ... Since freedom coincides in every respect with morality and contains in itself every moral obligation, there is no task of such nature lying outside its reach. (Croce, 1943 [1988]; my translation)

Croce's freedom is strictly the freedom not of the individual but of the mind; it is the life of the mind, because in idealistic philosophy it is the mind – the spirit – that is real, not the physical world. His freedom underplays the physical dimension of personal identity. Bringing such physical dimension back into the concept preserves the validity of his intuition (the identity between consciousness, freedom and morality), and at the same time strengthens its philosophical foundation and social implications.

THE SOCIAL ROLE OF SECULAR ETHICS: SOCIAL SOLIDARITY

Social Solidarity and Social Responsibility

By social solidarity I mean the fact of having respect and care not only for one's own interests, as one does by definition, but also for the interests of all other members of the same human family, recognizing such interests to have in principle the same value as one's own. It is the same thing as social generosity or altruism, where 'social' means that it must hold for every other human being as such. It must be distinguished from the respect and care for people with whom a person has bonds of a personal nature, such as partner, family, friends, and so on, which is simply an extension of one's care for oneself. And also from the so-called 'group solidarity', restricted to people sharing certain characteristics (ethnic, cultural, social, and so on).

Possessing social solidarity so defined has radical implications in terms of a person's social responsibility and behaviour. First, an uncompromising commitment to personal honesty in one's social life (absolute personal honesty is indeed the first and foremost expression of social generosity, but not surprisingly this is widely overlooked in non-secular cultures, which tend to identify generosity and altruism with 'giving' to others and 'direct dedication' to their needs). Second, a sense of the state, meaning the capacity of a person to perceive and value his public interests (his non-rival, common interests shared in his political capacity with the other members of a political community) no less than his private interests (his rival ones, conflicting with those of others). Third, a willingness to participate in social redistribution, both privately and when acting in one's political role, this meaning precisely a willingness to 'pay' for the satisfaction of other people's interests by forgoing the satisfaction of his or her own.

Since social solidarity, in order for the concept to make sense, must be defined in terms not of values but of interests, it has no moral status in its own right. Indeed, as already explained, it does not require morality for its existence. A person may have respect and care for the well-being of his fellow men, and act in a socially responsible way, and yet have no beliefs in moral values.

However, social solidarity does acquire an indirect moral status when it descends from moral beliefs. It is, in particular, an obvious implication of secular ethics that if a person believes in the unique secular value of individual freedom-independence, then he or she must possess social solidarity as a necessary consequence. It is another of my central contentions that the distinction between social solidarity as a well-defined non-moral, interest-based concept, and the unique secular value of individual freedom-independence generating it, is far more than a point of logic. The sentiment and practice of social solidarity descending from the belief in individual freedom-independence as the absolute secular meaning of human life have a special, unique power and depth, which, if they did not descend from it, they could never have. Indeed, and more dramatically, a cultural milieu where they do not descend from it contains the seeds of two far-reaching social consequences.

The Non-Moral Message of Personal Well-Being, Social Success and Power

First, a person who recognizes himself de facto in the secular view (whatever the degree of his rational awareness of it[3]) but fails to understand its powerful ethical dimension is, strictly, a person without moral beliefs. Any sentiment of social solidarity he may have, however deep and genuine, is bound to remain confined to the domain of human interests, whose non-moral nature is not converted into morality by virtue of their social nobility. As such it would be intrinsically weak, not in any practical or psychological sense, but in the cultural-moral one, because it would lack the strength of moral beliefs, and would therefore be easily displaced by more powerful behavioural incentives. The world of critical reason is – in itself – a valueless world. In contemporary liberal capitalist societies the valueless secular view has become the dominant ingredient of culture, customs and institutions, though widely disguised under the cover of contrary (and sometimes well-meaning) protestations If the appreciation of its powerful ethical dimension is insufficient, or shared by too few people, the room left empty by the absence of a true (secular) morality will inevitably be occupied by the secular non-morality of the drive for personal well-being, social success and power, pursued with all means as the primary reason of life. In the resulting moral vacuum it will be impossible to prevent the assertion of the self over the others, the overwhelming of individual and group interests over each other and over the citizens' public interests, the wealth-destructive compounding of economic and political rent power, from becoming the only actual standard of morality. Under such conditions it is naive to expect even an ideally perfect system of incentive-based rules for markets, the non-market (public) economy, and political institutions, ever to succeed in protecting society from being dominated by the incentive for rent-exploitation. The incentive to bend markets and politics for the pursuit of rent-exploitation has been proved to be always enormously stronger than all the efficiency-oriented ones devised by well-meaning economists. It is equally naive to expect any such good system of incentive-based rules ever to be established, because there are no reasons why the logic of rent-exploitation should remain constrained within any such system, as if it were superimposed on society from the outside. Any such system will inevitably be distorted by the same logic.

The Violation of the Individual's Moral Freedom-Independence by Religions and Ideologies

Second, if the sentiment and practice of social solidarity are based not on the secular value of individual freedom-independence but on religious or ideological values, then they will be perfectly capable of coexisting with the actual violation of the moral freedom-independence of the single human beings as individuals. Ethical beliefs derived from religious or ideological views may not recognize individual freedom-independence as a moral value. If so its violation lies *in re ipsa*. But even when they do recognize it, they do so in a fictitious way. In non-secular views the absolute meaning of human life lies in transcendence, or in facts and conditions of the social world transcending individual existence. Even if individual freedom-independence may appear to be compatible with such absolute meanings, it cannot possess the absolute primacy pertaining to a moral value in its own right because it is ideally and practically subordinated to superior transcendent or social principles. Any absolute meaning of human life set in transcendence or in facts and conditions of the social world contains the premises for the actual violation of the secular moral freedom-independence of the single human being as an individual. This claim is supported not only by logic, as explained, but also by an overwhelming historical evidence.

The Secular Bond between Human and Non-Human Life

Under the secular view all forms of life on earth share with each other the natural bond of life itself, and no primacy is conferred from the outside on any one of them. It is in this sense that the secular absolute meaning of human life carries over to the totality of the living world. It endows this natural life-bond with a secular moral dimension, extending the individual's unique moral responsibility towards his or her fellow men to the living world in general of which he or she is a part. The secular bond binding humans to the totality of the living world, and the related secular morality of a human responsibility towards it, have been investigated by many contemporary scientists, and most notably by Edward O. Wilson (2006, 1998, 1984). They are with full right an essential component of secular ethics.

THE SOCIAL ROLE OF SECULAR ETHICS: SOCIAL FREEDOM

Social Freedom

The concept of freedom used so far is a moral concept, defined in terms of the individual's personal experience of his or her own consciousness and self-consciousness, with no reference to any other fact of the physical and social world. It must not be confused with the non-moral concept of 'social freedom' used in the social sciences. This I take from Isaiah Berlin (1969, pp. xlvii, 122 ff.), who in turn draws it from the 'the most celebrated of its champions', John Stuart Mill.

Social freedom has two equally necessary social dimensions: a negative and a positive one. 'Negative' freedom is a well-defined specification of the concept of freedom of action. It is the freedom of a person in society to act in 'the pursuit of his own good in his own way', and must be conceived in terms of the degree to which no social coercive power constrains his activity. It is the social answer to the question: 'How much am I to be governed?' and is practically determined by the existing laws and institutions establishing, regulating and ensuring civic and economic freedoms.

'Positive' freedom as a distinct concept arises from the fact that a complete absence of social coercive interference is unthinkable, because the negative freedom of someone must not displace an equivalent negative freedom of somebody else. Therefore the need arises to conceive a positive freedom in terms of the possibility of a person to participate in the choice and dismissal of the political authority having the coercive power to constrain (regulate) his negative freedom. It is the social answer to the question: 'By whom am I to be governed?' and is practically determined by the existing laws and institutions concerning the formation and exercise of the political coercive power of government (in particular the institutions of political democracy, where they exist). A liberal social order is one based on laws and institutions ensuring both dimensions of social freedom to everybody to some maximum feasible degree, which of course cannot be fixed in the abstract, but only in relation to contingent social and cultural conditions. The distinction between the moral and social concepts of freedom has, in parallel to the previous one between moral beliefs and social solidarity, two implications concerning the foundations of the social fabric.

The Necessity of a Liberal Social Order

Firstly, neither the concept of social freedom nor its institutional counterpart of a liberal social order have the status of moral values in their own right, because they are defined in terms of facts and states of the social world. The laws and institutions of a liberal social order are however a necessary condition, though not a sufficient one, for the safeguarding and promotion of the secular value of individual freedom-independence. A non-liberal social order is one explicitly aimed not at protecting and extending the negative and positive freedom of the individual, but at restricting or eliminating them. As such it is explicitly founded on the disregard and violation of a person's moral freedom-independence, or sentiment of self-respect.[4]

Public vs Private Values: Social Fundamentalism

Secondly, since the belief in non-secular views and values is legitimate, and must be respected and guaranteed in a liberal social order, the well-known problem arises of what type of coexistence is possible in it between the unique secular morality and the many different moral values derived from non-secular views. A logical coexistence is clearly impossible, but this does not prevent the possibility of a political coexistence, based on separating public (or objective) from private (or subjective) values.

A value becomes public when it enters the ethical foundation of the system of rules and government of the political community. It is private when it does not. If a social order is to be liberal not only in form but also in substance, its system of rules and government must carry the secular morality of individual freedom-independence as its only ethical foundation. For this to happen that unique secular morality must be understood and recognized as the only morality acceptable as public by the people from all walks of life, irrespective of their social status, religious or ideological convictions, or degree of rational awareness of it. The fact that certain values must remain private does not mean that they must be prevented from having circulation and visibility in society, but that the modes of such circulation and visibility must face a non-trespassable barrier. It means that those values can enter the ethical foundation only of the life of those who accept them, who in turn can transmit them to others only through the cultural exchange of the reasons and sentiments supporting them, but never through the exercise of the political coercive power of government, however deep the democratic legitimation of such power may be.

A social order in which values derived from non-secular views enter the ethical foundation of its system of rules and government becomes non-liberal in substance, even if it preserves the forms of a liberal one. It becomes in fact a fundamentalist social order which, for this very reason, constitutes a violation of the moral freedom-independence of every individual. The theoretical foundation of these propositions needs to be emphasized. If the world of critical reason were a meaningless and valueless world, then the system of rules and government of a liberal social order would, strictly speaking, have no ethical foundation. If moral values could only be derived from non-secular views, then also the injection of an ethical foundation into that system could only come from non-secular views. The form of a liberal social order would then be the same thing as its substance. Its form would completely fulfil its liberal role by ensuring the practical coexistence of different non-secular public values with each other and with the secular absence of values, within some 'largest' feasible area of negative and positive social freedoms. The rationale of this role would completely exhaust itself in establishing a viable compromise between different behavioural codes. It would be utterly devoid of any moral substance.

It is a further central contention of this chapter that this view is wrong. The world of critical reason is neither meaningless nor valueless. It holds in its core a powerful secular ethics as strong as, and indeed stronger than, any ethics derived from non-secular views. The substance of a liberal social order is far more than its form, because it consists precisely of this unique secular ethics. A liberal social order's system of rules and government is not a moral vacuum in need of being filled with religious and ideological values. Since it does have its own ethical foundation, theoretically exhaustive and logically incompatible with any other, it demands that all other values be kept out of the public ground.[5]

SOCIAL AND MORAL JUSTICE

Related to the distinction between a moral and a social (non-moral) concept of freedom is the distinction between a moral and a social (non-moral) concept of justice. By logic, moral justice must be defined in terms of values, and social justice in terms of interests. Having reduced economic interests to a subspecies of the more general concept, for the sake of simplicity I shall talk of social justice using the 'reduced' concept of economic justice as a proxy. Following Carl Christian von Weizsäcker (2005), who in turn goes as far back as Aristotle, social justice can be further decomposed into two types: commutative and distributive.

Commutative Justice

Commutative justice is ensured when economic transactions between agents take place under conditions of total absence of power (of one or more agents over one or more of the others). In standard economics this is equivalent to saying that they are taking place under perfectly competitive conditions. Of course in the real world power is never absent, but ideal conditions make perfect sense as a benchmark for judging actual ones. Technically, the concept of perfectly competitive transactions applies only to private economic interests, satisfied through trading. Its extension to public economic interests and collective-political action requires some adaptation because shared interests cannot by definition be satisfied through trading. The extension is provided by another standard concept of economics. Collective-political decisions entail by definition the exercise of some kind of power (by some agents over some others), namely the political coercive power of government forming the core of a political community. Even under an ideal perfectly working direct democracy, collective-political decisions must be taken according to some kind of majority rule, entailing the exercise of power by the majority over the minority. Nevertheless an abstract no-power benchmark holding for the political scenario is the so-called Lindahl shares model, in which the exercise of political power would virtually vanish through its reduction to the unanimity condition.

An equivalent, perhaps more suggestive definition of commutative justice uses directly the concept of rent-exploitation power (Olson, 2000). All societies are exposed to the rent-exploitation power of single agents or organized groups to secure benefits for themselves by engaging not in the creation of additional social wealth, but in the distributional struggle aimed at subtracting an equivalent amount of benefits from others, out of a given output of social wealth. Exercising such rent power alters the distribution of benefits among the people of a community relative to what it would be if such rent power did not exist (it actually also destroys potential wealth creation in the process, but this is here irrelevant). The level of economic well-being enjoyed by an individual is the degree to which he or she can satisfy his or her economic interests through the access to private and public goods – including primary ones like health care, education and culture, which contribute more than others to his or her private and public human capital (Olson, 1996) – thereby enhancing his or her opportunities for self-realization and social participation. Any distribution of economic well-being – however measured and however unequal – among individuals satisfies the requirements of commutative justice when there is total absence of rent acquisition as defined.

Distributive Justice and Equality

The very essence of distributive justice is its egalitarian content. Ideally it should be defined in terms of the equality, or degree of inequality, in the distribution of general well-being among different individuals, where the general well-being enjoyed by an individual is the degree to which he can satisfy his interests of all kinds. Many economists and psychologists, adherents of the fashionable science of happiness, claim that this degree can be precisely identified with a fact of the natural world called experienced utility or happiness, which can be scientifically treated as an observable, measurable and interpersonally comparable quantity.

Physical and psychological pain and pleasure are certainly facts of the natural world accompanying every instant of one's life, but in my approach, centred on the distinction between morality and economics, the true nature of interests is behavioural: they are no more and no less than the very actions and choices made because they are considered as useful means in the pursuit of some further end. This approach suggests that: (1) identifying them instead with some observable, measurable, comparable quantity of pain or pleasure is a mistake; (2) defining distributive justice-equality in terms of the equality/inequality between quantities of experienced utility-happiness of different individuals is meaningless and misleading; and (3) any empirical definition of distributive justice-equality ought to be based on observable, measurable and comparable things and facts of the natural world representing people's outward conditions and behaviour rather than their inward physical, emotional and mental states.[6]

However, whatever our position on the treatment of happiness as a measurable quantity, or on the relationship between happiness, economic well-being, income–consumption–wealth, and other external multidimensional welfare indicators, my point here is another one. I claim that any concept of social justice-equality, however amply defined to include both commutative and distributional aspects, an emphasis on human capital, capabilities and opportunities for self-realization, and experienced utility-happiness over external welfare indicators, remains intrinsically confined to the domain of interests, and of material interpersonal distribution. It therefore does not possess in itself the status of a moral value, nor does it acquire one by the fact of being deemed desirable for all sorts of beneficial social effects.

The work of John Rawls (1971), Ronald Dworkin (2000) and Amartya Sen (1999), as well as of the many students of the science of happiness, has certainly deepened our current understanding of the notion and social impact of social justice-equality, but insofar as it treats the issue as a moral one in its own right, it runs into the ideological trap of giving to facts and conditions of the social world a status of moral values in their own right, thereby loading itself with potentially far-reaching socio-political consequences. Since moral values are universal principles giving an absolute meaning to human life, there is no rational support for the claim that any such absolute meaning may be related to the level of an individual's well-being, let alone the quantity of his or her happiness or good mood, and even less so to some relationship between his or her own well-being and that of others, irrespective of the way in which level and relationship are defined.

Moral Justice

If the concept of justice is to have any moral status, it must be defined using values. Following Avishai Margalit (1996) I shall say that a society is morally just not insofar as it guarantees some degree of socio-economic equality, however defined and measured, but insofar as it avoids and prevents any sort of behaviour, condition and rule that may cause a person, and especially the most disadvantaged, to suffer that particular human spiritual pain which is humiliation, consisting precisely in the injuring of one's sentiment of self-respect (which – as already argued   coincides in every aspect with the sentiment of his or her moral freedom-independence). Thus it seems appropriate to conceive a morally just social order more in a negative than in a positive sense, as one that avoids and prevents the injuring of a person's sentiment of self-respect, dignity and honour, or moral freedom-independence. The moral injustice of a social order or state may be caused by facts and conditions lying within and without the province of economics.

Within that province the obvious instance of moral injustice is that of people who are in a state of absolute poverty and social exclusion, particularly when combined with extreme socio-economic inequality. If the degree to which a person can live his own life by his own means falls below some minimum physical-social level of subsistence, his sentiment of self-respect may not be destroyed, but is certainly damaged, and hindered in its potential development. Other instances are all sorts of discriminations based on requisites not related to the nature of some particular job or transaction.

However, moral injustice occurs also, and in fact primarily, outside the province of economics. In my discussion of social freedom I have already demonstrated the moral injustice of a non-liberal social order, and of a fundamentalist social order liberal in form but hosting non-secular values in its ethical foundation. But I want to emphasize how far the secular concept of moral justice reaches beyond economics, because this helps in bringing out the full meaning (i) of Margalit's concept, and more generally (ii) of distinguishing justice as a moral issue from justice as a non-moral (social) one.

A recent discussion of the subject of embryo research regulation by the philosopher Jürgen Habermas (2001) is particularly suited to the purpose. The current state of embryo research already allows people, under existing liberal regulations, to recognize embryos with fateful hereditary diseases and to destroy them (negative eugenics). It is likely that further research will soon make it possible to treat such hereditary diseases at the embryonic stage (positive eugenics), and then furthermore for parents to programme children according to their wishes. This would put the relationship between two human beings, the designer and the designed, in a state of fundamental imbalance, and the designed might come to regard his own identity-independence to be existentially diminished, in a totally different way from any kind of conditioning sustained through the exposure to social and educational influences. It is for these reasons – Habermas claims – that a liberal regulation of the manipulation of the genetic endowment of embryos for such constructive purposes should be rejected. Whether one agrees or not with him on the specific issue of acceptance vs rejection, his reasons do not depend on any belief in a supposed non-secular supernatural status of the embryo, and would be in no contradiction with the acceptance of a liberal regulation of abortion. To me they are precisely the reasons of the unique secular ethics placed in the centre of this chapter.

NOTES

1. I wish to thank an anonymous referee, whose tough criticism has forced me to raise, hopefully, the standard of logic and clarity of the arguments in support of my central tenets.
2. Specific references to the technical literature of these research fields are outside the scope of this chapter. My reflection here draws on Lewontin (2005, pro secular view, but not much sympathy for the ambitions of sociobiology), Wilson (1998, 1984) and Searle (1997).
3. I emphasize this point on purpose. When stressing the importance of certain conceptual distinctions (absolute meaning vs conditionality-contingency; secular vs non-secular world-views, and so on) I certainly do not mean that in order to perceive them people need some kind of professional training in philosophy. I think of them as distinctions characterizing the intimate attitude towards life of every self-conscious human being, quite independently from his literacy, formal education, temperament or intelligence.

4. It is worth remembering that Croce himself did not endorse the claim of some necessary relationship between the promotion–protection of moral freedom and a particular social order. This was an 'honest mistake' imputable to idealistic philosophy which, by regarding freedom as the essence of the universal 'mind', has little room for the physical dimension of personal identity.

5. In discussing this chapter Bruno Frey suggested that more emphasis should be given to people's 'demand' for this secular value. Granted that individual moral freedom-independence is the unique secular value, what can be done if the demand for it by people were non-existent or insufficient? My answer lies in the social consequences and implications outlined above. Educating people to recognize in every person's moral freedom-independence the only source of public morality is a difficult task, facing powerful adversaries. Unfortunately nothing can be done to avoid the social and moral costs of its failure.

6. The study of physical, emotional and mental states (including for instance such diseases as depression and bipolar disorder) belong to the research programmes of medicine, psychiatry and psychology, not to those of sociology and economics; in the same way as the study of the volatility of stock market prices belongs to the research programme of finance, and not to that of physics. This does not mean that a research programme cannot benefit from interacting with another. It only means, more modestly, that there is nothing to gain, and much to lose, by confusing one with the other.

REFERENCES

Albert, Hans (1980), *Traktat über kritische Vernunft*, 4th edn, Tübingen: J.C.B. Mohr.

Berlin, Isaiah (1969), *Four Essays on Liberty*, Oxford: Oxford University Press.

Croce, Benedetto (1943), 'Revisione filosofica dei concetti di "libertà" e "giustizia"', *La Critica*, **41** (5), pp. 276–84; reprinted in B. Croce and L. Einaudi (1988), *Liberismo e liberalismo*, 2nd edn, Milan-Naples: Riccardo Ricciardi Editore, pp. 85–97.

Croce, Benedetto (1908), *Filosofia della pratica. Economica ed etica*, 6th revised edn 1950, Bari: Laterza.

Dworkin, Ronald (2000), *Sovereign Virtue: The Theory and Practice of Equality*, Cambridge, MA: Harvard University Press.

Habermas, Jürgen (2001), *Die Zukunft der menschlichen Natur. Auf dem Weg zu einer liberalen Eugenik?* Frankfurt a.M.: Suhrkamp Verlag.

Lewontin, Richard (2005), 'The wars over evolution', *New York Review of Books*, **52** (16), 51–4.

Margalit, Avishai (1996), *The Decent Society*, Cambridge, MA: Harvard University Press.

Olson, Mancur (1996), 'Distinguished Lecture on Economics in Government: Big Bills Left on the Sidewalk. Why Some Nations are Rich and Others Poor', *Journal of Economic Perspectives*, **10** (2), 3–24.

Olson, Mancur (2000), *Power and Prosperity*, New York: Basic Books.

Popper, Karl R. (1945), *The Open Society and its Enemies*, 5th edn 1966, New York: Routledge & Kegan Paul.

Rawls, John (1971), *A Theory of Justice*, Cambridge, MA: Harvard University Press.

Searle, John M. (1997), *The Mystery of Consciousness*, The New York Review of Books.

Sen, Amartya (1999), *Development as Freedom*, Oxford: Oxford University Press.

Spaemann, Robert (1976), 'Sinnstiftung in einer hypothetischen Zivilisation. Antwort auf eine Herausforderung der Gegenwart', *Neue Zürcher Zeitung*, Literatur und Kunst, 10.12.1976.

Spaemann, Robert (2007), *Der letzte Gottesbeweis*, Munich: Pattloch Verlag.
von Weizsäcker, Carl Christian (2005), 'Gerechtigkeit, Freiheit und Wohlstand. Die Auflösung einer vermeintlichen Antinomie', *Neue Zürcher Zeitung*, Fokus der Wirtschaft, 14/15.5.2005.
Weinberg, Steven (1993), *Dreams of a Final Theory*, London: Vintage Books.
Weinberg, Steven (2001), *Facing Up: Science and its Cultural Adversaries*, Cambridge, MA: Harvard University Press.
Weinberg, Steven (2008),'Without God', Phi Beta Kappa Oration, Harvard University, June.
Wilson, Edward O. (1984), *Biophylia*, Cambridge, MA: Harvard University Press.
Wilson, Edward O. (1998), *Consilience: The Unity of Knowledge*, New York: Vintage Books.
Wilson, Edward O. (2006), *The Creation*, New York: W.W. Norton & Company.

4. Conceptual confusions, ethics and economics

Hartmut Kliemt

INTRODUCTION AND OVERVIEW

The neoclassical economist tends to believe that rational normative argument is confined to pointing out means–ends relationships. The ends must be those of somebody, and a rational normative argument is valid relative to given ends, aims or values shared by the addressee of the argument. Beyond this kind of justificatory relativism economists tend to subscribe to the metaphysical or ontological thesis that there are no objective values. This in turn leads to non-cognitivism since nothing can be known about what does not exist. Such an epistemological view about the structure of the world or at least the structure of appearance is often mixed up with justificatory relativism. But the two positions are distinct. At least conceivably, somebody could believe that there are some objective values in the world whose presence or absence could be ascertained like, say, the presence or absence of colors (secondary qualities), and at the same time maintain that whatever rationally compelling force a normative argument might have is relative to given ends, aims or values of the addressee of the argument.

The economist will typically believe that what matters is the assent of the addressee of the argument to some basic value statement or other. To the extent that the assent will not be forthcoming the economist as justificatory relativist can offer no rationally compelling argument in terms of given aims, ends or values of the addressee of the argument. His (or her) standard of a valid argument is not met even though he might believe in the existence of values that can in principle be 'objectively' ascertained. He, for instance, might accept that values have a status comparable to 'secondary qualities' like colors. He is a kind of cognitivist who accepts that some are 'ethically blind' just like others are 'color blind'. At the same time he may still be a justificatory relativist who assigns the specific status of being rationally justified only to those arguments that claim to be valid merely relative to aims, ends or values of their addressee.

Many economists will add to such statements that they think that there is some intersubjectivity even in normative judgment. The methodologically more conservative will insist that intersubjectively valid value judgments of economics are restricted to the diagnosis of Pareto improvements. The methodologically more daring go beyond the real unanimity that should be rationally forthcoming due to the fact that the Pareto criterion is applicable to the merely conceivable unanimity of contractarianism (presumably, most notably, Buchanan, 1999; Brennan and Buchanan, 1985). Practically all economists agree, though, that there is, first, subjective value in the sense that individual actors do desire certain states of affairs to emerge and, second, that these desires deserve to be respected by the economist as prima facie valuable.[1]

How the preceding concepts hang together I will try to clarify subsequently. I believe that, quite independently of how we answer the ontological questions concerning the existence or non-existence of (objective) value(s), it is wise to distinguish between explicitly relativist and allegedly non-relativist justifications. The meta-ethical perspective I will apply is critical rationalist in the sense of Hans Albert and akin to that of John L. Mackie.[2] But it is that of Robbinsian welfare economics as well. Economists who intend to go beyond traditional Robbinsian welfare economics may, of course, do so within an appropriately defined variant of normative economics. The adherents of justificatory relativism have no monopoly rights on defining what normative economics is. Competing concepts of normative economics are possible and may raise a claim to rational justification. It is illegitimate, however, to act as if the justificatory argument of such 'new normative economics' would be based on the same innocuous forms of normative argument as that of the old Robbinsian ways. Those who think that modern normative ethics should be brought to bear on normative economic problems should be honest enough to admit that they are doing something other than traditional Robbinsian welfare economics. It might also be noted that at least since the times of Hume a full-fledged ethical theory of moral institutions has been developed within the argumentative constraints of justificatory relativism.

Subsequently it will be illustrated in some more detail that Robbinsian normative economics is a twin of modern relativist ethics. First, I will try to show that it was quite natural for economists to come to relativistic conclusions about the possibility of a 'normative moral science'. Second, I will sort out what is and what is not plausible of the economists' relativism and explicate such terms as hypothetical and categorical imperatives, ethical particularism and ethical universalism and so on in ways that lay out the several fallacies that seem to occur here. Third, it is shown how the relativistic meta-ethical outlook on rational norm justification (justification in terms of hypothetical imperatives) so popular among economists ever since Robbins' essay on the nature and significance of economic science hangs together with substantive norms of tolerance towards others.

MORAL SENSE OR NO SENSE?

On Knowing Right and Wrong

Relativism and non-relativism each come in many different 'brands'. But specific distinctions are of minor interest here. Generally speaking the terms stand for meta-ethical categories. Using them we are talking about ethics rather than 'talking ethics'. They are 'meta-' in being one level up or above the substantive issues of whether or not we ought – or ought not – to do certain things.

Discussing the truth or falsehood of 'relativism' or 'non-relativism' we are not interested in defending or attacking specific normative ethical views as substantively true or false. We are not talking about such substantive questions as whether abortion is right or wrong, but rather about the question of whether or not the claim that abortion is right or wrong makes sense and, if so, what sense it makes. We consider how we can rationally discuss substantive normative claims at all. The relativist believes that we cannot have a valid normative argument or value judgment independent of what the addressee of the argument ultimately desires, wants or accepts. The non-relativist believes that we can know right from wrong in a way that is not relative to the addressee and his factual aims, ends or values. The relativist subscribes to what may be called 'addressee-relativity' while the non-relativist believes in 'addressee-independent' normative argument.

It seems that adherents of both meta-ethical non-relativism as well as of meta-ethical relativism have been around practically since systematic ethical discourse began. Even before the distinction between ethics and meta-ethics was more fully understood, ethical theorists always have been engaged in disputes concerning the status of knowledge claims in ethics. In that sense the controversy is not distinctively modern. But the controversy became more intense and also better understood in modern times – in particular in the twentieth century.

Facts and Values in Perception and Justification

At the turn of the twentieth century G.E. Moore had discussed the meaning of terms like 'good' and the difficulties attached to an adequate explication of the term. For example, a yellow banana and a yellow car exhibit the quality of 'yellowness' but can we say that a good banana and a good car 'share' the quality of 'goodness'? Is there a quality that is common to a good banana and a good car? If 'good' does not stand for a natural quality, like 'yellow' stands for 'yellowness', does it refer to a non-natural one? If 'good things' do not have any quality in common, what then, if there is any definite one at all, is the meaning of 'good'? Such were some of the questions discussed.

According to one view of the matter terms like 'good' are without descriptive meaning. This seems to rule out that the presence of the qualities underlying the judgment that something is 'good' can be directly observed (at least not as 'described'). Therefore, if science proper must be based on observation, then scientific research on what is good seems impossible. Since philosophers were reluctant to declare terms like 'good' meaningless altogether, it was speculated that such terms rather than serving descriptive functions might conceivably serve as indicators of approval and means of persuasion. According to some accounts using the word 'good' was perceived like shouting 'hurrah' in a crowd. But shouting approval (or disapproval) in a crowd seems to be rather different from our use of the word 'good' in other contexts. In many contexts at least we use the term 'good' not in the arbitrary way of expressing approval. Our common use is rather relying on criteria that are open to, or at least claim to be subject to, intersubjective discussion.

The standards and criteria to which we refer when using the term 'good' seem so strong to many laymen and theorists alike that they feel that there must be something like a 'sense of goodness'. Whenever we see somebody perform an act like rescuing a child out of a fire we spontaneously approve of the act and say that it was a good one. We tend to do so independently of any personal involvement or interest in the matter. It is almost inconceivable that somebody would judge otherwise, and if so there would have to be a very specific explanation for the dissent like racial hatred (which most of us on other accounts will classify as 'bad', of course).

There does not seem to be much difference between spontaneous judgments of good or bad and stating, say, that the banana in front of us is yellow. In all such cases our response to the stimuli of the situation is coming forward spontaneously. Direct observational statements of the 'value qualities' of certain situations seem alike in this respect. People make mistakes in both cases (for example somebody classifies something as yellow though it may be orange; somebody says they thought this was a good deed at first but then they came to a different conclusion). There is some uncertainty, but the degree of interpersonal stability and similarity of judgments may be about the same in both cases.

In view of the preceding, one might claim that either observational statements of fact are as dubious and weak as intuitive value judgments, or intuitive value judgments are as strongly intersubjective as observational statements of fact. This seems to raise an obvious question: if elementary statements of observational and evaluative qualities are of comparable intersubjective stability, why make so much fuss about the fact–value distinction? After all, what really seems to matter is intersubjective stability of basic judgments rather than their nature as observational or not. If we have this stable basis we seem to be able to test our general theories by confronting them with that basis.

Again, we seem to 'see' the color of yellow in a different way than we 'perceive' the quality of goodness. If there is any such quality at all, we do not 'see' the latter – at least not in any proper sense of the term. As opposed to our perception of yellow our perception of goodness is not of the kind of an act of seeing. But this may not be such an important difference to perceptions of value.[3] Many observations that we make are not of the primitive kind of seeing a color. And even in 'seeing' elementary things very strong conventional elements do play a role. For instance, people in the Western world who have been brought up in an environment in which rectangular objects are prevalent will fall victim to errors when confronted with parallelograms, while others like members of the Zulu tribe who are used to living in an environment in which circular forms dominate can be deceived by playing appropriate tricks on their observations concerning circular forms.

The human observation apparatus intuitively corrects for certain common distortions arising from different perspectives. For example, almost all Westerners intuitively judge a considerably shorter diagonal to be the longer of the two diagonals in the so-called Sander parallelogram (Figure 4.1).

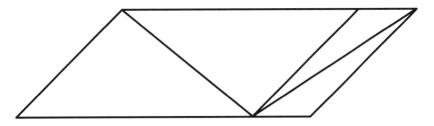

Figure 4.1   Sander parallelogram

Rectangular forms deceive us; certain elliptic forms lead the Zulus astray. Other cultures may have still other biases. And specific scientific cultures are no exception here.

Generalizing from the examples, we might say that we learn to observe in a certain way. We are trained to see things according to certain conventional ways of seeing them. Once the conventional 'constitution of observation' is in place, intersubjective control of judgment is possible.[4] Within the framework in which we have been brought up we pass judgments in ways that are interpersonally controllable. The judgments have a strong conventional or training component or, for that matter, are culturally formed.[5] They are not based on brute facts but on facts emerging only within certain 'ways of world-making'.

What holds for observational judgments may as well apply beyond. For instance among people who are brought up the same way some esthetic judgments may almost be as interpersonally reliable as statements about color. There may be people who are not cultivated enough or lack some natural ability to pass appropriate esthetic judgments. But how important is that? Though there obviously are some color-blind individuals around nobody would therefore doubt that observations concerning colors are quite unproblematic and intersubjectively convergent. Likewise, if there are some outsiders who just cannot perceive certain esthetic qualities, that does not signify much. As long as there are no other arguments casting doubts on the intersubjective validity of esthetic judgments, the existence of outsiders should not cast doubt on intersubjectivity. To give a final example, if we can find out that almost all knowledgeable people grade exams broadly the same way, leading to an intersubjectively stable ordinal ranking of relatively better or worse, what does it signify if there are some few people who do not apply the standards appropriately?

The upshot of all this seems to be that a rational and intersubjectively accessible discussion of value judgments may be possible in ways akin to discussions of matters of fact. In both realms, that of facts and that of values, a very strong conventional element is present in what we count as basic observations or judgments. In both cases theories are somewhat removed from direct observation. In both settings the general and more speculative systematic thinking can be controlled by individualized statements or judgments that are formed under the guidance of established conventions.

Nevertheless, admitting value judgments into science is routinely condemned as illegitimate and deemed a danger for scientific progress. Since it is obvious that value judgments do play a role when it comes to a characterization of scientific practice – by methodological 'do and do not' norms of the trade (see Lakatos, 1978) – not all value judgments may be ruled out from scientific practice. At the same time theorists insist that as far as the substantive content of science is concerned there is no room for value judgments. In particular, if a scientist utters a substantive value judgment concerning the world outside science he cannot do so with the authority of his science. It is a personal statement, not a scientific one, even though it is a statement of a scientist.

To put the reasoning behind this in Humean terms, the enterprise of science consists in scrutinizing 'relations of ideas' or analytical judgments, and 'relations of fact' or synthetic judgments. Since there is no way to derive values from either of these two it is clear within broadly Humean conceptions of science that values fall outside the justificatory domain of science. As it is impossible to define a term like 'goodness' in exclusively descriptive terms (the so-called naturalistic fallacy more narrowly conceived) and keep the evaluative content of 'good', so it is impossible to derive an 'ought' from exclusively non-normative premises (the naturalistic fallacy in the broader sense, see Hume, 1978 [1739]). Consequently, the contribution of science to the justification of norms and values as such is nil unless at least one basic value is brought in as a premise.

This seems particularly relevant for disciplines like economics that always had a very strong proclivity to enter the realm of value judgments and norms. For them the Humean criterion means purgatory (fitting Hume's suggestion to put certain kinds of books to the flames). And purgatory is what Lionel Robbins provided for classical welfare economics.

NORMATIVE JUSTIFICATION IN ETHICS AND ECONOMICS

Values in Robbinslan Economics

In 1932 economic self-criticism culminated in *An Essay on the Nature and Significance of Economic Science*. Lionel Robbins's effort to characterize the realm of economics proper is deservedly famous and still has a strong if somewhat indirect impact on economics.[6] As is well known, Robbins in his essay characterizes economics as scrutinizing the allocation of scarce resources (means) that have alternative uses to their most valuable purpose as evaluated according to some 'given' ends. In short, and as the famous line goes, economics can propose 'means to given ends' but 'on ends it must remain silent'.

To put it slightly otherwise, ends are exogenous to economic science while means are determined in ways endogenous to economic argument. Economics can issue intersubjectively valid statements of a normative kind insofar as it states what a person – who as a matter of fact pursues certain ends – should do under certain constraints if they intend to reach their ends. The appropriateness of suggested means can be intersubjectively assessed while such scrutiny of the ends themselves is impossible.

Whether somebody has a certain desire or not is ultimately a matter of fact and not of argument. If the subjective desire is what it is, then there is no way to argue about that 'brute' fact. It can be stated in intersubjectively valid ways whether or not the fact does exist, but there are no intersubjectively valid ways to assess whether or not it or the underlying convictions should exist. Though one can try to persuade or train another individual to develop other desires there is no scientific way to deal with the substantive issue of whether the ultimate ends are legitimate in some sense or other.

Since on ultimate ends economic science must remain silent, it comes as no surprise that Robbins also attacked the view that interpersonal utility comparisons could be possible in intersubjectively controllable ways. After all, if the ultimate subjective values are beyond the reach of scientific evaluation themselves, how could they be evaluated with respect to their relative importance and compared in an interindividually valid manner? There seem to be no standards of how trade-offs between ultimate ends either of the same or several persons should be made; for this would require some standard higher than the one that by assumption was to be regarded as ultimate. As opposed to that, the justification of imperatives expressing means–ends relations and the knowledge of the given ends need not be more arbitrary than the derivation of some statement of fact. Once the objective-function is specified and the constraints are known, we have a well-defined problem with an analytical solution. Whether a proposed solution – in view of 'the givens' – is correct can be checked by anyone who has the relevant information and is able to perform the relevant calculations.

But when we are discussing the relative weight of ultimate ends we are at a loss. Without a well-defined objective-function we cannot determine in intersubjectively valid form whether one of two ultimate values, ends, aims, goals and so on, is relatively more or less important. Though economics offers the tool of indifference curves by which, at least in a way, ultimate aims, ends or values can be represented in trade-off relations, the relative weight of such values in the trade-offs is nothing that can be scientifically ascertained – or so it seems.

There is no problem, though, with intra-personal comparisons of interpersonal welfare levels. We might, for example, ask a person A whether or not they would prefer, say, 10 units of X to, say, 5 units of Y. We might also ask the same person A whether they would prefer to make a person B better off by 10 units of a resource X to making a person C better off by 10 units of X. Assuming that X is divisible arbitrarily in full units, A could also consider the allocation of 5 units of X to B and of 5 units of X to C, of 4 to B and 6 to C, and so on. In each case A could compare the distributions of resources in the society 'B, C' and rank the distributions and their effects according to his or her aims, ends or values. These value judgments amount to intra-personal value judgments of person A, in which A compares the allocation of resources to B and C and ranks them according to better or worse as seen by him or her.

The problem of so-called 'interpersonal comparisons of utility' is a special, if important one in the methodology of normative economics. We may avoid that problem here, though. For, even if that problem were solved and we could with good reason drop the preceding reservations concerning the arbitrariness of interpersonal comparisons of welfare, it would still be an open question whether or not ethical judgment should be based on such comparisons and what the status of such judgments in terms of science would be. Problems of 'relativism', 'non-cognitivism' and 'skepticism' regarding rational norm justification are not automatically solved if there are non-arbitrary interpersonal welfare comparisons.

More on Means and Ends

As often in revolutionary or seemingly revolutionary developments in science, the initial criticism of previous positions was exaggerated. Robbins and his followers certainly sometimes did so. Obviously value judgments are not completely arbitrary. There may be an arbitrary and non rational component in the justification of value judgments, but it would be somewhat strange to assume that such judgments despite serious reflections are just arbitrary matters of taste. Controversies about, say, whether consumption or income taxes are preferable are different from mere tastes for, say, chocolate over vanilla ice cream.

One can concede so much but still insist that ultimately there is a fundamental difference between matters of value and matters of fact, at least when it comes to justifications of acts. It is also rather obvious that hypothetical imperatives that point out means–ends relationships, though normative in one sense, are fundamentally based on the normal scientific knowledge of facts and therefore seem much less arbitrary than claims to the effect that, say, something is ultimately 'right' or 'legitimate'.

Though in Robbins's view economics had to remain silent about ultimate values (ends), he believed that economists could justify value judgments relative to ends, aims or ultimate values once the latter were 'given'. Of course, 'technological' recommendations which are like recipes for, say, baking a cake are rationally possible. The normative advice, 'If you intend to bake a chocolate cake meeting certain requirements do x, y and z!' depends on our general empirical knowledge about baking cakes. But this knowledge of how to bake it does not tell anybody that she or he should bake a chocolate cake. Likewise, to say that a person who values x should therefore value y may be justifiable without being able to give a justification for valuing x itself.

If we say that beyond technological norms we cannot rationally go, this expresses a kind of relativism. We then maintain that all the normative justifications are relative to some kind of facts. These facts I will also refer to as 'normative facts'. Somebody must as a matter of fact want or desire something in order that something 'should' be done (or for that matter be valued). People as a matter of fact must desire certain things as ends if the use of certain means should be justified for them. If they do not desire to reach certain ends it does not make sense to tell them that they 'should' use means appropriate for the pursuit of their ends. Likewise, I may want others to do certain things in view of my ends. Then, depending on circumstances and my other aims, ends or values, such means as applying some force to make them do what I want them to do may make instrumental sense. According to the relativist any recommendation about what people 'should' desire ultimately boils down to what people 'would' desire. Likewise, there is no value unless there is an entity that as a matter of fact does value things.

If somebody can address another person with a normative statement to the effect that the addressee has endorsed the end to which the normative statement points out the means, he seems to be in command of a fairly appealing argument. We can convincingly criticize a person who intends to bake chocolate cake if they take vanilla instead of chocolate. As long as the person sticks to their end, they 'should' be convinced that they chose the wrong means. Of course, the addressee of a 'wrong means to given ends' statement may still say that they have changed their mind and are now pursuing different ends (that is, baking a vanilla cake). However, if and as long as the person sticks to their ends, any argument that points out optimal means[7] towards the ultimately decisive ends should be rationally (if not as a matter of fact) convincing to them.[8]

If somebody claims that there are aims, ends or values that they are rationally obliged to pursue independently of what they as a matter of fact pursue, this is an argument on a different plane. It is clear that the appeal to the aims, ends or value that the person as a matter of fact pursues will have a force different from the force of an appeal to aims, ends or values completely alien to their own. This does not preclude efforts to persuade them to adopt aims, ends or values other than those they in fact have adopted. But persuasion does not exert the same type of influence on its addressee as an argument relative to already given aims, ends or values of the addressee.

I do not claim that the appeal to the given aims, ends or values that an addressee as a matter of fact has is always behaviorally stronger than some other persuasive appeal. Nor do I claim that only 'means-to-ends appeals' can motivationally be effective. For the time being I insist only that different kinds of appeals should be distinguished from each other if confusion is to be avoided.

Universalism, Particularism and Cultural Relativism

Since means–ends arguments apply only to the particular group of people who as a matter of fact are willing to accept the ultimate normative premises of the arguments, the justifications based on them are not only relative to the aims, ends or values, they are also 'particularistic' in applying only to a particular group. A particularistic claim holds good only for those 'to whom it concerns'. Addressees of the arguments are a self-selected group (in a way). All and only those belong to the relevant addressees who share certain aims, ends or values to which the arguments are 'moored' or 'anchored' as the relevant 'normative facts'.

Contrary to justificatory particularism, justificatory universalism maintains that certain norms are justified for each and everyone of an exogenously defined group of 'all'. To whom it concerns is not a matter for concern of the addressees of the argument. Normative facts do not play a role here.

Very closely related to the preceding distinctions is that between hypothetical and categorical imperatives. Hypothetical imperatives would be otherwise if the aim, end or value to which they are 'moored' were as a matter of fact not present (that is, if the normative facts were missing). A hypothetical imperative is compelling for every person who as a matter of fact endorses some aim, end or value that is presupposed 'hypothetically' in the imperative. The validity of the imperative is contingent on the presence of appropriate aims, ends or values. Grammatically the imperative may have any form. However, its justification has but one form: means to given aims, ends or values.

As opposed to that, a categorical imperative claims to be validly justified independently of such contingent facts as the presence of aims, ends or values among the addressees of the justification. It claims to have a valid justification even if the addressee of the justification of the imperative does not share certain aims, ends or values. Grammatically it may be contingent on the presence of certain conditions. But there is no self-selection concerning the justification in the sense pointed out before.

An ethical theory that does not claim to be valid for people other than those who have as a matter of fact accepted particular values does not maintain any universal claim to validity as towards all and everybody. It concerns only those who 'have joined the club'. An ethical theory based on categorical imperatives need not be universal in the sense of addressing all individuals, either. It can exclusively address members of a specific group independently of their aims, ends or values. The crucial point is that it does not let individuals' factual endorsement of values be decisive about its range of application. The addressees are defined by the norm itself but they need not be all individuals (or all rational beings or whatever). On the other hand, an ethical theory may justify moral requirements in terms of hypothetical imperatives and as a matter of (very unlikely) fact claim to apply universally.

Table 4.1   Types of norm justification

Norm justifications and Norms	Particularistic	Universalistic
Hypothetical	1	2
Categorical	3	4

In Table 4.1 all cells may conceivably be occupied. The main diagonal contains the typical forms of norm justification. As far as cell 1 is concerned, practically nobody would have any doubts that there are such norm justifications and that they are rational justifications in a limited rational sense. As far as other cells are concerned, doubts may apply. For instance, followers of Lionel Robbins would assume that beyond the first row we cannot rationally go in economics, and skeptical philosophers might claim that not only for the justificatory enterprise of normative economics but rather for all normative argument across the board.

As opposed to that, most people would think that there are at least some categorical imperatives that do apply universally. They go beyond row one. For instance, that one should not kill innocent little babies seems to most people to be a norm with a claim to validity (rational justification) that is independent of the contingent aims, ends or values of the addressees of the justificatory argument. It seems somewhat bizarre to argue that 'one should not kill innocent babies' and then add a proviso linking the norm to given aims, ends or values. But those who believe that there cannot be justifications of norms other than hypothetical ones must say exactly this. They need not say that they are not willing to hinder those who intend to kill babies. They may be quite willing to fight for their divergent aim of protecting the babies. They acknowledge, though, that it is ultimately a matter of fight rather than compelling argument once they run out of the hypothetical arguments commending certain types of prudent behavior. In view of the preceding discussion of the Sander parallelogram they may also be aware that there possibly were societies like that of Carthage in Roman times where it was deemed a morally desirable act of sacrifice to throw babies into some holy fire or other. Though these reports may in part derive from Roman propaganda it is in no way impossible that human beings would develop norms like those. And Aristotle and the Greeks supported infanticide.

More generally speaking, even norms that seem to be necessary to secure survival in and of a society like those to which Herbert Hart referred as 'the minimum content of natural law' (see Hart, 1961) are, according to the view that sees itself confined to row one, validly justified only for those who as a matter of fact do want to survive. For instance, a suicide club might be formed. For members of the club it may be essential not to secure survival but rather to enhance the chance of, say, unforeseen death. They have different aims than securing survival and therefore advice other than that which furthers survival is to be given to them by the ethical theorist.

Two Traps of Justificatory Argument

Only few people as a matter of fact would not want to survive. But it is of importance for the status of the justificatory argument in favor of institutional rules securing survival to understand that its validity may depend on contingent facts about what people do want and what they do not. At the same time one must be careful to understand in the means–ends framework what this view of the hypothetical character even of the most fundamental norms means and what it does not. Two points deserve to be emphasized in particular. Both of them concern fallacies of sorts. One may be called the 'universalistic fallacy', the other the 'justificatory fallacy'.

The 'universalistic fallacy' is broadly the following: 'From the fact that practically everybody wants to survive it follows that the norm to universally protect survival is justified'. But even if everybody shares the same interest in, say, survival it is in no way implied that everybody must share an interest in providing universally for the means of survival. For instance, in Fascist Germany non-Jewish Germans could have been willing to concede that their Jewish compatriots were as interested in securing their own survival as they themselves. However, the non-Jew might have said he or she was not as interested in securing the means of survival for the Jewish Germans as the German Jews were. One should also note that the most awful of the Nazis (think of a swine like Himmler) have claimed that they personally suffered from the 'necessity' to commit atrocities in pursuit of their high moral standards of improving the genetic stock of the 'Arian race'. They did not what was prudent, but what they regarded as 'moral' according to their perverse standards. They endorsed the self-image of an unselfish supporter of a great cause.

Quite independently of the abominable historical background, the argument is perfectly general. That some interest is universally shared is not sufficient to show that the enforcement of a norm protecting that interest universally is justified for everybody. Though the conclusion from 'a universally shared interest' to 'a universally shared interest in protecting that interest' is widespread, it nevertheless amounts to a fallacy. Whether or not what is universally in the interest of everybody should be protected by everybody, for everybody, depends. We need to refer to still other aims, ends or values to justify to each the enforcement of what is in the interest of each in terms of hypothetical imperatives.[9]

The 'justificatory fallacy' is broadly speaking the following: 'If some norm is categorically requiring something then the norm must be categorically justified.' But even if some norm is categorical in its requirements it is not necessarily categorically justified (if it is justified at all). A hypothetically justified norm may very well require that promises be kept without further ado. It does not say that you should keep your promises because you should be prudent with respect to your long-term prospects and reputation. It may just state that promises should be kept, as in 'Keep your promises!' This is a categorical norm in that it does not appeal to given aims, ends or values of its addressee. Nevertheless the addressee of a norm needs to be distinguished from the addressee of the justification of the norm. And once the two are distinguished, the relevant difference emerges.

In particular many institutional norms as well as norms of custom, habit or everyday mores involve categorical requirements towards their addressees. One might even be of the opinion that it is a defining characteristic of moral norms that they appeal in a categorical manner to their addressees. But this does not imply that the requirements are also categorically justified or that the norms need to make any claim to such a categorical justification. The latter may or may not be the case.

We can give a hypothetical justification for implementing a categorical requirement like that of promise-keeping. One could for instance argue that practically everybody in a society has an interest in the institution of promise-keeping. Therefore practically everybody should also desire that an institution exists that requires categorically that promises be kept. It is mistaken to infer from the categorical character of the requirement that its justification must be non-hypothetical, too. As the argument shows, we may have a good reason to wish that the institution exists and that it be categorical, without necessarily being of the opinion that it is categorically justified.[10]

Though both the universalistic and the justificatory fallacy seem to be rather obvious mistakes, they seem to be fairly widespread. In a way it seems indeed 'natural' to think of categorical norms as categorically justified. But this is much less compelling once we think of moral norms in terms of moral institutions and practices that guide us in our social lives. Then we are speaking of normatively relevant facts like the conventions of our daily lives, and we may naturally wonder whether there are good reasons why we should desire them to be in place or not.

If we are able to justify the thesis that we have good reason to wish that an institution exists – in terms of hypothetical imperatives concerning its desirability as serving our ends – then this may in itself contribute to the stability of the institution. In this sense in a means–ends framework there is a role for moral theories that deal with moral institutions: if it is psychologically true that the theories make individuals more inclined to play by desirable rules then 'preaching', the theories may themselves contribute to reaching certain ends.

Interestingly enough, the ethical discussion is entirely within reach of the means–ends paradigm of economics as characterized by Lionel Robbins. In particular economics can justify in terms of hypothetical imperatives some categorical – typically institutional – requirements of certain forms of behavior that universally address everybody. In this spirit the norm, 'Promises must be kept!' may be hypothetically justified as an institutional rule for addressees who happen to share appropriate ends. This norm itself requires obedience categorically and universally, yet is justified hypothetically or relative to some normative fact.

RELATIVISM, TOLERANCE AND HIGHER IDEALS IN ECONOMICS

Often it is said that views like the preceding are 'too' relativistic. And relativistic justifications are deemed 'insufficient'. It is claimed that even if it leads to relativistic justifications of categorical institutional rules, we should reject relativism.

This kind of argument seems to be rather unclear at closer scrutiny. The complaint of insufficiency can mean many things. Logically speaking, the hypothetical justifications are not insufficient if they show in a valid way that the means–ends relations exist. It is also untrue that means–ends justifications must necessarily be motivationally less potent than other arguments in supporting moral institutions. So what remains is simply a desire that the ultimate justifications be non-relativistic. Nobody is prevented by a relativistic justification from providing a non-relativistic one, if one exists. In that sense the non-relativist should greet the accomplishment of the relativist as complementary if it leads to the same consequences as their own justifications. If the relativistic justification leads to consequences other than the non-relativistic one, the foe of relativism has to deal with the problem that there obviously are normative facts, aims, ends or values that lead to consequences other than their own preferred normative theory. Then they will tend to attack the relativistic justification on the basis of their own ethics. The meta-ethical views of justificatory relativism will become a natural target for such a theorist. Yet one should not mix things up here: the controversy is not about substantive ethics.

Different from meta-ethical relativism but closely related to it is the thesis of cultural relativism, which amounts to the view that individuals in different cultures as a matter of fact endorse different ultimate aims, ends or values dependent on their culture. But even if that were wrong and there were cultural universals, this does not mean much. Recalling the universalistic fallacy, this in particular does not mean that groups which all internally share the same aims, ends or values should not get into conflict. Quite the contrary may be the case if the pursuit of the aims leads to competition in access to the means to reach the aims. At the same time there need not be consent amongst individuals in each group and there is no rationally compelling reason why that should be so. Moreover, the (allegedly) non-relativistic justifications of norms differ widely in form and content regardless of the necessities of group survival and so on.

If there should as a matter of fact exist a common core of aims, ends or values 'universally' shared by all human groups this does not, of course, amount to a refutation of justificatory relativism. Something may universally apply without having a non-relativistic justification. The controversy about knowledge of matters of right and wrong cannot be decided on grounds of cultural non-relativism. To put it slightly otherwise, we may in particular be convinced that meta-ethical justificatory relativism is right, and at the same time reject cultural relativism since we believe in the existence of cultural universals or universals in human nature that give rise to the common structures of our cultural environment.

Against the background of the preceding discussion we can characterize more precisely what relativism and non-relativism, respectively, amount to in practical terms. A relativist claims that there are no valid categorical justifications of norms; that is, there are no norm justifications that have a convincing claim to validity independently of the aims, ends or values of the addressee of the justificatory argument. A non-relativist believes that there can be some valid justifications of normative precepts that are categorical in that they do not ultimately rest on means–ends relations; that is, they are justified in ways that are not relative to the presence of contingent aims, ends or values.

Robbinsian economics qualifies as meta-ethically non-cognitivist. Economists should be very careful not to draw too strong conclusions from their meta-ethical convictions, though. For instance, many economists seem to believe that being a non-cognitivist implies that one should be a subscriber to norms of tolerance and interpersonal respect. However, assuming that this conclusion can be drawn amounts to fallacious reasoning. If it so happens that I do share certain aims, ends or values that as a matter of fact clash with the opposing aims, ends or values of another person then, as a relativist, I have every reason to see to it that I get my way rather than my opponent theirs. It is all a matter of finding means to reach my ends. Unless there are other aims, ends or values which the relativist happens to share and which render peaceful intercourse and tolerance desirable as means to their own ends, they have no reason to respect other persons' efforts to realize their own goals, nor to keep the peace and so on.

Quite unsurprisingly the meta-theoretical view on what kinds of justificatory arguments lead to valid justifications of norms cannot yield norms with a specific substantive content like norms of tolerance. To admit that one does not know that one's own as well as other individuals' goals are rightly or wrongly pursued does not imply that one should treat all goals of all individuals as equally justified. Quite to the contrary, such a view is perfectly in line with giving precedence to one's own aims, ends or values, and the intention of forcing them on others. But given suitable aims, ends or values, it is coherent with the opposite view as well. And, given the way the world in fact is, the latter seems to be overwhelmingly the case.

In part, a misreading of Robbins and a misinterpretation of the implications of his meta-ethical position has been responsible for the view that a meta-theoretical conception of how substantive value judgments can be justified has implications for the substantive norms so justified. The argument that is still frequently offered by economists is basically the following one. Meta-theoretical reasons show that we cannot objectively, that is, with scientific methods, know what is good. We therefore have a scientific reason why we should respect the wishes of all individuals equally. To put it slightly otherwise: since we as economists can justify norms only relative to the given aims, ends or values of the addressees of a norm justification we should not recommend interference with the pursuit of happiness by others; we rather have 'economic science' reasons to favor tolerance.

Those who reason that way seem to be unaware that they are assuming that a norm can be derived from factual statements of a meta-theoretical nature. They implicitly deny the thesis that meta-ethics is neutral with respect to substantial norms, and violate the principle that we cannot derive 'ought' from 'is'. The statement that one cannot know right from wrong in a scientific way is a factual claim. The norm that we should (on behalf of a lack of knowledge) tolerate the desires of others is a normative statement. How can we derive the one from the other?

Vice versa, economists seem to believe that those who claim to know right and wrong in matters practical would have a good reason to impose their views on others. But it is hard to see why such a knowledge claim as such should have the practical implications assumed. A person who knows or believes they know right from wrong can at the same time be of the opinion that they should not impose their views on others. As long as the person believes in the latter substantive norm of toleration and is motivated to do what they believe they know, he or she has a good reason to tolerate others.

There may, of course, be psychological reasons why people who believe they know the truth in matters practical are more prone deliberately to exert externalities on others by imposing their own will on them. But there is no convincing systematic reason why that should necessarily be so.

The non-relativists who believe in knowledge in moral matters are wrong in claiming that a relativist could not have a good reason to go against a Hitler, Mao or Stalin or any other of the 'great humanists'. The person who has aims, ends or values that make it desirable to go against such – and other – gangsters has a good reason to ask for the means to get rid of them. And this holds good independently of whether or not they believe that there are non-relativistic justifications.

If we want to form a theory based on substantive norms of mutual respect we have to introduce and to justify such norms as what they are: substantive norms requiring substantive normative argument or substantive normative assumptions. For instance, if we intend to respect other individuals as persons who have an equal right as we ourselves to pursue their own ends, aims or values, then we have to introduce that norm explicitly – or some substantive norm that implies the substantive norm of respect.

This is in particular true also for the Pareto principle which is sometimes used to serve that function. More specifically, an individual A who in their personal welfare function w_A for the collectivity intends to respect the values of others in a fundamental way will be inclined to require that a state X can be ranked before a state Y in their personal ranking for the collectivity only if it makes everybody strictly better off (the weak Pareto principle). To require that change is legitimate only if each and everybody is better off in the state of affairs X than in an alternative state Y is a version of a Kantian norm of interpersonal respect. But it is a substantive normative assumption that brings some economists to that conclusion, and not any claim concerning the justifiability of norms. In particular the justification of the Pareto principle as a necessary condition of legitimate collective action cannot be based on an inability to make intersubjective comparisons of welfare levels or an inability to know what is right or wrong in practical matters.

Those who think that the belief that we know the badness of what is bad objectively or scientifically will add to our willingness to fight against it, may try to argue just the other way round. If the psychological claim is right, they might argue, there is a convincing reason for a relativist to adopt a non-relativist meta-ethical view. But there are strong reasons against that argument. First of all we should not believe that the convenience of the belief in something should ever be accepted as a convincing reason for adopting it – at least if there are arguments indicating that the belief may be mistaken. If we believe in the truth of non-relativism we should accept that as a fact, at least so long as we share methodological ideals that rule out certain forms of wishful thinking. Second, it does not seem viable to eliminate strong arguments to the contrary from any discussion, and therefore we should not think that as a matter of fact inculcating the belief in some non-relativist position would be a good means towards ends, aims or values that we and others share. Finally, instilling belief in non-relativist views is a tricky thing. For if it be so that those who believe that one can know right from wrong are more willing to fight for the substantive beliefs that they endorse, who would guarantee that they will tend to believe in 'good causes' (at least causes that we accept as good)? It may well be that people can be brought to believe that they know that it is right to be tolerant and respectful towards others. Still, there is no guarantee that they will endorse such benign beliefs rather than, say, claim that they know of the superiority of a specific 'race' or other foolish and dangerous things.

It may be worth noting that in all the great crimes of human history – and in particular in the twentieth century there is no scarcity of such crimes – the appeal to individual interest and to the individual desire to reach personal aims, ends or values was conspicuously absent. Economic means–ends reasoning in general, and egotism in particular, upon which so much is blamed by philosophers and well-intentioned laymen, can hardly be the culprit (on this tradition, see Levy, 2001). What was center stage almost everywhere was an appeal to some great cause, the rightness of which could be known by all who were willing to see or to listen to their leaders. All too often the peculiar unselfishness of the masses ran its course in pursuit of allegedly self-evident moral truths (see Arendt, 1951) and the outcomes were the several disasters that emerged.

It is an open question what the overall practical consequences of certain forms of meta-theoretical convictions will be. I personally happen to be convinced by several arguments in favor of non-cognitivism and justificatory relativism. At the same time I believe that rational argument concerning practical matters is possible. The differences between critical practical and critical theoretical dispute should not be overemphasized. The so-called reflective equilibrium method or metaphor is applicable independently of how we interpret the normative facts on which the search for reflective equilibrium is based (see Daniels, 1979; Hahn, 2000).

NOTES

1. But note also that the strict justificatory relativists cannot coherently claim that they know that aims, ends or values should be respected. Since a valid normative argument can be made only in relation to given aims, ends or values shared by somebody it is a contingent fact – and not a logical implication of relativism – that the justificatory relativists as a matter of fact share appropriate desires.
2. See Mackie (1977, 1980), Albert (1985).
3. An argument well put by von Savigny; see Savigny (1983).
4. The Denkstil of Ludwik Fleck; see Fleck (1980 [1935]).
5. The ability of people living in Arctic regions to distinguish several kinds of snow where we cannot discriminate between them may serve as a further illustration, if any may be needed. They have learnt to see and to observe.
6. See for the following the second revised edition (Robbins, 1935).
7. Optimal relative to their aims, ends or values.
8. The 'should' in this sentence is not an ethical one.
9. It may be noted that the worst of the Nazis conceived of themselves as unselfish and motivated by non-hypothetical moral interests that transcended the pursuit of their own given aims, ends or values, like that of furthering the interest of the race.
10. This is exactly what the Hobbesian hypothetical imperatives do: they oblige us to desire that certain institutions exist, yet not necessarily to act to make the desire come true; see Hobbes (1968 [1651], § 15).

REFERENCES

Albert, Hans (1985), *Treatise on Critical Reason*, Princeton, NJ: Princeton University Press.

Arendt, Hannah (1951), *The Origins of Totalitarianism*, New York: Harcourt.

Brennan, Harold Geoffrey and James M. Buchanan (1985), *The Reason of Rules*, Cambridge: Cambridge University Press.

Buchanan, James M. (1999), *The Logical Foundations of Constitutional Liberty*, Indianapolis, IN: Liberty Fund.

Daniels, Norman (1979), 'Wide reflective equilibrium and theory acceptance in ethics', *Journal of Philosophy*, **76** (1), 265–82.

Fleck, Ludwick (1980 [1935]), *Entstehung und Entwicklung einer wissenschaftlichen Tatsache: Einführung in die Lehre vom Denkstil und Denkkollektiv*, Frankfurt: Suhrkamp.

Hahn, Susanne (2000), *Überlegungsgleichgewicht(e). Prüfung einer Rechtfertigungsmetapher*, Freiburg i. Br.: Karl Alber.

Hart, Herbert L.A. (1961), *The Concept of Law*, Oxford: Clarendon.

Hobbes, Thomas (1968 [1651]), *Leviathan*, Harmondsworth: Penguin.

Hume, David (1978 [1739]), *A Treatise of Human Nature*, Oxford: Clarendon.

Lakatos, Imre (1978), *The Methodology of Scientific Research Programmes*, Cambridge: Cambridge University Press.

Levy, David M. (2001), *How the Dismal Science Got Its Name*, Ann Arbor, MI: University of Michigan Press.

Mackie, John L. (1977), *Ethics: Inventing Right and Wrong*, Harmondsworth: Penguin.

Mackie, John L. (1980), *Hume's Moral Theory*, London: Routledge.

Robbins, Lionel (1935), *An Essay on the Nature and Significance of Economic Science*, 2nd rev edn, London: Macmillan.

Savigny, Eike von (1983), 'A modest concept of moral sense perception', *Erkenntnis*, **19** (1–3), 331–44.

PART II

Money and medals: the role of motivations in collective choices

5. Awards: a view from economics

Bruno S. Frey[1] and Susanne Neckermann[2]

AWARDS ARE WIDELY USED

Awards are ubiquitous in all countries of the world irrespective of whether a country is a monarchy or a republic, a democracy or a dictatorship, a traditional or modern society or governed by a party with a left-wing or right-wing ideology. As is well known, in the United Kingdom the Queen and the government bestow many lordships and knighthoods (with the title 'Sir') each year. But many people are unaware that also in the United States the President and Congress bestow orders in the form of medals, namely the Presidential Medal of Freedom, the Presidential Citizens Medal and the Congressional Gold Medal, as well as a great number of military awards such as Purple Hearts, Bronze and Silver Stars. A flood of orders, medals and titles was handed out in communist countries, such as the Soviet Union or the German Democratic Republic.

Awards are also popular in the corporate sectors of market economies. Firms honor their employees as 'Employee of the Month'. The media also supports this activity and regularly chooses the 'Person of the Year' (*Time*), or at least 'Best Managers' (*Business Week*) or 'CEOs of the Year' (*Financial World*).

In sports, athletes receive the honor of being chosen 'Sports Personality of the Year' (the BBC has no less than seven categories), and of being admitted into one of the many Halls of Fame. In the arts, culture and the media, awards are also of central importance. A few prominent examples are the prizes handed out by the film festivals in Cannes, Venice or Berlin, as well as the Academy Awards (Oscars), the Grammy awards for artistic significance in the field of recording and the Prix Goncourt in literature or the Pulitzer Prize. In the world of science awards are held in particularly high esteem. Universities and academies have an elaborate and extensive system of awards. They bestow titles such as Honorary Doctor, Professor or Senator, and professional associations award an enormous number of awards such as the Fields Medal in mathematics and, most importantly, the Nobel Prizes.

THE SOCIAL SCIENCE LITERATURE ON AWARDS

Most of the existing literature is devoted to presenting the historical facts about individual orders as well as the rules according to which an order is handed out. Few works cover orders across several countries. Awards or related issues have to some extent been discussed in sociology. Examples are Bourdieu (1979), Elster (1983), Braudy (1986), Marmot (2004) and de Botton (2004). However, with few exceptions, these works address awards and distinctions in a general and abstract way (and not as incentives). The psychological literature provides important insights into the mechanisms through which awards work on the individual level. However, this literature mainly focuses on isolated stimuli and is largely silent about the types of tasks and situations for which one can expect awards to be successful motivators.

Despite the importance of awards in society, economists have largely disregarded them, with the exception of the early contribution by Hansen and Weisbrod (1972) whose lead was not taken up by other researchers until recently.[3] Some literature in economics provides insights into specific aspects of awards. A typical way for (standard) economists to look at awards would be in terms of the signal emitted (see Spence, 1974), in terms of the competition induced (for example Lazear and Rosen, 1981), and in terms of incentives in a principal–agent relationship in a firm (a survey is provided by Prendergast, 1999). In psychological economics, combining economic methods with insights from psychology will produce several useful approaches illuminating special aspects of awards. Of particular relevance are the works on esteem, identity, status and reputation. Examples of recent economic works addressing aspects related to awards are analyses of status incentives (for example Auriol and Renault, 2001; Dubey and Geanakoplos, 2005; Ederer and Patacconi, 2004; Loch et al., 2001 and Fershtman et al., 2001), of rewards as feedback (Sururov and van de Ven, 2006), of social recognition (Brennan and Pettit, 2004; English 2005), of reciprocity (for example Fehr and Gächter, 2000; Fehr and Schmidt, 2004), of identity (Akerlof and Kranton, 2005), of conventions (for example Young, 1993), of superstars, and of positional goods (Hirsch, 1976; Rosen, 1981; Frank, 1985).

There may be various reasons why economists have so far neglected awards:

- They are not fungible; compared to monetary compensation awards may therefore be considered inferior instruments to induce effort.
- Awards may just be one result of high motivation and success and not a contributing cause.
- Awards may not be perceived as different from monetary incentives. It could be assumed that they are only valued by the recipients for the ancil-

lary bonus connected to them or to the extent that they may induce increases in future income. This assumption certainly has some truth to it. However, it has also been demonstrated in experiments that people value status independently of any monetary consequence; they are even willing to incur material costs to obtain it (Huberman et al., 2004).

One of the goals of this chapter is to demonstrate that awards have many characteristics that make them different from monetary rewards, and that they are therefore a useful subject to study.

DIFFERENCES BETWEEN AWARDS AND MONETARY COMPENSATION

There are important differences between awards and monetary compensation. These make it worthwhile to analyze awards separately. Consider the following differences between awards and monetary compensation:

First, accepting an award establishes a special relationship, in which the recipient owes (some measure of) loyalty to the donor. However, the respective contract is tacit, incomplete and difficult or impossible to enforce by the donor. Monetary compensation in contrast typically does not demand loyalty. Quite the opposite is true: payments can easily be used as justification to work for an organization that one publicly denounces.

Second, awards are superior incentive instruments to monetary payments when the recipients' performance can be determined only vaguely. The qualification criteria for awards are typically broad and not clearly specified. Therefore, performance can be globally evaluated *ex post*. Monetary compensation on the other hand almost always needs to be clearly specified contractually *ex ante*. Hence, the principal has no room to take other than the stipulated performance dimensions into account or to adjust the weights of the different performance criteria in determining the winner according to realized business needs. This is often perceived as unfair or inadequate when performance is difficult to contract and measure.

Third, awards are always made public. In the case of companies, award recipients may be announced on the intranet, displayed on bulletin boards or celebrated in a specially arranged ceremony. In contrast, the size and details of monetary compensations (that is, salaries), tends to be covert.

Fourth, awards are less likely to crowd out the intrinsic motivation in the recipients than monetary compensation. Typically, awards are perceived as supportive rather than controlling. This lies in the social nature of awards, and the fact that the associated *ex post* performance measurement is less intrusive and allows for the consideration of input factors such as motivation and working morale as well as a broad assessment of performance dimensions that are hard to measure. Further, unlike pure monetary payments, awards are less likely to destroy the signal value of actions requiring special commitment, or of actions beyond what is typically expected. When payments are involved it is not clear for observers whether the behavior was driven by dedication and commitment or solely by the money. In principle the same is true for awards because they are also extrinsic incentives. However, awards are less powerful extrinsic incentives, so that the signal value of special behaviors is reduced less.

Fifth, the material costs of awards may be very low or even nil, for the donor, but the value to the recipient may be very high.[4] In contrast to monetary compensation, award givers need to take into account that the value of an award decreases with the number of awards in circulation since the prestige associated with winning an award depends on it being scarce.

Sixth, awards are not taxed, while monetary income is. In countries with high marginal taxes it is therefore relatively more attractive to receive an untaxed award than to receive a highly taxed monetary compensation.

These considerations make clear that there are indeed many major differences between awards and monetary compensation that are well worth inquiring into.

THE CHARACTERISTICS OF AWARDS

Awards work as incentives via a number of channels that have been shown to influence human behavior. Among other reasons, awards motivate because:

- Winning an award makes the recipient feel good about himself or herself irrespective of monetary or status consequences, hence even without others knowing about the award.
- Awards are typically conferred by a principal whose opinion the agent values.
- They generate social prestige and bring recognition within the peer group.
- Awards are typically set up as tournaments and many persons enjoy competing; that is, working towards an award generates process utility (for example Frey et al., 2004), and hence pleasure irrespective of the outcome.
- There are monetary compensation or other material or immaterial benefits associated with winning the awards. However, awards do not only work as incentives; they also work *ex post*. Awards create and establish role models, they distribute information about successful and desirable behavior and create loyalty. Depending on the specific award analyzed the

various award channels mentioned above are salient in differing degrees. While the general term 'award' implies that the different existing honors and prizes pertain to the same group of incentives, specific awards differ vastly from one another in terms of what component is most salient. Some awards are clearly competition prizes, while others more closely resemble feedback or praise. Some awards are valuable in monetary terms, while others come with neither monetary nor other material benefits. Enormous differences exist between state orders that are governmental or monarchical acts, and prizes granted by non-profits, foundations or clubs, and awards in for-profit companies such as the title 'Employee of the Month', to name just a few. But even within this large realm of awards there are considerable differences. They differ greatly with respect to the social recognition and prestige they will bring to the recipient.

These considerations show that awards are omnipresent in all spheres of life, which suggests that they perform important functions, and that awards can be defined according to a set of criteria despite the myriad of specific forms they take. Thus, awards can and should be studied as a unique phenomenon in psychology as well as in economics.

AN INTERNATIONAL COMPARISON OF AWARDS

The prevalence of awards can be analyzed across countries. Specifically, it is interesting to identify the factors that render an award important or unimportant in a country, be it as an incentive, as a visible symbol of social recognition or as a signal. A major problem confronting researchers trying to analyze awards systematically across countries is the lack of internationally comparative data. Wikipedia is the only source we found that offers an extensive list of prizes, medals and awards across many different countries.[5] This source is of a somewhat doubtful quality, and it is quite obvious that some countries are covered more completely than others. In view of this data problem we turn to individuals' own reports to identify how many awards they possess. We use the awards specified by individuals in the *International Who's Who* (IWW) (Neil, 2006), a work of reference comprising a list of the most important personalities in 212 countries. The persons included are, for example, every head of state, all directors of international organizations, heads of leading universities, chief executive officers (CEOs) of the Global 500 and Fortune 500 companies, prize winners of distinguished awards (such as the Nobel Prize and the Pulitzer Prize) and important sports personalities, as well as prominent individuals from the film and television industry. The data source provides information on person-specific characteristics such as nationality, occupation and age as well as information

Table 5.1   Average number of awards per individual per country

	Total awards		Domestic state awards		Business awards
Mean	2.66	Mean	0.43	Mean	0.06
Variance	1.96	Variance	0.11	Variance	0.01
Top 5 countries in each category					
Canada	6.82	Poland	1.78	Canada	0.52
UK	6.78	France	1.32	Singapore	0.46
Poland	6.16	Tunisia	1.05	USA	0.34
Australia	5.66	Egypt	1.02	Saudi Arabia	0.27
Senegal	5.30	Malaysia	1.00	Australia	0.26
Lowest 5 countries in each category					
Honduras	0.83	Nicaragua	0.05	Trinidad & Tobago	0.00
Bangladesh	0.78	Honduras	0.04	Uganda	0.00
Uganda	0.76	Uruguay	0.04	Ukraine	0.00
Tanzania	0.62	Switzerland	0.02	Uruguay	0.00
El Salvador	0.30	El Salvador	0.00	Venezuela	0.00
Information on 7 additional countries					
USA	3.80		0.22		0.34
Canada	6.82		0.86		0.52
UK	6.78		0.78		0.04
France	3.60		1.32		0.04
Germany	2.46		0.48		0.06
Spain	4.20		0.70		0.06
Italy	1.96		0.22		0.04

Source: Own calculations using data constructed from the *International Who's Who 2007* (Neil, 2006).

about the number and kinds of awards each person has received. For a subsample of 82 countries, we coded the available information for a random sample of 50 individuals per country.

In order to document the importance of awards in a globalized world, Table 5.1 shows the average number of awards handed out per country per individual sampled. The table lists the total number of awards as well as two specific, and very different, types of awards: domestic state awards (often called 'orders' or 'medals') and business awards (such as 'Manager of the Year' or 'Business Executive of the Month'). In addition to the average and variance over all 82 countries, the five countries with the highest average, and the five countries with the lowest average, are listed. In addition, information on all three categories is provided for the United States and Canada, and for the United Kingdom, France, Germany, Spain and Italy. This 'elite' (as defined by the *International Who's Who*) lists, on average, between two and three awards per person. The largest number of awards per person is given for three Anglo-Saxon countries (Canada, the UK and Australia) as well as for Poland and Senegal, averaging between five and seven awards. The lowest average number of awards per person are reported for some small South American, African and Asian countries (such as El Salvador and Tanzania) with substantially less than one award per person.

The average number of awards per member of the elite (3.8) in the United States is considerably higher than the average of 2.7 over all 82 countries. Americans thus seem to enjoy bestowing and receiving awards. Awards enjoy a similar importance in France and Spain (3.6 and 4.2, respectively). This is surpassed by Canada and the United Kingdom (6.8). As can be inferred from the high number of awards handed out in such staunch republics as the United States and France, awards are not only a matter of tradition or monarchic regimes. Rather, the data indicate that awards are of importance and general relevance today in many countries of the world.

The ranking of the countries with respect to the average number of awards changes when awards bestowed by national governments (in particular national orders, medals and decorations) are considered. Not surprisingly, the average number of national government awards received by the individuals listed in the *International Who's Who* is much lower (less than every second individual sampled received such an award). Also, different countries now lead the list of handing out the highest numbers of awards per person (except for Poland which heads the list in this award category). The top five are now comprised of Poland, France, Tunisia, Egypt and Malaysia. The smallest numbers of these awards are bestowed by a similar set of nations as the overall number of awards. Switzerland joins the ranks because the nation is the only country in the world not to bestow any governmental awards (not even to its soldiers). There is one individual in the data set with an honorary citizenship from Lausanne, Switzerland that causes the coefficient to be greater than zero.

Business awards have, of course, a quite different character from national government awards. They refer to awards handed out for private sector activities and comprise honors such as 'Most Powerful Woman', 'Manager of the Year' or 'Arabian Business Achievement Award'. On average, only a few persons in the *International Who's Who* elite have such awards (the average number of business awards per person is 0.06 over all countries).[6] The largest number of business awards goes, on average, to persons in three Anglo-Saxon countries – Canada, the United States and Australia – and to individuals in Singapore and in Saudi Arabia. In a considerable number of countries (33 of the 82 countries in the sample) no business awards are reported.

In the United States, the awards are divided very unequally between national governmental awards and business awards: with respect to domestic state awards US-Americans are clearly below average in international comparison, but for business awards they are nearly at the top. With an average number of awards per person far above the worldwide average, this suggests that in the US the large number of business awards compensates for the small number of state awards. A different pattern holds, for instance, in Canada. In that country, both the number of domestic state awards as well as the number of business awards a person in the *International Who's Who* has are above average. In Europe, France, Germany, Spain and the UK rank above average with respect to national government awards (between 0.5 and 1.3), and below average with respect to business awards (between 0.04 and 0.06). These findings are consistent with the notion that in the United States business affairs are of central social importance, while in European and Commonwealth countries awards bestowed by the state are held in great esteem.

Awards are handed out for activities in many different areas. This shows that the relevance and importance of awards is not limited to certain narrow fields or spheres in a society. Three areas comprise the largest share of the awards handed out in the 82 countries of the sample. The two major sectors are social welfare and academia, followed by culture. The remaining sectors (armed forces, sports, media, business and religion) make up only 10 per cent of all rewards bestowed.

The largest share of awards is bestowed to persons for activities that can be broadly summarized as belonging to the category of social welfare (37 per cent). This category includes awards such as state orders and peace prizes. This large proportion of awards for social welfare can be attributed to the fact that these activities – while being socially desirable – are often not or only inadequately compensated in monetary terms. Often, monetary compensation could even be counterproductive as means of rewarding these kinds of activities (see for example the literature on motivation crowding: Frey, 1997; or Bénabou and Tirole, 2004). Hence, awards work better to motivate and reward persons active in these kinds of activities. Individuals working in academia receive the second-highest share of awards (32 per cent). These data suggest that individuals in the scientific sector, though a place of rational discourse, are quite happy to receive awards. A significant, but clearly lower, share of awards (19 per cent) is bestowed in the cultural sector. Similar arguments explaining the intensive use of awards in this sector as in the case of social welfare may be adduced. In addition, the cultural sector, which includes film, television and writing, is particularly skillful in using the media to promote its own importance. This is reflected in the great attention received by the award ceremonies such as the Oscar, the Grammy and Emmy or the Pulitzer or Brooker prizes.

AWARDS AS MOTIVATORS IN FIRMS

This section presents a survey experiment in the form of a vignette study on awards as incentives in principal–agent relationships (for a more extensive discussion of the methodology, the theories guiding the design, details of the design and the results see Neckermann and Frey, 2007).

The vignette study was conducted online during a two-week period in January and February 2007 with the employees of the IBM research laboratory in Rüschlikon, Switzerland. The facility has 255 employees, 177 of which are researchers from more than 20 different nations (primarily from European countries). The lab in Rüschlikon is one of the eight labs that IBM operates worldwide, with about 3550 employees in total. In collaboration with clients and universities, researchers at these labs conduct basic as well as applied research in chemistry, information technology, physics, electrical engineering and materials science, among others. To date (2009), four researchers have been awarded Nobel Prizes in physics for research they conducted during the time they were employed at the IBM lab in Rüschlikon.

The management hands out the approximately 20 different awards that are available in all IBM research labs. The awards are broadly divided into two main categories: formal and informal awards. Formal awards recognize outstanding scientific contributions and innovations and they are rewarded with substantial monetary compensations. Recipients of these awards are always announced on the worldwide intranet of IBM research and have the possibility to move up on the award ladder, culminating in either the admission into the IBM academy (about 500 persons worldwide) or in the nomination as an IBM Fellow (about 40 persons worldwide).

Informal awards, on the other hand, honor exceptional motivation in general; examples are contributions to teams, knowledge-sharing, passion for work and customer service. According to the human resource manager at IBM Rüschlikon, informal awards are also used to motivate researchers during times in which no major scientific breakthrough is pending. Informal awards are typically rewarded with smaller monetary bonuses or gifts such as vouchers for dinners or weekend city trips. Only the more important informal awards are publicized on the local intranet of the Rüschlikon lab.

Given this large number of established awards at IBM, the respondents to this study can be assumed to be familiar with their own behavior and feelings with respect to striving for and receiving awards. This is an advantage for this study, since it increases the reliability and predictive power of our findings.

The survey focused on the quantitative effect of introducing an award on work behavior and analyzes which award characteristics determine the size of the effect. The behavioral response of the employees was measured via a question asking about the willingness to share an important finding immediately with their team[7] in their current work environment, as well as in four different scenarios, each of which represented the introduction of a new award for international cooperation at IBM. The awards differed with respect to whether they were accompanied by cash bonuses or gifts, the monetary value of the bonus or gift, the number of award recipients and the degree of publicity associated with winning the award. Further, we simulated a situation in which the respondents were informed that they either did or did not receive the award. This addresses the question about the behavior of both winners and losers upon the receipt of an award.

Each vignette describes the introduction of a new incentive for all employees at the IBM research lab in Rüschlikon. All vignettes – that is, reward descriptions – are identical in their basic set-up; they only differ in the realized values of the five different reward characteristics, which we analyze. Those five independent reward characteristics have been chosen according to what seems to be vital to the effectiveness of a reward.

First, the incentive is framed either as a purely monetary bonus or as an award. The difference is that the former is almost completely deprived of a social component. In this scenario, the management decides who will receive the bonus without any employee participation in the nomination process. The money is subsequently transferred to the selected employee's bank account together with the next paycheck. The winners are neither specifically notified nor congratulated by the management. If the incentive, however, is designed as an award the opposite holds. Since we assume that the social approval associated with winning an award matters greatly, we expect to find a larger behavioral response to the introduction of an award as compared to the introduction of a monetary bonus.

Second, the reward is randomly described as being accompanied with a cash payment or a gift. Where the reward was framed as a monetary bonus it always came with cash. For this factor there are two opposing behavioral predictions. On the one hand, standard economic theory predicts that cash should work better than a gift because it is fungible (Waldfogel, 1993). On the other hand, the psychological and management literature cites a number of reasons why a gift should work better than cash (Jeffrey and Shaffer, 2007). Examples of such reasons are evaluability (the perceived value of the gift is higher than its actual value) and justifiability (recipients value the gift more than the equivalent payment in cash, but would not have bought it for themselves; for example luxuries).

Third, the degree of publicity is varied among three different types. First, the list of recipients remains undisclosed. Second, the list of recipients is published on the intranet. Third, in addition to publicizing the list of recipients on the intranet, the company arranges a formal ceremony in which the award is handed to the recipients. Where the incentive is framed as a monetary bonus, the third type of publicity involving the ceremony is excluded, as this would not have been realistic. Since status and social recognition can only be gained when others know about the reward, we hypothesize that the effect of a reward is greater when it is publicized. Further, the effect should be even greater when there is a ceremony in addition to the announcement of the winners on the intranet.

Fourth, the value of the accompanying cash payment or gift was varied between CHF 0 and CHF 10 000. In line with standard economic theory and psychological reinforcement theories, we hypothesize that the behavioral impact of the reward increases with its monetary value.

Fifth, the maximum number of award recipients per year was varied between 1, 2, 6, 10, 16 and 20. The number of recipients is an interesting variable because the value of an award changes with its scarcity. The effect of a reward should therefore decrease with an increased number of recipients. However, there is a countervailing effect as an increase in the number of reward recipients *ceteris paribus* increases the chances of an individual employee being a winner. Therefore, we hypothesize an inversely U-shaped relationship between the number of recipients and motivation. As long as the quality of the award is not diluted by too high a number of recipients, additional recipients will increase effort by raising the perceived chances of winning the award. Beyond a certain threshold number of recipients, the negative effect of decreased reward quality outweighs the positive effect of an increase in chances to win.

After specifying the dimensions (award characteristics) and their values, the vignettes can be constructed by choosing one value of the variable for each of the independent dimensions.

Following the scenarios introducing the rewards, the subjects were asked to indicate their behavior in a public-good situation, that is, a situation in which subjects face a trade-off between individual and collective benefit. In particular, we asked about their willingness to share an important finding with their team before publishing it under their own name. They were told that sharing the finding now would increase the quality and speed of the team project, but expose them to the personal risk that the finding could be used and published without giving them the appropriate credit for the discovery. Alternatively, they could wait and publish the finding in a scientific journal under their own name before sharing it with the team colleagues. Respondents marked their willingness on a ten-point scale ranging from 1 meaning 'I definitely would not share now' to 10 meaning 'I would certainly share now'. Employees were familiar with this type of public-good situation in their everyday work life, as was confirmed in interviews preceding the study. In the survey about 84 per cent of the respondents rated the situation description as realistic or very realistic.

To control for individual specific effects we generated multiple observations per person by presenting each subject with four different reward scenarios. First, however, we asked the respondents to state their willingness to share the finding assuming they were working in their current work environment (status quo). This gives us the baseline motivation of each respondent. Then subjects were confronted with the vignettes – that is, the reward introduction scenarios – and were asked to indicate for each of them their willingness to share their finding. The rewards were granted for extraordinary efforts with respect to cooperation on international teams. Hence, the behavior in the public-good situation described above was relevant for winning the award. The descriptions of rewards 1, 2, 3 and 4 were different for each respondent. The individual subject was presented with a random set of four reward descriptions out of the total pool of over 100 different reward descriptions.[8] The total pool was comprised of all possible combinations of values in the five dimensions that characterize each reward. After having stated their motivation in the public-good situation after the fourth award vignette, we described a scenario in which the individual either did or did not receive the reward that was described to them as reward 4. Then we asked them again to indicate their willingness to share the finding when they knew whether they had received reward 4 or not. The questionnaire ended with a survey section in which respondents were asked questions about their perception of the role of awards in organizations and the determinants of award effectiveness in motivating employees. Further, we inquired about personal characteristics such as gender, age and award history at IBM. These questions were the same for all participants.

During the survey period, 52 researchers completed the online questionnaire, resulting in a rate of return of 30 per cent. The respondents were representative of the workforce with respect to all objective criteria available from the company.[9]

The results described in the following refer to the *ceteris paribus* impact of individual award characteristics. These impacts were calculated using the responses of the subjects to the different reward descriptions, each of which contained a multitude of different award characteristics. Our design therefore closely resembles 'real-world' organizational reward programs, where rewards always consist of more than one incentive dimension (such as monetary compensation, feedback, social recognition).

The monetary value of the reward has a robust, significant and positive impact on the willingness to share the finding. It turns out that CHF (Swiss franc) zero and small monetary values do not have a significantly different impact on motivation. The same is true for medium and high values. Compared to the latter, CHF zero or small monetary values lead to a motivation that is approximately half a point lower on a ten-point scale. This difference is significant. In the qualitative survey conducted after the vignette study, the responding employees confirmed the importance of the monetary value of rewards. Almost all indicated that they considered it to be essential for an award to be accompanied by a substantial monetary bonus.

Publicity has a significant positive effect on stated contributions to the public good. As compared to a situation with no publicity, contributions are on average 0.44 points higher when publicity is involved, which is substantial. Naming the recipients and having a ceremony increases contributions by as much as increasing the value of the award from CHF 0 to about CHF 1000. The coefficient of having a ceremony and announcing the winners on the intranet is substantially larger than the coefficient of an announcement on the intranet alone. Hence, the larger coefficient on the combination of intranet and ceremony indicates that employees value the ceremony per se.

For a given monetary value, gifts do not work as well as payments in cash. Holding the value of the reward constant, a gift leads to a willingness that is 0.3 points lower than the willingness induced by an equivalent payment in cash. For a gift to induce the same willingness to share as does a payment in cash of CHF 50, it needs to increase in value from CHF 50 to CHF 2000. This is in line with remarks by the respondents in the last part of the questionnaire. In the comment section a substantial number stated that they preferred money or a paid vacation to other kinds of prizes.

We do not find a significant effect of the factor 'type of reward'. The pure framing of the reward as a bonus or an award *ceteris paribus* does not make a difference on the motivation of the employees. This insignificance might be due to the fact that bonuses in our design were very similar to awards. Since each reward description presents a combination of values for all characteristics, bonus scenarios also contain a maximum number of recipients and in half of the cases an announcement of the recipients on the intranet. This is very uncommon for monetary bonuses at IBM and might have rendered them too similar to established IBM awards for us to find a significant effect. Also the number of recipients does not have an effect that is significantly different from zero. We hypothesize that an increase in the number of recipients has two countervailing effects on motivation: an increase reduces the scarcity value of the award, but raises perceived chances of winning. This could cause the insignificance. The baseline motivation has a highly significant positive effect on the willingness to share the finding. The coefficient of 0.9 implies that a person with a one-point higher willingness to share the finding in the current work environment is about 0.9 points more willing to share the finding after incentives have been introduced. Demographic variables such as age, gender and experience with international teams do not play a role. The same holds for the award history of the participants: that is, the number and value of the IBM awards received in the past.

Hence, the analysis shows that in a public-good situation that participants were very familiar with in their work experience, awards have significant and systematic effects on the stated contributions of employees. Specifically, we find that the effect of rewards is increased by the degree of publicity associated with winning the award and by the monetary value of the reward. Rewards at IBM work better when they are accompanied by a payment in cash rather than a gift. The study shows that it is important also to consider the effect of awards after conferral, as it was shown that non-recipients substantially decrease their contributions even if the award is granted yearly and is hence open to them in the future. Winners, on the other hand, increase their contributions even further.

CONCLUDING REMARKS

Awards are a relevant phenomenon deserving the attention of economists. This chapter has presented several approaches to beginning to understand the phenomenon of awards. Awards cannot be equated with monetary compensation. We have presented two different empirical avenues to the study of awards. The first is an international comparison based on the information provided by the recipients. The second is a vignette study in a particular firm showing that awards substantially and systematically change stated work behavior. The economics of awards is only at its beginning, but it has already become clear that it deals with an important phenomenon. It allows us to see motivation in a broader context than considered so far, ranging from the extremes of extrinsic monetary compensation to intrinsic motivation, with awards as extrinsic but non-material incentives in between.

NOTES

1. Bruno S. Frey is Professor at the University of Zurich, Institute for Empirical Research in Economics and research director at CREMA – Center for Research in Economics, Management and the Arts, Switzerland.
2. Susanne Neckermann is Researcher at the University of Zurich, Institute for Empirical Research in Economics.
3. See the contributions by Frey (2005, 2006, 2007), Frey and Neckermann (2006, 2008), Neckermann and Frey (2007, 2008), Neckermann et al. (2009).
4. Often, there is some monetary compensation tied to winning an award that entails corresponding costs to the giver. However, these costs are typically very low when compared with wage payments and can also be deducted from taxable profits.
5. http://en.wikipedia.org/wiki/List_of_prizes%2C_medals%2C_and_awards, accessed 30 November 2007.
6. This may be due to the way the *International Who's Who* defines its 'elite'. Business persons, and hence the persons most likely to receive business awards, may be under-represented since only CEOs and chief financial officers (CFOs) of the top 500 companies worldwide and the top 500 US companies are included in the book.

7. Specifically, we inquired into their willingness to share an important finding in their work with their work group. Sharing increases team productivity, but entails the risk of losing part or all of the personal scientific credit that a researcher would certainly receive when publishing the finding first and only sharing it with the team later.
8. Vignettes were sampled without replacement from the pool of all possible vignettes for a given subject. It is not important that all possible vignettes are actually answered as long as the levels are uncorrelated and there is sufficient variation in the vignettes drawn. In the sample of vignettes drawn in our study both of these conditions were met. While the attribution of vignettes to individual respondents was random, we ensured that the four award descriptions each subject was confronted with differed sufficiently in the realized values of the factors (that is, we ensured that each person received awards with zero, small, medium and high monetary value). Further, each person received at least one bonus, one award that came with a cash payment and one award that came with a gift. This was necessary to ensure that subjects were not confused by the potential close similarity of award realizations caused by a purely random assignment. Further, we randomized the order in which the different factors appeared in the award description to control for order effects (only the type of reward – bonus or award – always remained at the beginning of the vignette).
9. Average age, percentage of female workforce and length of employment at IBM were 41 years, 13.2 per cent and 12 years, respectively, among the workforce of the IBM lab in Rüschlikon and 42 years, 10 per cent, and 12 years, respectively, in our sample of respondents.

REFERENCES

Akerlof, G.A. and R.E. Kranton (2005), 'Identity and the economics of organization', *Journal of Economic Perspectives*, **19**, 9–32.
Auriol, E. and R. Renault (2001), 'Incentive hierarchies', *Annales d'Economie et de Statistique*, **63**, 261–82.
Bénabou, R. and J. Tirole (2004), 'Incentives and prosocial behavior', Princeton Economics Discussion Paper No. 230, Princeton University.
Bourdieu, P. (1979), *La Distinction. Critique Sociale Du Jugement*, Paris: Les editions de minuit.
Braudy, L. (1986), *The Frenzy of Renown: Fame and its History*, New York: Oxford University Press.
Brennan, G. and P. Pettit (2004), *The Economy of Esteem: an Essay on Civil and Political Society*, Oxford: Oxford University Press.
De Botton, A. (2004), *Status Anxiety*, New York: Pantheon Books.
Dubey, P. and J. Geanakoplos (2005), 'Grading in games of status: marking exams and setting wages', mimeo, Cowles Foundation, Yale University.
Ederer, F. and A. Patacconi (2004), 'Interpersonal comparisons, status and ambition in organisations', mimeo, Department of Economics, University of Oxford.
Elster, J. (1983), *Sour Grapes: Studies in the Subversion of Rationality*, Cambridge: Cambridge University Press.
English, J.F. (2005), *The Economy of Prestige: Prizes, Awards, and the Circulation of Cultural Value*, Cambridge, MA: Harvard University Press.
Fehr, E. and S. Gächter (2000), 'Fairness and retaliation: the economics of reciprocity', *Journal of Economic Perspectives*, **14**, 159–81.
Fehr, E. and K. Schmidt (2004), 'Fairness and incentives in a multi-task principal–agent model', *Scandinavian Journal of Economics*, **106**, 453–74.
Fershtman, C., Y. Weiss and H.K. Hvide (2001), 'Status concerns and the organization of work', mimeo, Eitan Berglas School of Economics, Tel-Aviv University.

Frank, R.H. (1985), *Choosing the Right Pond: Human Behavior and the Quest for Status*, Oxford: Oxford University Press.

Frey, B.S. (1997), *Not Just for the Money: An Economic Theory of Personal Motivation*, Cheltenham, UK and Lyme, NH, USA: Edward Elgar.

Frey, B.S. (2005), 'Knight fever: towards an economics of awards', IEW Working Paper No. 239, University of Zurich.

Frey, B.S. (2006), 'Giving and receiving awards', *Perspectives on Psychological Science*, **1**, 377–88.

Frey, B.S. (2007), 'Awards as compensation', *European Management Review*, **4**, 6–14.

Frey, B.S., M. Benz and A. Stutzer (2004), 'Introducing procedural utility: not only what, but also how matters', *Journal of Institutional and Theoretical Economics*, **160** (3), 377–401.

Frey, B.S. and S. Neckermann (2006), 'Auszeichnungen: Ein vernachlässigter Anreiz', *Perspektiven der Wirtschaftspolitik*, **7**, 271–84.

Frey, B.S. and S. Neckermann (2008), 'Awards: a view from psychological economics', IEW Working Paper No. 357, University of Zurich.

Hansen, W.L. and B.A. Weisbrod (1972), 'Towards a general theory of awards, or do economists need a hall of fame?', *Journal of Political Economy*, **80**, 422–31.

Hirsch, F. (1976), *Social Limits to Growth*, Cambridge, MA: Harvard University Press.

Huberman, B., C. Loch and A. Oncüler (2004), 'Status as a valued resource', *Social Psychology Quarterly*, **67**, 103–14.

Jeffrey, S.A. and V.A. Shaffer (2007), 'The benefits of tangible non-cash incentives', *Compensation and Benefits Review*, **39** (3), 44–50.

Lazear, E.P. and S. Rosen (1981), 'Rank-order tournaments as optimum labor contracts', *Journal of Political Economy*, **89**, 841–64.

Loch C.H., M. Yaziji and C. Langen (2001), 'The fight for the alpha position: channeling status competition in organizations', *European Management Journal*, **19**, 16–25.

Marmot, M.G. (2004), *The Status Syndrome: How Social Standing Affects Our Health And Longevity*, New York: Times Books/Henry Holt.

Neckermann, S. and B.S. Frey (2007), 'Awards as incentives', IEW Working Paper No. 334, University of Zurich.

Neckermann, S. and B.S. Frey (2008), 'Social incentives: determinants and consequences of awards in companies', mimeo, University of Zurich.

Neckermann, S., R. Cueni and B.S. Frey (2009), 'Making them rich or proud? A managerial perspective on employee awards', mimeo, University of Zurich.

Neil, A. (ed.) (2006), *International Who's Who*, London: Routledge.

Prendergast, C. (1999), 'The provision of incentives in firms', *Journal of Economic Literature*, **37**, 7–63.

Rosen, S. (1981), 'The economics of superstars', *American Economic Review*, **71**, 845–58.

Spence, A.M. (1974), *Market Signaling*, Cambridge, MA: Harvard University Press.

Sururov, A. and J. van de Ven (2006), 'Discretionary rewards as a feedback mechanism', Working Paper 2006–16, Amsterdam Center for Law and Economics.

Waldfogel, J. (1993), 'The deadweight loss of Christmas', *American Economic Review*, **83**, 1328–36.

Young, H.P. (1993), 'The evolution of conventions', *Econometrica*, **61**, 57–84.

6. Assessing collective decision-making processes: the relevance of motivation

Philip Jones

INTRODUCTION

Collective decision-making processes attract criticism when the policies that communities adopt differ from policies prescribed to maximize citizens' welfare (Cullis and Jones, 1998). Differences are often attributed to biases introduced by voting rules and to distortions introduced by self-serving actors (for example politicians and bureaucrats). But what if differences arise because voters prefer policies that differ from those prescribed?

Public finance textbooks are critical of in-kind provision of services (for example education, medical care) but in Western economies budgets are dominated by the requirement to finance in-kind provision (Brennan and Pincus, 1983). Textbooks prescribe policies that provide the cash equivalent of services delivered in kind (because citizens can allocate cash to maximize welfare). Textbooks demonstrate that it is possible to achieve the same increase in welfare with lower levels of government spending. But what if voters express a preference for services provided in kind? In the UK, Le Grand (2003, p. 161) cites evidence that citizens are 'most proud of ... the NHS' and 'persist in their pride despite their perception of the service's ongoing difficulties'. If voters prefer these policies, have collective decision-making processes failed citizens by deferring to their preferences?

The first objective in this chapter is to consider the impact of the motivation that brings voters to the ballot box. How are preferences expressed at the ballot box? How will policies be designed to win voters' approval?

The second objective is to consider how collective decision-making processes should be assessed. Can they fail even when they deliver the policies that voters approve? If choice at the ballot box reflects more than instrumental evaluation of outcomes, how should the performance of collective decision-making processes be evaluated?

CHOICE AT THE BALLOT BOX

It is usually the case that voters are described as taxpaying-consumers in a 'political market'; a market in which politicians 'sell policies for votes' (Peacock, 1992, pp. 49–58). Gemmell et al. (2003, p. 793) refer to this 'standard approach' as one in which 'consumer–voters can identify … implicit tax prices and treat them analogously to market prices'. The approach focuses on *Homo economicus* (an egoistic individual whose motivation to take action is to change outcome).[1] The approach ignores the observations of the architects of utility theory (for example Bentham, 1789 [1970]) that individuals also derive utility from action. Theorists have focused narrowly on outcome (Lowenstein, 1999) but empiricists remind theoreticians that an individual is 'intrinsically motivated to perform an activity when one receives no apparent reward except the activity itself' (Deci, 1971, p. 105).

Downs (1957) focused on outcome when considering the decision to vote. If welfare derived from one electoral outcome rather than another is b (in utility), and the probability that a voter will influence an electoral outcome is p, the expected utility from voting is pb. If the costs of voting (that is, acquiring information and turning out to vote) equal c (in utility), an individual decides to vote if the net expected utility (*NEU*) is positive:

$$NEU = pb - c > 0. \tag{6.1}$$

But if citizens are expected to abstain when p is minuscule, turnout is high even in national elections (Aldrich, 1993).

For many, the 'paradox of voting' is testament to a different motivation. Riker and Ordeshook (1968) and Ashenfelter and Kelly (1975) show that voters turn out to fulfil civic duty. Fiorina (1976) and Brennan and Lomasky (1993) argue that voters take action to express preference. Both of these explanations share a common theme. Individuals take action to express identity (with the community and with preferred electoral alternatives).[2]

Wallis (2003, p. 227) shows that individuals 'define who they are in terms of the people they interact with and how they interact'. Individuals also act to affirm identity when identity is already preordained (by race, nationality, and so on). Akerlof and Kranton (2005) review an extensive empirical literature that explains behaviour in terms of willingness to express identity. If 'a person's identity describes gains and losses in utility from behaviour that conforms or departs from the norms for particular social categories in particular situations' (Akerlof and Kranton, 2005, p. 12), how will this affect choice at the ballot box?

If voters turn out to express identity, the choice they register will depend on their perception of their identity. The motivation that brings voters to the ballot box is relevant when explaining the choice that voters express. Elster (1986, p. 26) criticizes the argument that choice is separable from the motivation to vote:

> to explain *that* people vote, an appeal to civic duty or similar normative concepts seems inevitable; to explain *how* they vote, the appeal to self-interest is usually deemed sufficient (Barry, 1979). It is as if the voter, upon entering the voting booth, sheds the social motivations that had carried him there. Surely, this cannot be the right conceptualisation ...

To ignore the motivation to participate is to assume 'motivational schizophrenia' (Brennan and Lomasky, 1985, p. 194). Empirical studies support the proposition that the motivation to participate matters when voters express choice. Individuals act more collectively the more they feel part of a collective process (Pommerhene et al., 1997; Jones and Dawson, 2008). The question is not whether expressive action is relevant; the question is how relevant is expressive action.

Compare the choice that a consumer reveals with the choice a voter registers. Consider a consumer who prefers a large-engined motor car to a small-engined model (the large-engined model yields additional utility equal to B at an additional utility cost of C). The consumer also derives intrinsic value (E) by choosing the small-engined model and expressing identity with the community (the large-engined model increases pollution). The 'price' of expressive choice is the cost of foregoing a preferred outcome (in this case $B-C$).[3]

Now consider choice registered at the ballot box. The same individual decides whether large-engined motor cars should be banned (because of their environmental impact). The voter can express identity with the community (and derive E) by voting 'yes'. If legislation is passed there is no opportunity to acquire this automobile (the loss is $B-C$) but the 'price' of expressive choice depends on the expectation that one vote will alter the majority decision, and the probability (p) that a vote will be significant in a national election is very small (other things being equal). The price of expressive choice is $p(B-C)$ and this approaches zero as p approaches zero.

This comparison illustrates why an analogy between choice revealed by consumers and choice registered by voters is spurious.[4] It also highlights the relatively low price of expressive action when voters signal self-image (to themselves and to others).[5] If public policies differ from policies prescribed for *Homo economicus* it is because the motivation to participate in collective decision-making processes is not solely instrumental.

POLICIES APPROVED AT THE BALLOT BOX

Politicians 'formulate policies in order to win elections, rather than win elections in order to formulate policies' (Downs, 1957, p. 28). In this section of the chapter the focus falls on the way policy is designed when voters identify with the process by which services are supplied. When considering welfare-state provision of services, voters' incentive is to express a 'generous' identity, by signalling (to themselves and to others) that 'as a matter of ideological principle ... [they] ... *believe* in the welfare state' (Brennan, 2001, p. 227, emphasis added).

Empirical studies reveal that individuals are not simply outcome-regarding (motivated by 'the quantity and quality of goods and services that they possess and consume'); individuals are also 'process-regarding' (Bowles and Gintis, 2006, p. 172).[6] If voters were solely outcome-regarding they would assess institutions and processes 'in terms of the outcomes produced' (Brennan and Hamlin, 2002, p. 310). Institutions would be assessed 'in a manner analogous to that in which market institutions are judged' (that is, with 'reference to the allocation of resources that they induce'). But, as individuals are also process-regarding there is an incentive to identify with 'what those institutions "stand for"' (Brennan and Hamlin, 2002, p. 310). As processes 'have inherent value in their own right', voters' preferences differ from preferences premised on 'a narrow consequentialist view' (Dolan et al., 2007, p. 159).

If voters' incentive is to turn out to express identity (as 'generous' citizens committed to equal access to services) this motivation is relevant when politicians design public policy. Voters might see very little cost in expressing identity at the ballot box but the relevant price when designing public policy is the price that will be paid by politicians. In this section of the chapter the focus falls on the pressures that politicians must accommodate when designing public policy.

In many communities primary education is supplied to all children (with the proviso that parents must pay to supplement provision, for example for additional music tuition). Medical care may also be supplied with equal access (with the proviso that patients pay for treatment deemed non-essential, for example cosmetic surgery). What determines the extent to which policy relies on welfare-state provision of services?

When voters consider the signal they emit they are conscious of the inherent virtues associated with policy process. The draftsman of the UK National Health Service (Aneurin Bevan) argued: 'No society can legitimately call itself civilised if a sick person is denied medical aid because of a lack of means' (Foot, 1975, p. 103). Voters' incentive is to signal self-image and, for some, there is a predilection to express identity this way.

In Figure 6.1, MV_E is marginal (expressive) vote gain if voters identify with the process of equal access. Acting expressively, voters approve an increase in

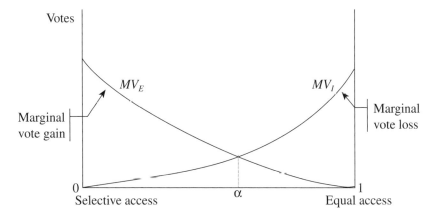

Figure 6.1   Designing public policy

the proportion of medical services supplied with equal access (along a spectrum that runs from 0 – only selective access – to 1). Votes are won at a diminishing rate because voters are also sensitive to attributes associated with selective access. In the 1980s selective access to services was exhorted as nurturing self-reliance and personal responsibility (see Kavanagh's 1990 analysis of Mrs Thatcher's speeches). As more services are supplied with equal access, marginal vote gain diminishes.

The incentive to politicians is to design policy to accommodate expressive pressures but there is a price if instrumental pressures are also articulated. Figure 6.1 also illustrates marginal vote loss (MV_I) if:

1. Some voters (mistakenly) assume that their vote counts. Following Marmolo (1999), marginal vote loss increases when self-interested instrumental taxpayers are reluctant to increase 'equal access provision' because they perceive tax as a payment to supply services to others. [7]
2. Some citizens exert pressure via lobby groups. Lobby groups offer electoral campaign contributions that can be used to win votes (Brennan and Buchanan, 1984). In this context, producers (as a 'small' group) exert pressure instrumentally (Olson, 1965). If equal access is to be provided when services are supplied by bureaus, producers fear that they will experience losses because bureaus might act as monopsonist purchasers of their services (Mueller, 2003).

In Figure 6.1 votes are maximized when the degree of equal access is α (that is, when the proportion of all medical services with equal access is α). Figure 6.1 offers a framework for analysis of the design of public policy. This framework can be refined to explain why different communities place different emphasis on the provision of welfare-state services. For example:

1. MV_E shifts to the right the more that individuals identify with collective processes. When comparing reliance on welfare-state processes, Alesina et al. (1999) highlight the importance of ethnic fragmentation within the community. Alesina and Glaeser (2004) argue that 'welfare state' expenditure is lower in the USA than in European countries because ethnic fragmentation is greater (Americans 'like most people ... prefer giving money to people of their own race, religion and ethnicity', p. 6). Willingness to identify with recipients of services is relevant when explaining support in the USA (Poterba, 1997; Alesina et al., 1999; Luttmer, 2001), in other Western democracies (Lindert, 1996) and in developing countries (La Ferrara, 2002). The greater the weight that voters give to expressive voting the more they identify with collective provision of services in kind (and the more that MV_E shifts to the right).

2. MV_I shifts to the right when producers see opportunities to achieve improved working conditions by collaboration with budget-maximizing government bureaus (Tollison and Wagner, 1991).

Policies presented to the electorate will be policies designed to accommodate expressive and instrumental pressures. Policies differ systematically from textbook prescriptions because textbook policies are prescribed for instrumental *Homo economicus*. Differences can be explained with reference to the way that expressive and instrumental pressures are articulated. As 'producers of mass participation' (Schuessler, 2000, p. 91), politicians rely on a 'symbol-intensive, expressive-attachment-inviting approach' (Schuessler, 2000, p. 87).[8]

POSITIVE AND NEGATIVE 'MOTIVATION SPILLOVER'

With evidence that the motivation to participate in collective decision-making processes is the intrinsic value of expressive action, it is no surprise that public policies differ systematically from policies prescribed for instrumental citizens. If government spending differs from levels predicted for instrumental *Homo economicus*, these differences are not indicative, in and of themselves, of failings in decision-making processes. But are collective decision-making processes always commendable if they deliver the policies that voters approve?

The starting point, once again, is the price of expressive action. This 'price' ($p[B-C]$) is so much lower than the cost each voter will experience ($B-C$) if, collectively, voters forego prescribed outcomes. Public finance texts predict that there will be 'deadweight loss' if voters rely on equal access to services (services supplied 'free' at the point of delivery). Textbooks predict deadweight loss (and excessive levels of government spending) because each recipient of the service has an incentive to consume beyond the point at which the marginal benefit of the service is equal to marginal resource cost. Will policy be welfare-enhancing if these concerns are discounted?

While each individual expresses choice at the ballot box with little or no concern for outcome, collectively voters change outcomes (Jones, 2008). 'Motivation spillover' occurs when citizens do not consider outcome but take action that (collectively) will affect outcome.

Positive Motivation Spillover

Positive motivation spillover occurs when expressive action proves consistent with the attainment of a preferred outcome. Consider a representative citizen who is the equivalent of £100 better off if a collective good is provided. If the individual were purely instrumental there would be no incentive to vote for the policy (as a single vote has virtually no impact on the 'will of the majority') and there would be no incentive to design this policy. However, if the representative citizen also derives intrinsic value (E) from expressive action (for example expressing identity with the action government proposes) there is an incentive. If the expressive voter is representative there is positive motivation spillover because, collectively, voters will redress 'undersupply' (in terms of individuals' own preferences).

Focusing on services supplied with equal access, public finance textbooks consider deadweight loss for self-interested *Homo economicus*. However, if voters choose equal access to services because they are altruists, a collective good (altruism) is likely to be supplied more efficiently. With utility interdependence, the marginal benefit of a service supplied with equal access exceeds the marginal benefit derived by recipients of the service. Altruists also derive marginal benefit from consumption by others. Hochman and Rodgers (1969) explain why government intervention is required (for if each altruist focused only on outcome, each altruist's incentive would be to 'free ride'). Equal access to tax-financed services ('free' at the point of delivery) can prove to be exactly the process that yields an efficient allocation of resources (for example Culyer, 1971).

Motivation spillover is positive because in the absence of the motivation to turn out to express identity (with process) there would be no incentive to design a policy that will deliver this collective good. Motivation spillover redresses the 'undersupply' of a collective good (altruism) that would occur if individuals' only incentive to act were instrumental (to change outcome) – instrumental citizens are 'rationally apathetic'.

Negative Motivation Spillover

The difficulty is that preferred outcome may be incompatible with preferred process (and a misleadingly low price of expressive action creates an incentive to dismiss evaluation of outcome). If an expressive voter ($E > 0$) derives negative net benefit (B-C) from a collective good, equivalent to −£100, there is an incentive to discount such instrumental evaluation of outcome (because a single vote is unlikely to change the majority decision).

Returning to the example of equal access to services, self-interested taxpayers experience costs as a consequence of increased consumption by others. If voters' only gain is intrinsic value when signalling identity (with this process), they experience costs as government spending differs from the levels they would prefer as self-interested citizens (just as public finance textbooks describe). When process and outcome are incompatible there is concern that a misleadingly low price of expressive action creates an incentive to dismiss these costs.[9]

In this case a great deal depends on the existence of constraints to limit 'excessive' expressive action in political processes. If in Figure 6.1, MV_E fully reflected marginal benefit (derived from provision of equal access) and MV_I fully reflected efficiency costs, α would represent a welfare-enhancing trade-off. Following Becker (1983), those who feel better off from preferred process would (potentially) be able to compensate those who suffer deadweight loss. Brooks (2002) illustrates the impact on welfare when considering reliance on regulation to reduce pollution. If the electorate 'find more appeal in the command-and-control approach' as compared with more 'instrumentally efficient' policies (such as taxation) regulation might be 'Kaldor–Hicks preferred' (pp. 161, 171).

When considering the USA's decision to renew 'Most Favored Nation' trading status for China in 1994, expressive voters objected because the Chinese government had not made sufficient progress with human rights. This expressive pressure was constrained by 'strong pressure from the business community' (Baldwin and Magee, 2000, p. 85). Excessive expressive pressure is also constrained if citizens vote for more than one policy. Tullock (1971) argues that this constrains expressive inclination for any one policy. Clark and Lee (2006) argue that expressive voting is constrained because voters eventually become cynical of politicians' reliance on expressive-attachment-inviting policy. If these constraints are operative, voters are less vulnerable than they would be if expressive action were unbridled. These constraints are relevant when determining the relative positions of MV_E and MV_I in Figure 6.1.

A misleadingly low price of expressive action may be constrained if instrumental actors resist expressive voting. The problem arises when instrumental actors' interests are served by encouraging (and manipulating) expressive voting. Negative motivation spillover is more likely under the circumstances described below.

Rent-seekers' incentive is to increase voters' vulnerability

Rent-seeking occurs when producers incur costs to press for payments in excess of payments they would receive in a competitive market (Tullock, 1965) but rent-seeking costs are much lower than anticipated (for example, for estimates of rent-seeking costs experienced, see Ansolabehere et al., 2003). Tullock (1997, 1998) repeatedly asks why. Magee (1997, p. 545) comments: 'Tullock has posed an underdissipation puzzle on the question of rent seeking: Why is so little expended, relative to benefits ... ?'.

The likelihood of negative motivation spillover increases when there is pressure to design policies to deliver rent. Policies are designed to accommodate seemingly disparate groups. Focusing on regulation, Yandle (1989, p. 39) noted that: 'regulation of the Sunday sale of booze ties together bootleggers, Baptists and the legal operators of liquor stores' (p. 34). Regulation of the Sunday sale of alcohol delivers a direct 'consumption' gain to Baptists (expressing identity) and rent to 'bootleggers' (who experience higher profits when the legal supply of alcohol is regulated). But Baptists are vulnerable if their preoccupation with expressive action means that they ignore the finer points of policy (if they fail to question whether regulation might be designed more efficiently). Rent-seeking costs are lower than expected because resistance to rent-seekers is lower than anticipated.

Consider policy that accommodates expressive pressures from citizen groups for international aid (Kaul and Conceição, 2006) and instrumental pressures from producers of export goods for international aid (Burnell, 1991). 'Tied aid' requires that recipients import from donor countries. Tied aid aligns both groups, but if expressive voters assessed policy in greater detail, it would be evident that tied aid is less efficient than aid without these import constraints (Jones, 1996).[10]

Turning to policies that offer equal access to services, the National Health Service in the UK won greater support when the concerns of highly paid medical consultants were addressed (Eckstein, 1960). Equal access to services is more prevalent when producers are able to create rent-seeking opportunities (Tollison and Wagner, 1991).[11]

Negative motivation spillover is more likely (and rent-seeking costs are systematically lower) when expressive voters are manipulated, that is, when 'the power expressive voting grants government to pursue noble goals is captured by interest groups for nefarious purposes' (Clark and Lee, 2006, p. 27).[12]

Voters rely on representation

Negative motivation spillover may also be more likely the more that voters identify with personalities. Representative democracy offers an even more tenuous 'contract' and the voter has a further incentive to discount instrumental evaluation of outcome. When it is left to political representatives to assess outcomes and make decisions, voters' inclination is to express identity with personality traits (exalted in political representatives). McLean (2001) is critical that public choice analysis ignores the charismatic impact of leadership. Jones and Hudson (1996) estimate the impact when voters identify with a candidate's personality. Studies estimate citizens' response to ethical posturing by leaders (Vitell and Davis, 1990, measure this response). Voters are likely to be more vulnerable to negative motivation spillover the more they rely on expression of identity with politicians' personalities.

Voters rely on ideology
When discussing stable expression of identity, Pizzorno (1986, pp. 368–9) argues that social action is motivated by expression of 'interpersonal horizontal connectedness' (with different groups within the community) and 'vertical connectedness' (with perceptions of a future self). Loyalty to 'a common circle of recognition' increases the more individuals rely on 'strong ideological commitments'. However, the more that politicians rely on strong ideological commitments to win loyalty, the more they are able to manipulate expressive voters and the greater the likelihood of negative motivation spillover.

Brennan and Lomasky (1993) discuss extreme examples of costs experienced by negative motivation spillover when they reflect on the impact of expressive motivation in pre-World War II Germany. Outcomes experienced were far worse because individuals relied so heavily on identity with personality and ideology.

CONCLUSIONS

This chapter began with two objectives. The first was to explore the impact of motivation on choice. If voters derive intrinsic value from action, it matters how they act (it matters how they express identity – to themselves and to others). If citizens participate to derive intrinsic value from expressive action, public policy differs from policy prescribed for instrumental *Homo economicus.*

This chapter offers a framework for policy analysis. Policy is designed to accommodate expressive and instrumental pressures. While the analytical framework has been applied to explain why communities rely on tax-financed services ('free' at the point of delivery), it can be applied generally to explain why policy differs from policy prescribed for *Homo economicus.*[13]

The second objective was to explore the relevance of motivation when assessing the performance of collective decision-making processes. When voters turn out to derive intrinsic value from action, a low price of expressive action may create a positive motivation spillover. When preference for outcome is congruent with preference for process, the incentive to turn out to express identity with preferred process corrects an 'undersupply' of collective goods (in terms of individuals' own preferences). In this chapter expression of identity with the process of in-kind provision corrects an 'undersupply' of altruism.

Problems arise when expressive action and preferred outcome are incongruent. The question is whether 'excessive' (expressive) action will be constrained. If those who act instrumentally (for example interest groups) are able to correct the distortions that would otherwise occur, the conclusion is that one distortion (created by a misleadingly low price of expressive action) may be mitigated by another (for example disproportionate action by pressure groups).

In the absence of such 'safety net' features there is negative motivation spillover. If those who act instrumentally find their interests are better served by manipulating (rather than resisting) expressive action, negative motivation spillover is even more likely. Negative motivation spillover is more likely if the problem of a misleadingly low price of expressive action is compounded because rent-seekers' interests are served by expressive action and because voters focus on personalities and ideologies.

The overarching conclusion is that assessments of the performance of collective decision-making processes depend on analysis of motivation spillover. However it is important to note that negative motivation spillovers are not unique to collective decision-making processes. Recent studies of the determinants of 'happiness' (for example Layard, 2005) highlight the significance of relative income. Market failure is created by expressive action (by 'conspicuous consumption'). Consumers are trapped in an expressive acquisition race (spending more and more on larger houses, more powerful motor cars, and so on). Negative motivation spillover means that the collective good (that Frank, 1997, refers to as a 'frame of reference') is oversupplied because 'ordinary people end up spending too much time earning money to buy private goods' (Frank, 1997, p. 1841).[14]

In summary, any evaluation of the performance of collective decision-making processes is sensitive to the behavioural assumptions upon which it is premised (Jones, 2008).[15] If evaluation is premised on instrumental motivation (to change outcome) it is possible to compare policies that are delivered with policies prescribed for instrumental citizens. But if individuals also derive utility from action (Bentham, 1789 [1970]), this benchmark is no longer appropriate. Any evaluation of the performance of collective decision-making processes must be premised on a comparison between the policies that collective decision-making processes deliver and the policies that citizens would approve if they were faced with an accurate price of expressive voting. Collective decision-making processes may fail citizens even when they deliver the very policies voters approve.

NOTES

1. Brennan and Lomasky (1993) provide a comprehensive description of *Homo economicus*.
2. Downs referred to the importance of civic duty for instrumental individuals. He argued that they vote because democracy will not survive if they fail to fulfil their civic duty. However this long-term goal is a public good and instrumental voters would not incur cost to provide this outcome (Aldrich, 1997). This chapter focuses on the intrinsic value of expressive action.
3. Choice can be expressive in markets. Consumers are willing to pay more for 'eco-labelled' products to express environmental concern (Zarrilli et al., 1997); investors sometimes prefer ethical investments with lower monetary rates of return that eschew certain production processes (Lewis et al., 1998). But market choice is usually to acquire goods and services.
4. Satisfaction from expressive approval (E) might differ in the two examples (in one case by purchasing and in the other by voting) but the 'choice' expressed will always depend on differences in the 'price' of expressive approval in each forum.
5. For evidence that voters express choice with reference to symbols (rather than with reference to instrumental valuation) see Sears et al. (1980) and Jones and Dawson (2007). For surveys of studies that report differences in voting patterns between those premised on 'pocket book' voting and those premised on expressive voting see Brennan and Lomasky (1993) and Hudson and Jones (1994).
6. For further evidence that individuals are prepared to trade-off preferred outcome for preferred process see empirical studies by Kahneman et al. (1986), Lind and Tyler (1988) and Kramer and Tyler (1996).
7. Quattrone and Tversky (1986) argue that some voters confuse the causal impact of action with the diagnostic signal (they vote because they know that if sufficient numbers voted for a preferred outcome, this outcome would be achieved and, in so doing, they confuse diagnosis with causal impact of a personal vote). Drinkwater and Jennings (2007) provide an empirical analysis of the differences between those who vote expressively and those who vote instrumentally.
8. This example explains the existence of in-kind provision of services with reference to expressive voting. There are alternative explanations. Normative analysis prescribes equal access for public goods because it is costly to exclude access to public goods (Samuelson, 1954) but Marmolo (1999, p. 29) emphasizes that, in practice, services are seldom 'non-excludable'. It is possible to offer other explanations premised solely on instrumental motivation but these are also far from satisfactory. 'Merit wants' are supplied when consumers are unable to judge what is 'good' for them (Musgrave, 1957). Voters defer to experts in government (Mooney, 1979). But when are services 'merit wants' (individuals are seldom fully informed)? Who are the 'experts'? And why do experts not simply supply information? Another explanation is set in terms of Director's Law. The middle class are wooed by the poor and by the rich to support redistribution (Stigler, 1970; Tullock, 1971) and, in practice, the middle class gain if services are provided 'free' at the point of delivery (Le Grand, 1982; Dixon et al., 2003). But this explanation ignores the argument that not all redistribution favours a majority (minorities sometimes gain at the expense of a majority; Mueller, 2003) and fiscal preferences (across different income cohorts) are not as predicted (for example Gramlich and Rubinfeld, 1982).
9. In the *Theory of Moral Sentiments*, Adam Smith (1790 [1982], I.i.2.1. p. 14) distinguished between expression of sympathy (with preferred values) and pursuit of self-interest; when 'both the pleasure and the pain are always felt so instantaneously ... it seems evident that neither of them can be derived from ... self-interested consideration'. If it is desirable that voters act as 'impartial spectators', a low price of expressive voting is attractive. J.S. Mill argued that the voter 'is called upon ... to be guided ... by another rule than his own private partialities' (Mill, 1991 [1861], p. 255). However, there is cause for concern if willingness to identify 'sympathetically' with a preferred 'rule' (to derive the 'consumption' gain from expressive action) means that voters' incentive is to dismiss consideration of the impact the 'rule' exerts on outcome.

10. Similarly, consider policy designed to exert trade sanctions. Such policy is a reflection of expressive disapproval but policy is also designed to accommodate instrumental pressures from producers for import protection (Kaempfer and Lowenberg, 1988). However, policies designed to accommodate both pressures deliver trade sanctions that 'seldom achieve their goals' (van Bergeijk, 1994).

11. There are many other examples. Körber (1998) questions alignment in the USA between environmentalists and producers of canned tuna (pressing for legislation to protect the dolphin). Legislation offered environmentalists an expressive gain and US producers achieved a competitive advantage (because by the 1980s the supply of tuna to US producers was from dolphin-free waters).

12. Olson (1965) argued that large groups will be exploited by small groups and such exploitation is likely to increase if individuals dismiss instrumental evaluation of outcome in large group situations.

13. It was noted that differences can be explained with reference to: (a) differences in the scope for expressive and instrumental pressures in political processes (for example differences in the influence that pressure groups might exert); and (b) differences in socio-economic variables that determine the likelihood that voters will derive intrinsic value when identifying with collective processes (for example the degree of ethnic fragmentation; Alesina et al., 1999). It should also be emphasized that the positions of MV_E and MV_I in Figure 6.1 also depend on p, the probability that a single vote will change an outcome (see Sobel and Wagner, 2004) and on signals that expressive action is acknowledged (Frey, 1997).

14. Table 6.1 illustrates the incentive to spend 'excessively'. An individual decides whether to spend £4 acquiring a good purely as a status symbol (which yields a private gain of £5 when others are unable to acquire the good). The payoff from acquisition is (£5–£4) if others do not acquire this symbol but, if others purchase the good, the status gain of £5 is 'cancelled'. On the other hand, if the individual does not acquire the good, the individual is £5 worse off when others purchase the good (but no worse off if no one purchases the good). The individual's incentive is to express identity even though the outcome when all act expressively (−£4 in the top left-hand cell) is worse than if no one acquired the good (0 in the lower right-hand cell).

Table 6.1   Collective action and 'frames of reference'

	'Others' acquire a symbol	'Others' do not acquire a symbol
acquire a symbol	−5 + 5 −4 = −4	+5 − 4 = 1
not acquire a symbol	−5	0

15. A new literature referred to as 'behavioral public finance' (for example McCaffery and Slemrod, 2006) is relevant when assessing the way that collective decision-making processes serve citizens who differ systematically from instrumental *Homo economicus*.

REFERENCES

Akerlof, G. and R.E. Kranton (2005), 'Identity and the economics of organizations', *Journal of Economic Perspectives*, **19** (1), 9–32.

Aldrich, J. (1993), 'Rational choice and turnout', *American Journal of Political Science*, **37** (1), 246–78.

Aldrich, John (1997), 'When is it rational to vote?' in Dennis C. Mueller (ed.), *Perspectives on Public Choice*, Cambridge: Cambridge University Press, pp. 373–90.

Alesina, A., R. Baqir and W. Easterly (1999), 'Public goods and ethnic divisions', *Quarterly Journal of Economics*, **114** (4), 1243–84.

Alesina, Alberto and Edward L. Glaeser (2004), *Fighting Poverty in the US and Europe: a World of Difference*, Oxford: Oxford University Press.

Ansolabehere, S., J.M. de Figueiredo and J. Snyder Jr (2003), 'Why is there so little money in US politics?' *Journal of Economic Perspectives*, **17** (1), 105–30.

Ashenfelter, O. and S. Kelly Jr. (1975), 'Determinants of participation in presidential elections', *Journal of Law and Economics*, **18** (4), 695–733.

Baldwin, R.E. and C.S. Magee (2000), 'Is trade policy for sale? Congressional voting on recent trade bills', *Public Choice*, **105** (1–2), 79–101.

Barry, Brian (1979), *Economists, Sociologists and Democracy*, rev. edn, Chicago, IL: University of Chicago Press.

Becker, G.S. (1983), 'A theory of competition among pressure groups for political influence', *Quarterly Journal of Economics*, **98** (3), 371–99.

Bentham, J. (1789), *The Principles of Morals and Legislation*, edited by J.H. Burns and H.L.A. Hart (1970), London: Athlone.

Bowles, Samuel and Herbert Gintis (2006), 'Social preferences, *homo economicus* and *zoon politikon*', in Robert. E. Goodin and Charles Tilly (eds), *The Oxford Handbook of Contextual Political Analysis*, Oxford: Oxford University Press, pp. 172–86.

Brennan, G. (2001), 'Five rational actor accounts of the welfare state', *Kyklos*, **54** (2–3), 213–33.

Brennan, G. and J.M. Buchanan (1984), 'Voter choice: evaluating political alternatives', *American Behavioral Scientist*, **28** (2), 185–201.

Brennan, G. and A. Hamlin (2002), 'Expressive constitutionalism', *Constitutional Political Economy*, **13** (4), 299–311.

Brennan, G. and L. Lomasky (1985), 'The impartial spectator goes to Washington: toward a Smithian theory of electoral politics', *Economics and Philosophy*, **1** (1), 189–211.

Brennan, Geoffrey and Loren Lomasky (1993), *Democracy and Decision: The Pure Theory of Electoral Preference*, Cambridge: Cambridge University Press.

Brennan, G. and J.M. Pincus (1983), 'Government expenditure growth and resource allocation', *Oxford Economic Papers*, **35** (3), 351–65.

Brooks, M. (2002), 'Lowering the cost of pollution control versus controlling pollution: a comment', *Public Choice*, **110** (1–2), 163–72.

Burnell, Peter (1991), *Charity, Politics and the Third World*, London: Harvester Wheatsheaf.

Clark, J.R. and Dwight R. Lee (2006), 'Expressive voting: how special interests enlist their victims as political allies', in Giuseppe Eusepi and Alan Hamlin (eds), *Beyond Conventional Economics: The Limits of Rational Behaviour in Political Decision Making*, Cheltenham, UK and Northampton, MA, USA: Edward Elgar, pp. 17–32.

Cullis, John and Philip Jones (1998), *Public Finance and Public Choice*, 2nd edn, Oxford, Oxford University Press.

Culyer, A.J. (1971), 'The nature of the commodity health care and its efficient allocation', *Oxford Economic Papers*, **23** (2), 189–211.

Deci, E.L. (1971), 'Effects of externally mediated rewards on intrinsic motivation', *Journal of Personality and Social Psychology*, **18** (1), 105–15.

Dixon, Anna, Julian Le Grand, John Henderson, Richard Murray and Emmi Poteliakhoff (2003), 'Is the NHS equitable? a review of evidence', London School of Economics, Health and Social Care Discussion Paper No 11.

Dolan, P., R. Edllin, A. Tsuchiya and A. Wailoo (2007), 'It ain't what you do it's the way that you do it: characteristics of procedural justice and their importance in social decision-making', *Journal of Economic Behavior and Organisation*, **64** (1), 157–70.

Downs, Anthony (1957), *An Economic Theory of Democracy*, New York: Harper & Row.

Drinkwater, S. and C. Jennings (2007), 'Who are the expressive voters?' *Public Choice*, **132** (1–2), 179–89.

Eckstein, Harry (1960), *Pressure Group Politics: The Case of the British Medical Association*, London: Allen & Unwin.

Elster, Jon (1986), *The Multiple Self*, Cambridge: Cambridge University Press.

Fiorina, M.P. (1976), 'The voting decision: instrumental and expressive aspects', *Journal of Politics*, **21**, 601–25.

Foot, Michael (1975), *Aneurin Bevan 1945–1960*, London: Paladin.

Frank, R.H. (1997), 'The frame of reference as a public good', *Economic Journal*, **107** (445), 1832–47.

Frey, Bruno S. (1997), *Not Just For the Money: An Economic Theory of Personal Motivation*, Cheltenham, UK and Lyme, NH, USA: Edward Elgar.

Gemmell, N., O. Morrissey and A. Pinar (2003), 'Tax perceptions and the demand for public expenditure: evidence from UK micro-data', *European Journal of Political Economy*, **19** (4), 793–816.

Gramlich, E.M. and D.L. Rubinfeld (1982), 'Micro estimates of public spending demand functions and tests of the Tiebout and median voter hypothesis', *Journal of Political Economy*, **90** (3), 536–60.

Hochman, H.M. and J.D. Rodgers (1969), 'Pareto optimal redistribution', *American Economic Review*, **57** (3–5), 542–57.

Hudson, J. and P. Jones (1994), 'The importance of the "ethical voter": an estimate of "altruism"', *European Journal of Political Economy*, **10** (3), 499–509.

Jones, P. (1996), 'Rents from in-kind subsidy: "charity" in the public sector', *Public Choice*, **86** (3–4), 359–87.

Jones, P. (2008), 'Motivation spillover: tax policy designed to mobilise collective action', *Public Finance and Management*, **8** (2), 234–64.

Jones, P. and P. Dawson (2007), 'Choice in collective decision-making processes: instrumental or expressive approval?', *Journal of Socio-Economics*, **36** (1), 101–17.

Jones, P. and P. Dawson (2008), 'How much do voters know? An analysis of motivation and political awareness', *Scottish Journal of Political Economy*, **5** (2), 123–42.

Jones, P. and J. Hudson (1996), 'The quality of political leadership: a case study of John Major', *British Journal of Political Science*, **26** (2), 292–44.

Kaempfer, W.H. and A.D. Lowenberg (1988), 'The theory of international economic sanctions: a public choice approach', *American Economic Review*, **78** (4), 786–93.

Kahneman, D., J.L. Knetsch and R.H. Thaler (1986), 'Fairness as a constraint on profit seeking: entitlements in the market', *American Economic Review*, **76** (4), 728–41.

Kaul, Inge and Pedro Conceição (2006), *The New Public Finance: Responding to Global Challenges*, New York: Oxford University Press.

Kavanagh, Dennis (1990), *Thatcherism and British Politics*, Oxford: Oxford University Press.

Körber, A. (1998), 'Why everybody loves Flipper: the political economy of the US Dolphin Safe Laws', *European Journal of Political Economy*, **14** (3), 475–509.

Kramer, R.M. and T.R. Tyler (1996), *Trust in Organizations*, Thousand Oaks, CA: Sage.

La Ferrara, E. (2002), 'Inequality and group participation; theory and evidence from rural Tanzania', *Journal of Public Economics*, **85** (2), 235–73.

Layard, Richard (2005), 'Rethinking public economics: the implications of rivalry and habit', in Luigino Bruni and Pier Luigi Porta (eds), *Economics and Happiness: Framing the Analysis*, Oxford: Oxford University Press, pp. 147–69.

Le Grand, Julian (1982), *The Strategy of Equality*, London: Allen & Unwin.

Le Grand, Julian (2003), *Motivation, Agency, and Public Policy*, Oxford: Oxford University Press.

Lewis, A., P. Webley, A. Winnett and C. Mackenzie (1998), 'Morals and markets: some theoretical and policy implications of ethical investing', in P. Taylor-Gooby (ed.), *Choice and Public Policy: The Limits to Welfare Markets*, London: Macmillan, pp. 164–83.

Lind, E. Allan and Tom R. Tyler (1988), *The Social Psychology of Procedural Justice*, New York and London: Plenum Press.

Lindert, P.H. (1996), 'What limits social spending?' *Explorations in Economic History*, **33** (1), 1–34.

Lowenstein, G. (1999), 'Because it is there: the challenge of mountaineering for utility theory', *Kyklos*, **52** (3), 315–44.

Luttmer, E.F.P. (2001), 'Group loyalty and the taste for redistribution', *Journal of Political Economy*, **109** (3), 500–528.

Magee, Stephen P. (1997), 'Endogenous protection: the empirical evidence', in Dennis C. Mueller (ed.), *Perspectives on Public Choice: A Handbook*, Cambridge: Cambridge University Press, pp. 526–61.

Marmolo, E. (1999), 'A constitutional theory of public goods', *Journal of Economic Behavior and Organization*, **38** (1), 27–42.

McCaffery, Edward and Joel Slemrod (2006), *Behavioral Finance: Towards a New Agenda*, New York, NY: Russell Sage Foundation.

McLean, Iain (2001), *Rational Choice and British Politics: An Analysis of Rhetoric and Manipulation from Peel to Blair*, Oxford: Oxford University Press.

Mill, J.S. (1991 [1861]), 'Considerations on representative government', in *On Liberty and Other Essays*, Oxford: Oxford University Press, pp. 205–476.

Mooney, Gavin H. (1979), 'Values in health care', in Kenneth Lee (ed.), *Economics and Planning*, London: Croom Helm, pp. 23–44.

Mueller, Dennis C. (2003), *Public Choice III*, Cambridge, Cambridge University Press.

Musgrave, Richard A. (1957), *The Theory of Public Finance*, New York: McGraw Hill.

Olson, Mancur Jr (1965), *The Logic of Collective Action: Public Goods and the Theory of Groups*, Cambridge, MA: Harvard University Press.

Peacock, Alan (1992), *Public Choice Analysis in Historical Perspective*, Cambridge: Cambridge University Press.

Pizzorno, Alessandro (1986), 'Some other kinds of otherness: a critique of "rational choice" theories', in Alejandro Foxley, Michael S. McPherson and Guillermo O'Donnell (eds), *Development, Democracy and the Art of Trespassing: Essays in Honor of Albert O. Hirschman*, Notre Dame, IN: University of Notre Dame, pp. 355–73.

Pommerhene, W.W., A. Hart and L.P. Feld (1997), 'Steuerhinterziehung und ihre Konrtolee in unter-shiedlichen politischen Systemen', *Homo Oeconomicus*, **14**, 469–87.

Poterba, J.M. (1977), 'Demographic structure and political economy of public education', *Journal of Public Policy Analysis and Management*, **16** (1), 48–66.

Quattrone, George A. and Amos Tversky (1986), 'Self deception and the voter's illusion', in Jon Elster (ed.), *The Multiple Self*, Cambridge: Cambridge University Press, pp. 35–58.

Riker, W.H. and P.C. Ordeshook (1968), 'A theory of the calculus of voting', *American Political Science Review*, **62** (1), 25–42.

Samuleson, P.A. (1954), 'The pure theory of public expenditure', *Review of Economics and Statistics*, **36** (4), 387–9.

Schuessler, Alexander A. (2000), *A Logic of Expressive Choice*, Princeton, NJ: Princeton University Press.

Sears, D.O., R.R. Lau, T.R. Tyler and H.M. Allen Jr (1980), 'Self interest vs. symbolic politics in policy attitudes and presidential voting', *American Political Science Review*, **74** (2), 670–84.

Smith, A. (1790) *The Theory of Moral Sentiments*, edited by D.D. Raphael and A.L. Macfie (1982), Indianapolis, IN: Liberty Classics.

Sobel, R. and G.A. Wagner (2004), 'Expressive voting and government redistribution: testing Tullock's "Charity of the Uncharitable"', *Public Choice*, **119** (1–2), 143–59.

Stigler, G. (1970), 'Director's Law of public income redistribution', *Journal of Law and Economics*, **13** (1), 1–10.

Tollison, R.D. and R.E. Wagner (1991), 'Self interest, public interest and public health', *Public Choice*, **69** (3), 232–43.

Tullock, G. (1965), 'The welfare costs of tariffs, monopolies and theft', *Western Economic Journal*, **5** (3), 224–32.

Tullock, G. (1971), 'The charity of the uncharitable', *Western Economic Journal*, **9** (4), 379–92.

Tullock, G. (1997), 'Where is the rectangle?' *Public Choice*, **91** (2), 149–59.

Tullock, G. (1998), 'Which rectangle?' *Public Choice*, **96** (1–2), 405–10.

van Bergeijk, Peter A.G. (1994), *Economic Diplomacy, Trade and Commercial Policy*, Aldershot, UK and Brookfield, VT, USA: Edward Elgar.

Vitell, S.J. and D.L. Davis (1990), 'The relationship between ethics and job satisfaction: an empirical investigation', *Journal of Business Ethics*, **9** (6), 489–94.

Wallis, John J. (2003), 'The public promotion of private interest (groups)', in J. Heckelman and Dennis Coates (eds), *Collective Choice Essays in Honor of Mancur Olson*, Berlin: Springer-Verlag, pp. 219–46.

Yandle, Bruce (1989), 'Bootleggers and Baptists in the market for regulation', in Jason S. Shogren (ed.), *The Political Economy of Government Regulation*, London: Kluwer, pp. 29–54.

Zarrilli, Simonetta, Veena Jha and Rene Vossenaar (1997), *Eco-Labelling and International Trade*, London: Macmillan.

7. Positive constraints on normative political theory[1]

Geoffrey Brennan and Alan Hamlin

INTRODUCTION

What should be the relationship between positive political theory and normative political theory? This is the large question towards which this chapter edges. The answer to this large question will depend, in part, on our understanding of the purposes of positive and normative political theory, respectively. We will not dwell for long on discussing the range of potential purposes and will simply stipulate that a primary purpose of positive political theory is to explain observed political behaviour. We will make no attempt to explain what we mean by 'explain', or the differences between explanation, prediction and other related ideas, but we will stress that the central idea of explanation goes beyond mere description while leaving open a wide variety of approaches to positive political theory.[2]

With respect to normative political theory, we identify three possible aims. First, analysing normative concepts, categories, ideals and intuitions aimed at revealing their true features and interrelationships (if any). Call this the formal aim of normative theory. Second, deploying normative criteria or ideals to evaluate particular actions, policies, practices, reforms and institutions. Call this the evaluative aim of normative political theory. Third, justifying and advocating particular actions, policies, practices, reforms and institutions in the real world. Call this the practical aim of normative political theory.[3] Clearly these three aims interact, in that the practical aim requires formal and evaluative consideration, and equally clearly normative political theory might be valuable even if the practical aim were not achieved – although we would suggest that its value would be sharply reduced. At first glance it may seem that the evaluative and the practical aims overlap, but it is what divides the practical from the evaluative that is crucial for our purposes: for this is precisely where 'positive political theory' connects with normative theory.

Almost everything we say in this chapter relates to the practical aim of normative political theory and its relationship with positive political theory. This immediately reduces the scale of the big question that we started with, and makes our task more manageable, but we do not mean to imply that the relationships between positive political theory and the formal and evaluative aspects of normative political theory are either unimportant or secondary. Indeed we believe that something of what we say here carries over to these other areas, and that there is more to be said. But we shall not pursue those issues here.

Indeed, the specific trigger for this chapter is still more limited in its range, and is provided by a recent essay by Christiano (2004) focusing attention on the relationship between the positive (explanatory) and the normative (practical) aspects specifically of rational choice political theory. A sharp statement of Christiano's thesis is that the explanatory theory advanced by mainstream rational choice theorists, if true, undermines the normative stance adopted by rational choice theorists, so rendering the overall theoretical position 'self-defeating'. Christiano goes on to argue that the attempt to escape this problem by 'revisionist' rational choice theorists – exemplified in Christiano's characterization by Brennan and Hamlin (2000)[4] – fails.

We wish to examine several aspects of Christiano's thesis in the process of developing a more general argument. In particular, we will advance three propositions. Our first proposition is that the problem identified by Christiano is overstated: the central issue is not, in our view, best thought of in terms of the categorical distinction between theoretical positions that are self-defeating and those that are not. Rather, the nature of the relationship between positive and normative theory is one in which the positive constrains the normative to a greater or lesser degree. And while we agree that the degree to which the positive constrains the normative is indeed significant, this fact does not undermine either the positive or the normative aspect of rational choice theory. Second, we will argue that this issue is in no way restricted to the rational choice approach to political theory. The issue arises with only minor modification and with equal force in all plausible approaches to political theory. Third, we will argue that the 'revisionist' moves laid out in earlier work and summarized below can be expected to reduce the degree of tension between explanatory and justificatory aspects of rational choice theory and therefore to open up an increased, but still limited, practical role for normative theorizing in the rational choice tradition.

While we differ from Christiano on many details, we agree with him that the nature of the relationship between positive and normative theory – whether in the rational choice tradition or more generally – is a topic of great significance that is too often ignored by theorists, of both positive and normative stripe. Our overall aims, therefore, are to refine Christiano's arguments and to generalize them.

Before embarking on developing and supporting these three propositions, it is appropriate to sketch out the basic terrain – much of which is common ground between all parties to the debate. As a first step in doing so, it may be appropriate to locate our central concerns in relation to another debate. Critics of 'ideal theory' often allege that ideal normative theory has become too remote from practical reality: that normative theory devotes itself to the analysis and specification of the ideal at the expense of the consideration of applications of normative thinking to practical problems or issues in the real (non-ideal) world. We would agree that this criticism has some force, but this point relates more obviously to the discussion of the formal aim of normative political theory and it is not the point that we wish to make here.

Our point is closer to a second line of criticism of ideal theory: that normative theory depends crucially on facts about the world and so cannot be divorced from at least some descriptive or explicatory considerations. We are concerned with a rather special subset of facts about the world: those that, taken together, provide the basis for positive political theory. Our concern is with just one part of the move from the ideal to the practical: the relationship between normative theory and positive theory. Of course, both bodies of theory operate at a level of abstraction from the real world, but our point is that the two bodies of theory should be seen as interconnected in at least some respects.[5]

This interconnection is, we believe, best seen as bidirectional. A part of our argument will be to sketch out the case for incorporating normative concerns into positive political theory, even where that theory is approached from the rational choice tradition; but our primary concern in this chapter is the connection that flows from the positive to the normative. Stripped to the bare essentials, our argument is that, to the extent that the practical purpose of normative political theory is important, normative theory must take seriously the behavioural and motivational structure of political agents as summarized in positive political theory. Put otherwise, if normative theory is, at least in part, concerned with preaching, it should ensure that its message can have purchase with people like us.

THE TERRAIN

Rationality and Revisionism

A central point of relevance in relation to rational choice theory concerns the specification of the content of rationality. In Christiano's terminology, mainstream rational choice theory:

> adheres strictly to the thesis of *homo economicus*. In other words, it explains the operation of institutions and justifies the reform of those institutions under the assumption that individuals normally maximize their own utility in every action they undertake. (Christiano, 2004, p. 123)

What Christiano (along with many other commentators) has in mind by 'utility maximization' is the commitment to narrow self-interest as the basis for rational choice, and by its act-by-act application of this motivation.[6] Of course, one might characterize rationality by the formal, structural properties of 'utility functions' rather than by their content, but we broadly accept that Christiano identifies a clear theme in the rational choice tradition.

We will take the 'mainstream' position as one that emphasizes a relatively narrow conception of self-interest; and understand the 'revisionist' rational choice theory alternative as one that seeks to move away from the strict conception of *Homo economicus*. Christiano initially states that: 'revisionists think of individuals, at least in a large set of cases, as not maximizing utility in every action but as adopting dispositions to act that maximize utility for the person as a whole' (Christiano, 2004, p. 123).

We agree that this is at least part of what is at stake.[7] We conceive of a disposition as a piece of motivational apparatus that may be influenced by first- or higher-order desires in the long term, and which operates to condition or govern first-order desires and behaviour in the short term – so that dispositions are, at least to some extent, subject to agent influence in the long term, but serve to commit action in the short term.[8] But this move from act-rationality to dispositional-rationality is, we think, only part of the 'revisionist programme'.[9] We also want to argue for a rather broader concept of 'utility' than is typically assumed in the mainstream approach to rational actor politics, where utility is taken to be restricted to self-interest. Much of what we have in mind here is outlined in the opening chapters of Brennan and Hamlin (2000) which makes the move from preferences to dispositions and also introduces the possibility of what are termed 'somewhat moral motivations'. These moral motivations may be analysed in terms of desires and beliefs – the desire to act as morality requires and a set of beliefs about what morality requires in particular circumstances – and, clearly, since the desires and beliefs belong to the individual in exactly the same way as other desires and beliefs (for example, those that relate to mainstream self-interested preferences) there is no logical or formal difficulty in incorporating moral motivations within the framework of utility maximization.

However, while there is no formal difficulty, we should also recognize that the incorporation of such moral motivations might affect the substantive nature of utility maximization and, in particular, break the link to narrow conceptions of self-interest.[10] We make no strong claims about the precise substantive content of these moral motivations; indeed, we suggest that such motivations will be unevenly distributed in the population both in terms of their precise content and in terms of their strength (relative, say, to standard preferences). Motivational (and therefore behavioural) heterogeneity is a hallmark of our understanding of the revisionist position. On this account, individuals are both rational and somewhat moral, with different individuals taking rather different views on what morality requires. Moral motivations sit alongside other motivations within any individual; they do not pre-empt or otherwise dominate other motivations but, we argue, their presence can make a difference to action both directly, and indirectly through dispositions. Accordingly, once somewhat moral desires are admitted, dispositions may also be at least somewhat moral.

There is a third aspect to the revisionist position: namely, the move from purely instrumental action so as to allow for elements of expressive behaviour. This expressive move does not depend upon either the dispositional or the moral moves, but we argue that it may interact with them. Essentially, the expressive argument recognizes that there may be benefits (utility) from speech acts (or equivalent acts) that merely express an opinion or view or preference, even if that act has no further consequences; and, in particular, even if that act plays no causal or instrumental role in bringing about the act or state for which a preference is expressed, or in realizing the underlying view, or persuading others of the underlying opinion, and so on. Normally we might expect such expressive benefits to be small relative to instrumental benefits, and we might also expect the (speech) acts that realize the expressive benefits to be perfectly consistent with the acts that satisfy the underlying preference. But in at least some cases these connections come apart. The now standard example relates to voting in a mass election. The scale of the election makes the probability that your vote will have any instrumental impact vanishingly small, thus removing any instrumental reason for voting in any particular way, or indeed for voting at all. At the same time, it is easy to imagine that at least some individuals will derive expressive benefits from voicing political opinions or positions that are different from those that they would choose to bring about if they were instrumentally decisive. In these circumstances, we might expect expressive voting to carry implications for substantive political outcomes.[11]

In what follows we will take the revisionist position on rational actor political theory to include these three departures from the mainstream account – the dispositional, the somewhat moral and the expressive – and we will try to be clear as to which of these moves is doing the work at each stage of the argument.

Normative Rational Choice

The normative aspiration of rational choice political theory may be understood in terms of its recommendations for institutional design and reform. There is a contrast here between mainstream economics and rational choice political theory. Within mainstream economics the normative focus is often on the design of policies, understood as particular interventions by government or other agencies. A major aspect of the public choice critique of mainstream economics is that policies are properly understood as emerging from a political process, rather than as being directly chosen by an agent labelled 'government' that is assumed both to be motivated to serve (a specific notion of) the public interest and to have the power to implement whatever policies turn out to be optimal. In moving away from this 'benign despot' model of government, public choice theory and rational actor political theory more generally argues that the political process should be seen as the interaction of essentially rational individuals operating within a structure of particular institutional rules. Thus, attention is focused on the properties of alternative sets of such rules, and of the policies that might be expected to emerge from their operation.

Notice that the point here is not that rational choice theorists believe that policies are completely beyond the reach of normative advice; but rather that, until and unless one has an understanding of the policy-making process, its institutional context and the role of agency, it is impossible to understand the role that any such advice might play. Furthermore, there is the general point that normative recommendations about the institutional structure may be both more powerful and less idiosyncratic than normative theorizing about specific policies.

Basic Structure Determinism

We now come to what Christiano terms 'basic structure determinism': 'What I mean by "basic structure determinism" is the thesis that the development, maintenance, and decline of the basic structural institutions in society is determined by forces that are beyond the capacity of human beings to guide and design' (Christiano, 2004, p. 124).

So, basic structure determinism takes seriously the idea that institutions themselves (at least the basic institutions which include the institutions of politics) emerge as the unintended consequences of many actions by many individuals over time, so that the design or reform of such institutions is beyond the reach of any individual. In its pure or extreme form, basic structure determinism denies any genuine agency at all in the process of institutional evolution. Note that the case of basic structure determinism is, in at least some respects, similar both to the argument just sketched in relation to normative policy advice and to the case of expressive voting sketched above: just as the argument on policy advice points to the need to understand a complex policy-making process rather than assume a 'benign dictator', and the argument for expressive voting involves the claim that the outcome of a mass election is beyond the influence of any individual voter, so basic structure determinism involves the claim that the design or reform of basic institutions is beyond the influence of individual agents.[12]

The argument in support of basic structure determinism presented by Christiano is intended to reflect the mainstream rational choice position, and draws extensively on Hardin (1999). Essentially, the argument revolves around the conception of institutions as coordination equilibria in games involving many individuals. Such coordination points emerge in the course of repeated play, and become institutionalized just because they are self-enforcing. Notice that this account, which is broadly similar to Lewis's account of conventions (Lewis, 1969), takes the rational action of individuals within political games as a starting point. The coordination equilibria that emerge as institutions may or may not be justifiable in terms of any particular normative criterion, but the point is that, since they are equilibria, no individual can rationally depart from the institutionalized behaviour, nor expect to shift society to a different equilibrium (assuming that other equilibria exist). And this is true regardless of the normative status of the equilibrium.

We will return to more detailed discussion of some aspects of this line of argument later, but for the moment we merely note the difference between this argument and the more contractarian line of argument often associated with public choice accounts of politics following James Buchanan. On that account, there is a distinction between everyday or in-period politics, which might be thought of as the playing of the game, and constitutional politics where the rules of the game are considered and decided. On the more contractarian account, institutions do not simply emerge from repeated play, but may be directly influenced by individuals acting collectively. The difficulties faced by the contractarian account include explaining how individuals escape from the obvious regress of seeing the constitutional level of politics as just another in-period game.

Strategy

Christiano's strategy is first to argue that the explanatory aspect of rational choice theory supports the idea of basic structure determinism, and then to argue that if both rational choice theory (in its descriptive form) and basic structure determinism are true, then the practical normative aspect of rational choice theory is completely undermined – in the sense that its normative aspirations cannot be realized. Of course, it is still possible for rational choice theorists to use the normative framework to evaluate alternative states of the world, but there is no practical role for the normative theory to influence the world. The institutional and constitutional recommendations of normative rational actor political theory could not be effective – they could play no role in actually bringing about institutional change.

We agree with Christiano that the potential effectiveness of practical normative theory is an important focus of attention. If normative political theory, of whatever substantive content, were to be insulated from the world in the sense that it could not be action-guiding and so could have no impact on political behaviour or outcomes, this would seriously limit the value of normative political theory.[13]

We also agree with Christiano's argument in formal terms: if the strict, mainstream interpretation of rational choice theory and basic structure determinism were both true, there would be no room for an effective normative branch of rational actor political theory. However, we do not believe that Christiano's argument is successful in substantive terms, and much of the remainder of this chapter is devoted to exploring some of its shortcomings.

PROPOSITION ONE: CATEGORIES OR CONTINUITY?

Our first line of argument concerns Christiano's ambition to show that rational choice theory is 'self-defeating' – that is, to cast the question in terms of a categorical distinction between those theories that are self-defeating and those that are not. We argue, to the contrary, that the issue at stake is better conceived in terms of a continuum that indicates the extent to which the positive features of political reality (whatever they may be) constrain the practical effectiveness of normative theory (of whatever variety). In other words, the 'constraints' posited by positive political theory are to be seen as matters of degree. With this view in place, we suggest that while arguments such as those deployed by Christiano clearly indicate the constraining nature of the rational choice approach to positive political theory, they fall far short of demonstrating that the constraint is absolute, so that the practical effectiveness of normative rational choice theory is not undermined. For simplicity, in discussing this line of argument we will operate entirely within the mainstream tradition of rational choice theory, returning to our preferred revisionist account in later sections.

A starting point is that while Christiano phrases his basic claim and conclusion in absolute or categorical language, much of the argument is rather less cut-and-dried than that language implies. For example, on the one hand we have:

> unlike some forms of determinism, basic structure determinism is a hard kind of determinism. It is not merely the case that agency is determined by external forces; in basic structure determinism, there is no agency at all, in the sense that the development of these institutions is not guided by human design ... The development of political institutions is not up to human beings. (Christiano, 2004, p. 124)

Which indicates an absolute or categorical stance. While on the other hand we have:

> The thesis of basic structural determinism is also compatible with people making marginal changes to the basic structural institutions. One might attempt to change

aspects of the committee system in the United States Congress, for example, and in some cases succeed. And to this extent, there is still some room for rational choice theorists to make practically effective recommendations for change. But it is a highly limited space and certainly much more limited than rational choice theorists normally have in mind. (Christiano, 2004, p. 125)

Which is explicitly concerned with the extent of the determinism and the 'space' remaining for effective normative debate. In this way, Christiano seems to concede that it is appropriate to think in terms of the extent to which normative theory is constrained by features of the positive theory of political behaviour. And we are happy to agree that many rational choice theorists have assumed rather more 'space' than might actually exist. For the moment, we are content to accept the principle of continuity – that the constraining nature of positive political theory is a matter of degree and that these constraints do not entirely preclude the possibility of a space for effective normative debate. Later we will argue that this space may be larger than conceded by Christiano. But if there is any space at all, normative theory will have potential practical value.

But potential value is not actual value. Even if we all agree that there is some normative space remaining, normative rational choice theory might not be able to operate in that space. And there is at least one reason for supposing that this might be the case. Under the mainstream interpretation, the agents operating in the world are all motivated exclusively by a relatively narrow conception of self-interest, regardless of their positions in the political structure (whether voter, politician, bureaucrat, policy advisor or whatever). It might be that the recommendations made by normative rational choice theory for institutional reform are such that they carry no weight with such agents, so that they cannot be effective – it would be as if the recommendations were made in a language that no actual individuals can understand.

While the normative aspirations of rational choice theory are best understood in terms of its institutional recommendations, the fundamental normative criterion underlying rational choice theory might be crudely categorized as a form of normative individualism. By this we mean only that whether or not some particular institutional reform is considered, on balance, to be worthwhile will depend crucially upon that reform's impact on individuals and how well their lives go. We do not mean to place any specific limits on what is included in the set of things that make an individual's life go well (or better), and in particular we do not necessarily restrict this set to any particular notion of 'welfare', but we do suggest that a hallmark of normative rational choice theory is that it adopts an essentially individualistic approach to value, so that social or collective value supervenes on individual value.[14] Given this normative individualism it is of course likely that any normative recommendation made by a rational choice theorist is likely to be heard, understood and accepted by at least some individuals – those who benefit from the reform. But there is no assurance that these individuals will be positioned so that they can be effective in acting on the recommendation, and the fact that it is a recommendation from rational choice political theory carries no weight either with them or with others. After all, almost all reforms that might seriously be contemplated might be expected to benefit at least some individuals, and the mere fact that some individuals support a reform on these grounds neither makes that reform more likely to be effected nor justifies it to the rational choice normative theorist. In this way, one might suggest that the recommendations of the rational choice normative theorist, if not literally unintelligible to all real individuals, will have no special or distinctive voice in the babble of self-interested debate.

Of course, this issue has long been recognized by rational choice theorists in the tradition of James Buchanan.[15] There are (at least) two types of issue involved in the choice of institutional and constitutional rules. On the one hand, the very idea of the choice of rules is somewhat attenuated since an essential feature of a constitutional or institutional rule is its relative fixity – if such rules were not seen as fixed (at least in the short to medium run) it is difficult to see how they could play the required role of constraining and shaping choice and behaviour. On the other hand, if individuals rationally choose the rules under which they operate, an obvious regress beckons: if individuals are modelled as self-interested in their choice of actions, they will presumably be just as self-interested in their choice of rules, unless constrained by some deeper rules, and so on. And no normative advice from rational choice theorists will bear on this issue.

The basic response to these two issues from mainstream public choice theory has been to suggest that the former issue might help to resolve the latter. If rules are to be quasi-permanent, then in those rare moments when I face the choice of rules, I have to evaluate alternative rules over the long term when I cannot be sure of the impact that any particular rule may have on me or my interests. This uncertainty yields a veil of ignorance, which is argued to distance constitutional choice from self-interest by ensuring that each individual adopts a more impartial standpoint. This distinction between constitutional choice and in-period political choice is basic to the normative aspect of rational choice political theory in that it holds out the prospect of the relatively impartial choice of institutional and constitutional rules by which in-period politics and the choice of policy might be influenced.

Of course, we accept that the setting of constitutional choice falls a long way short of the full veil of ignorance that might be required to establish an entirely impartial standpoint. Christiano rightly reminds us[16] that even constitutions have a relatively short expected life, and are in any case open to interpretive change, and so may not always be regarded as once-and-for-all choices by constitution makers. Equally, the typical constitution maker will not necessarily imagine himself as occupying a potentially wide range of roles under the constitution to be chosen. Nevertheless, we believe that the shift to the constitutional perspective is a shift in the direction of impartiality – albeit a modest one.

And this shift to impartiality, however modest in scale, opens up the space available to the normative theorist. At its most basic, the theorist may consider which institutional reforms are desirable when seen from this more impartial perspective. To be sure this is mostly an analytic role based on an ability to analyse the operating characteristics of alternative institutional arrangements, but it will also require more obviously normative skills in articulating the relevant idea of impartiality. A clear example of this type of normative, analytic logic in action is provided by the Rae–Taylor theorem on majority voting (Rae, 1969; Taylor, 1969). This theorem sets up the problem as the choice of a voting rule by an individual who expects the chosen rule to be used on a range of issues where they are not certain of whether they support or oppose the individual propositions to be voted on.

So far, then, we have one role for the normative theorist: that of informing institutional choice or institutional reform from behind a veil of ignorance that shrouds the actual outcomes of those reforms, as they will play out into the future. We now turn to consider a rather different role: the role of political entrepreneur or professional politician.

In many areas of life we rely on the professional incentives faced by individuals rather than their personal preferences. This is the basic point of the famous Adam Smith quotation: 'It is not from the benevolence of the butcher, the brewer, or the baker that we expect our dinner, but from their regard to their own interest' (Smith, 1981 [1776], Book 1, Chapter 2). A butcher faces a professional incentive to build and maintain a reputation for quality and we can rely on this to at least some extent. And we might think that the same applies to professional politicians, at least in a tolerably democratic society: in striving to build a career as a politician, they will face incentives not to pursue policies or reforms that they particularly like as an individual, but rather to construct packages of policies and reforms that will advance their careers, and one leading possibility here is to offer advantage to significant groups of voters.

Now, the introduction of such professional politicians makes a difference to the way in which we conceive of the operation of positive political theory. On the account offered by Christiano, following and extending Hardin, social and political situations are seen as games in which all individuals participate in a broadly symmetric way: each pursuing their own self-interest, so that the resultant equilibrium could not be said to be substantially intended or brought about by any of them. But if we replace this picture with one in which some agents act as political entrepreneurs or professional politicians in shaping the agenda and structuring the game, we might conclude that these aspects of the game's formation were just as significant as the mere fact that the final outcome could be seen as a coordination equilibrium. In economic markets most individuals, most of the time, have no direct or intentional effect on the market outcome or equilibrium, but some individuals do have direct and intended effects on some markets: they are the entrepreneurs who offer something distinctive that creates, shapes or otherwise influences a market (for better or worse). In the same way, in a more structured political world it might be true that while most individuals, most of the time, have no direct or intentional impact on either policy choice or institutional reform, it might still be the case that some individuals do have such effects. This point further weakens the claim of basic structural determinism. The essential point here is that, while the idea of coordination equilibria as a source of institutions is a key part of a rational choice theoretic account, it is not the only part.

This point leads to a further line of concern with Christiano's argument and, in particular, with that part of Christiano's argument that revolves around what it might mean for a positive political theory to be 'true'. Recall that the form of Christiano's argument is that if both mainstream rational choice theory and basic structure determinism are true as descriptive theories, then normative rational choice theory is undermined. But this formulation places a considerable burden on the idea of a true theory – a burden that is, in our view, unwarranted. Most obviously, the form of Christiano's argument requires that the truth of the positive theory implies that the theory is a complete and accurate account of reality. Complete in the sense that there is no systematic residual political behaviour left unexplained by the theory; and accurate in the sense that the explanation offered cannot be improved upon by recourse to additional factors. This does not mean that the theory has to be capable of perfect prediction – the theory could (and presumably should) allow for any non-systematic or random elements that may be relevant, and randomness may be an important feature of at least some aspects of behaviour.[17]

But we do not recognize this idea of truth as the key ambition of rational choice political theory in general, or of that aspect of the theory used to support the idea of basic structure determinism in particular; and we would certainly deny that rational choice theorists must be committed to the descriptive truth of either theory in this sense. To the contrary, rational choice theory is grounded in the idea of theory as model, where a model – especially an idealized, theoretical model – is, by necessity, an abstraction from the truth. Rational choice theory is seen not as the embodiment of truth, but as a useful perspective on reality that focuses attention on an important feature of that reality without denying that other features may also play significant roles. So, while a rational choice theorist should be committed to the idea that their theory captures a significant aspect of the truth, they need not (and should not) take the view that it exhausts the truth.

If positive rational choice theory is understood in this way, as a useful but necessarily incomplete model of relevant aspects of the world, with the idea of

institutions as coordinating equilibria as a particular example of this approach
to theory, further space for the normative aspirations of rational choice theory
is opened up. Of course, this might be a slightly uncomfortable argument for
some rational choice theorists, since it suggests that the effectiveness of their
normative approach depends, at least in part, on factors not explicitly accounted
for in their positive models. But that is a different point, and one that we defer
until our discussion of proposition three below.

To return to the theme outlined at the start of this section, concerning the
language of constraints and feasibility and its interpretation in various settings,
we suggest that in the context of practical normative theory, constraints and
issues of feasibility are most often taken to operate as logical counters or requirements which are digital in nature, but we suggest that it is appropriate to
focus less on the digital, binary or on–off nature of such requirements and
rather see issues of feasibility more as analogue, continuous or 'plausibility'
counters. Once this shift of interpretation is accepted, so that the relevant debate
becomes one of determining the degree to which any particular constraint
binds, the importance of even mild relaxation in such constraints becomes
apparent.

PROPOSITION TWO: SAUCE FOR THE GOOSE

In this section we turn our attention to examine the relationship between the
linkages connecting the positive and the normative, and the particular case of
rational choice theory. After all, Christiano's claim is that rational choice political theory is self-defeating, not that all political theory is self-defeating. The
impression that Christiano's account may give is that the self-defeatingness
problem is unique to rational choice theory.[18] But we think all positive theories
are in the same boat here, and that the relation between the normative and positive strands of political theory is essentially independent of the content of the
positive account. We will proceed in several steps, first holding fixed the positive
account of politics to consider variations at the normative level, and then allowing alternative positive accounts of politics.

So, initially (and despite our arguments in the previous section) we want to
take as our starting point Christiano's extreme case in which both mainstream
rational choice political theory, and the hard version of basic structural determinism, are true in the strong sense. In these circumstances, it is difficult to see how
any variety of normative political theory could be effective in terms of its practical aim. Of course, as was the case with rational choice normative theory, it
would be perfectly possible for any variety of normative political theory to serve
as an evaluative criterion. There is no bar to theorists of the relevant variety
debating which actions, policies or institutional rules would be 'best' according

to the theory in question, but neither debates of this form, nor any other aspect of the normative theory could be effective in bringing about the identified actions, policies or institutional rules. The existence of the normative theory could have no political impact.

The point here is simple enough: the full specification of the nature of the political world in descriptive terms identifies all of the factors that can be effective in influencing outcomes[19] in that world. If we stipulate that the political world takes a specific form, and this specification involves the claim that no normative argument is relevant in determining political outcomes, we effectively undermine the practical relevance of normative political theorizing of all varieties.

It might seem that this claim is too strong, and that even a fully deterministic specification of political life would allow of normative theorizing of at least some type, a type that was in some relevant sense integrated with the nature of the positive specification. This is not so, but the point usefully underlines the distinction between the evaluative and practical roles of normative political theory. In the case in which descriptive rational choice theory and basic structure determinism together fully characterize the political world, the normative theory most obviously linked to, and integrated with, this underlying positive account would be a form of Paretianism. Within this normative scheme, alternative political outcomes A and B could be compared in terms of their impact on individual lives and how well they went, with A being better than B if and only if everyone's life went as least as well in A as in B, and some people's lives went better in A than in B. And it may well be the case that, at least under some circumstances, theorists could demonstrate that the political world as specified tended to produce outcomes that were, indeed, Pareto optimal in this sense. But even if all of this were true, it would still be the case that the Paretian normative theory would be ineffective in influencing action, simply because the fact that some action (or policy or institutional rule) would be recommended by the Paretian normative theory could not count as increasing the probability of that action (policy, rule) actually occurring in the world. No individual (or group of individuals, or office holder) would be influenced by the normative theorizing, even if they were fully aware of it.

The situation here is directly comparable to the standard discussion of the one-shot prisoner's dilemma. Each prisoner has a dominant strategy of defection, and this is so even on the assumption that each is fully informed about the game – including the fact that both prisoners would be better off if both cooperated. The information concerning the theoretical availability of a Pareto improvement has no weight in the actual play of the game, since the play of the game is already fully determined by other factors. We can use the Pareto criterion to label the equilibrium of the game as inefficient, but such labels do not in themselves offer practical or behavioural routes to efficiency.

Now, notice that this general problem is in no way dependent on the positive specification of the political world being based on rational choice theory. Any positive political theory that serves to identify the causes of political outcomes, to the extent that it succeeds, limits the scope for practically effective normative political theory. To put the same point in another way, unless a positive political theory explicitly includes some means by which appropriate normative political theory may operate, so that there is a clear operational linkage between the normative theory and the relevant descriptive political theory, the positive theory will constrain and, in the limit, undermine normative theory.

At one level, this should be obvious enough. The normative theories that build on the idea of equality, or of rights, for example, could hardly be thought to be effective if everyday political debate and decision-making did not also refer to equality or rights. But the issue is rather subtler than that. It is not sufficient for the appropriate normative language to be used in the real world: that language must be effective in normative terms. To revert, for a moment, to the case of mainstream rational choice theory at the descriptive level, it may still be the case that rational actors – including rational politicians – invoke ideas of equality or of rights in political debate. But, if the narrowly self-interested idea of rationality is taken to be 'true', such invocations must, by definition, simply provide a rhetorical screen for more narrowly self-interested or professional motivations by those concerned. It might be that rights are generally upheld, or that equalizing policies are supported, but the explanation for these facts would not lie in the existence of recognized normative theoretical claims surrounding equality or rights, but rather in the specifics of the (true, by assumption) positive model of political behaviour. Now, of course, rhetoric may actually play an effective political role – we do not mean to imply that rhetoric is necessarily empty – but we do want to argue that if rhetoric is effective, then this fact should be built into the relevant positive political theory, so that the rhetorical appeal to equality or rights might itself be explained.

Now, as we argued in the previous section, we do not believe that the rational choice model of politics at the descriptive level fully constrains normative theorizing, and more generally we do not believe that the best available model of politics at the descriptive level (regardless of the extent to which this model might be characterized as a rational choice model), fully constrains normative political theorizing. But we do believe that descriptive political theory substantially constrains normative political theorizing, and that this constraint imposes a duty on normative theory to demonstrate how it might be effective. This duty implies in turn that normative political theory needs to engage with positive political theory in an explicit manner.

PROPOSITION THREE: REVISIONISM RIDES AGAIN

So far, we have argued:

1. That Christiano's original case was overstated in claiming that normative rational choice theory is self-defeating, while agreeing that the content of rational choice theory at the descriptive level must constrain the effectiveness of normative theory in the rational choice tradition.
2. That the same general issue affects all approaches to political theory, and points to the generality of the positive theory–normative theory issue.

We now turn to our third and final proposition: that the move from mainstream to revisionist rational choice theory carries with it a reduction in the severity of the constraints imposed by descriptive theory, so expanding the space available for practically effective normative political theory. While the style of normative political theory that we have in mind is generally of the institutional and constitutional type already indicated as characteristic of the rational choice theory approach, our argument is more general: to the extent that something like a revisionist rational choice theory account of politics is a significant part of the truth in accounting for political behaviour, we argue that this opens up significant space for normative theory of any type, providing only that that normative theory engages in an appropriate way with the motivations of rational (in our revisionist sense) individuals in political settings.

The first and most obvious step in support of this proposition relates to the aspect of revisionist rational choice theory that incorporates somewhat moral motivations into the rational calculus of individual agents. This step directly connects the positive to the normative insofar as individuals' moral motivations line up with the structure of the relevant normative theory. Essentially, by incorporating a specifically normative perspective within individual agents we allow of the possibility that normative argument can be effective simply by persuading individual agents of what morality requires and so influencing their chosen actions.

But, once again, a possible effect is not necessarily an effect. We still have to overcome at least two further hurdles to transform the potential impact of somewhat moral motivations into an actual impact. The first hurdle is the possibility, noted earlier, that moral motivations may often be swamped by more self-interested motivations. Clearly, if moral motivations are present, but are so weak that they rarely, if ever, drive behaviour, they will not be sufficient to build an effective channel from the normative to the positive. The second hurdle is provided by the structure of the collective action problem that lies at the heart of both the argument concerning basic structure determinism (even in its softer and more acceptable form) and the more general rational choice interpretation of political life. The issue here is that, even if individuals are partly motivated by appropriate normative concerns, and this motivation impacts on their individual action, this may still not be sufficient to prove effective at the level of political outcomes. We will tackle these two hurdles in turn.

We have emphasized that our interpretation of the revisionist position places the desire to act as morality requires alongside other desires – indeed we might suggest that one could summarize desires into just a few similarly high-level desires, such as the desire to act as prudence requires, supported by sets of beliefs about what morality and prudence require in particular circumstances, rather than the indefinitely long list of specific desires and preferences that are more normally considered. Such a move might seem to shift the focus of attention from desires to beliefs, but actually we think that it illustrates the difficulty in constructing a clear dividing line between desires and beliefs. To have a desire provides some support for the belief that you have that desire; and beliefs often include a degree of intentionality: for example, to believe that something is good is closely related to believing that you should desire that thing. Anything like a satisfactory discussion of the structure of desires and beliefs would take us too far from our major theme, but we want to register the view that both desires and beliefs may be the subject of rational scrutiny as well as being the inputs to rational choice. This is not to say that certain desires and beliefs are rationally required (although we do not rule this out), but rather that we think that desires and beliefs may be subject to evaluation against both epistemic and structural criteria.

With this in mind, and bearing in mind our earlier indication that heterogeneity of desire and belief in relation to morality should be expected, it is by no means clear that our revisionist position requires us to accept that moral motivations will normally or typically be overwhelmed by prudential or other desires. This is essentially an empirical matter and one where we will not offer any real evidence. But we will argue that the two other moves associated with our revisionist position – the expressive and the dispositional – will systematically increase the effectiveness of moral motivations in the arena of politics, amplifying whatever basic moral motivation may be present.[20]

In the case of the dispositional move, the basic point is simply that the shift to the dispositional perspective removes political action from the domain of act-by-act evaluation against the full range of desires and admits the possibility that at least some actors will be committed to political dispositions that embody a moral perspective. At this point we need to say a little more about the nature of dispositions (drawing on Hamlin, 2006). We distinguish between three types of disposition: specific conditioning dispositions, general conditioning dispositions and modal dispositions, where the key issues are the nature and scope of the commitments involved.

In the case of specific conditioning dispositions, the commitment is substantive, but is essentially narrow and focused on a particular domain – an example might be the commitment to vegetarianism where the commitment clearly in-dicates the course of action to be taken but the range of decision situations in which the disposition is relevant is both clear and relatively small. In the case of general conditioning dispositions, the commitment is again substantive, but the domain is broad and perhaps even universal – an example might be the disposition to tell the truth, or the disposition to be cautious. In the case of modal dispositions, the commitment is procedural in the sense that the actor commits to adopt a particular decision-making perspective when confronted with choices in a particular domain, but does not commit to specific substantive actions. A moral disposition over some domain might be seen as a modal disposition in that it commits the individual to consider decisions in the relevant domain from a moral perspective, and act as morality requires.

Once the possibility of dispositions that privilege the moral calculus over the prudential calculus in a particular sphere of decision-making is recognized, it remains to argue that the political domain has characteristics that lead us to believe that specifically moral dispositions are likely to be particularly relevant there. This argument is provided by an application of the general idea of relative prices. In the arena of democratic politics, the impact of any single individual who is not a professional politician on the overall political outcome is, at best, very limited. This fact reduces the *ex ante* prudential impact (favourable or unfavourable) of any political action. Thus, compared to a situation in which the individual is decisive, prudential considerations will be backgrounded, so that moral considerations are likely to take on greater relative prominence. And this is true both at the level of disposition choice and at the level of action. We would expect moral dispositions – of the modal type – to arise more often in the domain of democratic politics than in other domains where individual action is more directly linked to outcomes. And we would expect moral motivations to play a greater role in action when the opportunity cost of behaving morally is reduced – as it characteristically is in large-number electoral settings.

So, both in the case of uncommitted action (that is, where dispositions do not apply), and in the case where dispositions replace act-by-act evaluation, we have good reason to believe that the setting of democratic politics will tend to reduce the relevance of individually prudential considerations and increase the rele-vance of moral considerations as guides to political behaviour. This is not to say that politics will be dominated by moral action, or that what counts as moral action in any particular political context is unambiguous; but the argument is sufficient, we believe, to indicate that the revisionist version of rational choice theory with its combination of somewhat moral motivations, expressive behav-iour and a dispositional approach to commitment can offer a coherent account of a connection between normative considerations and political behaviour.

So, we argue that we can clear the first hurdle by combining the various features of the revisionist account of rational choice theory. In effect the dispositional and expressive arguments serve to amplify the effectiveness of moral motivations in the particular context of democratic politics so that the 'space' for effective normative debate is enlarged.

The second hurdle we set ourselves was that even if individuals are motivated to at least some extent by appropriate normative concerns, with that motivation amplified so that it impacts on their individual action, this may still not be sufficient to prove effective at the level of political or social outcomes. We see this hurdle as the real testing ground for both positive and normative political theory. To some extent we can refer again to our earlier discussion of the idea of political entrepreneurs, and our earlier suggestion that the idea of coordination equilibria does not exhaust the set of political mechanisms – but these appeals do little more than suggest that the hurdle might be overcome at least sometimes, rather than offering any clear argument. Indeed, it would seem implausibly optimistic to think that there might be some general argument to indicate that such a hurdle can always be overcome – that normative ideas once agreed and appropriately internalized can always be translated into the relevant actions and social outcomes. So here lies the irreducibly political aspect of the interrelationship between positive and normative political theory: even when the normative argument is settled and the political agents are (reasonably) appropriately motivated, there is still the question of actually generating the normatively indicated outcome. Clearly, institutions (as well as individual motivations) matter here, and the focus on institutional design within the rational actor tradition reminds us of the way in which thinking normatively about our institutions can help us. But just as our actual individual motivations will not be perfect, so institutions will also be imperfect. The political problem is essentially a 'second-best' problem, and ideal theory is a poor guide.

CONCLUDING COMMENTS

Politics is a matter of the feasible and the desirable, with the interaction between feasibility and desirability identifying the best that can be achieved. Discussion of the feasible is provided by positive political theory (together with other physical and social sciences operating in explanatory and descriptive modes). But it is important to note that feasibility issues arise in a variety of forms; at the beginning of this chapter we distinguished between the debate on ideal versus non-ideal normative theory and our own concern with the relationship between normative and positive theory. These distinctions reflect two aspects of feasibility, one concerned with what might be termed the practical or pragmatic feasibility of normative theory, the other concerned with what we might term structural or theory-feasibility of normative theory. A particular ideal normative theory may be pragmatically feasible or applicable if it is capable of generating a policy recommendation that responds to a specific real-world issue. For example, a particular version of egalitarianism might be judged to be pragmatically feasible in a particular case just insofar as it produces a clear policy recommendation in respect of, say, the issue of the distribution of particular health care resources. But such a clear policy recommendation might still be theory-infeasible in our terms if that recommendation did not engage appropriately with the operation of the political system, so that the fact of the normative endorsement itself did no real work (and could do no real work) in bringing about the recommended policy. This is not a matter of the technical feasibility of the policy – it might be accepted that the recommended policy could be implemented – but rather it is a matter of the political will to act as the relevant normative theory requires: a 'will' that may be directly the will of individuals acting in political roles, or may be the product of the institutional structure.

Our general claim is simply that issues of theory-feasibility, the extent of coherence between normative and positive theory, are important, and that positive political theory (of whatever variety) therefore implies considerable constraints on normative theory if normative theory is to be effective in its practical, action-guiding sense. While these constraints are significant, they do not, even in the case of a positive political theory that is based in mainstream rational choice theory, completely undermine the role of normative political theory.

More specifically, we have argued that the revisionist account of rational choice political theory – which generalizes the mainstream analysis to allow of somewhat moral motivations, expressive behaviour and a dispositional approach to rational choice – offers a clear route by which normative political theory and positive political theory can be connected, with each constraining the other to an appropriate degree.

We finish with what we hope may be a helpful story. Imagine an anthropologist (A) studying a remote civilization – the X. Having studied the language, A notes that the X engage in normative political debate – debate, that is, about what should be done – although A also notes that not all of the X are engaged in this debate, that the debate includes a number of rather different positions, and that the substance of the X's moral debate seemed wholly alien to anything that might count as morality in A's own society. Let the dominant moral code of the civilization under study be M1 and the moral code of the anthropologist's own society be M2. In A's role as a field anthropologist, he or she studies whether the behaviour of individuals can be explained, at least in part, by the normative code M1. To the extent that M1 contributes to explaining behaviour, A might reasonably conclude that the X internalize their normative debate, so that the requirements of morality take on at least some motivational force. A might also note that this force varied across individuals and across circumstances. If, on the other hand, A found that M1 played no explanatory role in understanding the behaviour of the X, A might reasonably conclude that norma- tive debate among the X was practically ineffective, and might go on to suggest that the normative debate itself might be understood in other terms (including formal and evaluative terms). Note that A is engaged in an essentially positive or descriptive analysis throughout. It is true that the subject matter of A's study includes the normative debate among the X, but A's study is not itself normative. Specifically, M2 – A's own moral code – has played no role.

We see our discussion here as related to that of the anthropologist. Obviously, we are not concerned with a remote civilization, and we cannot pretend to be external observers. Nevertheless, our basic question has been the nature of the connection between normative political debate and actual political behaviour at the general level of abstraction at which general theories (positive and norma- tive) are constructed. The anthropologist was concerned primarily with the connection from the normative to the positive, with the animating question be- ing: do normative considerations contribute to the explanation of political behaviour? And one aspect of our revisionist rational choice position is to allow normative concerns to be considered for their explanatory power within a posi- tive model of political behaviour. But we are also concerned with the extent to which the understanding of positive political theory feeds back into and con- strains normative analysis. Here then we must reverse the direction of the anthropologist's study and investigate the extent to which the X's own under- standing of positive politics informs and constrains their normative debate and their political and moral code M1. To the extent that M1 attempts to take proper account of what is politically feasible in making its various recommendations, this feedback from the positive to the normative is, we think inevitable. And we think that the two directions of the relationship – from the normative to the positive, and from the positive to the normative – must be viewed together, if we are to arrive at an overall political theory that is coherent.

NOTES

1. This chapter grew out of discussion at a colloquium held at Duke University, USA in April 2005 and has benefited from discussion at a conference in Manchester, UK in October 2006, and at the Oxford Political Thought Conference, St Catherine's College, Oxford in January 2007. We thank participants in all of these discussions and particularly Tom Christiano, Russell Hardin, Loren Lomasky, Allen Buchanan, Doug Maclean, Jerry Postema, John O'Neill, Hillel Steiner, Jonathan Quong, Susan Mendus, Alex Voorhoeve, Chandran Kukathas, Keith Dowd- ing, David Owen and David Miller for their comments. Normal caveats apply.
2. For a discussion of positive political theory and its relationship to both political science and rational choice theory, see Forbes (2004).
3. Further distinctions are, of course, possible. For example, within the practical aim of normative theory we might distinguish between action-guiding and attitude-guiding roles; see Brennan and Southwood (2007).
4. See also Brennan and Hamlin (2008).

5. The argument that normative theorizing is (or should be) independent of any issues of feasibility is put in the context of theories of justice by Cohen (2003). For discussion and an argument that at least some 'facts' about human nature may constrain normative theorizing, see Mason (2004).
6. Christiano exemplifies sophisticated mainstream rational choice theory by reference to Hardin (1999).
7. We note that even in strictly self-interested modelling in the game-theoretic tradition, it is not individual actions that are considered as the options of choice but rather 'strategies' that may be complex combinations or actions contingent on the behaviour of others. Nevertheless, we believe that the move from 'acts' to 'dispositions' is distinct from the move from 'acts' to 'strategies'.
8. For a fuller account of dispositions, see Hamlin (2006).
9. And Christiano agrees; later in his essay he discusses other aspects of the revisionist position, although it is not clear that he sees them as constitutive features.
10. We should stress that we do not see morality in sharp contrast to self-interest in all circumstances.
11. For more detailed discussion of the expressive argument see Brennan and Lomasky (1993), Schuessler (2000) and Brennan and Hamlin (2000). For empirical investigations of expressive voting behaviour see Copeland and Laband (2002) and Tyran (2004).
12. Note that the important aspect of basic structure determinism is its denial of agency; it is not part of basic structure determinism to deny that political structures may evolve in a manner that is stochastic rather than determinative in the statistical sense.
13. We repeat that we do not intend to imply that the action-guiding aspect of normative political theory is necessarily the most important aspect. We would also underline our view that most normative theorists act as if they expect or hope that their theories may have some impact in the world.
14. For related discussion see Broome (1991), whose 'principle of personal good' is individualistic in this sense since if something is good, it must be good for (at least) someone.
15. At least since Buchanan and Tullock (1962); for an extended treatment see Brennan and Buchanan (1985).
16. In private correspondence, see also Christiano (1996), especially Chapter 4.
17. So that the theory may be stochastic rather than deterministic in the statistical sense, see note 10 above.
18. This thought is encouraged by the fact that elsewhere Christiano pursues the idea of bringing positive political theory to bear on the elaboration of a normative political theory; see Christiano (1996).
19. Here and in the following discussion, we use 'outcomes' in a broad sense to include procedural and other aspects of political life such as whether certain decisions were made democratically, or the extent to which rights are respected, and so on.
20. A further addition to the set of revisionist ideas might be the idea of 'esteem' as motivator; see Brennan and Pettit (2004).

REFERENCES

Brennan, G. and J.M. Buchanan (1985), *The Reason of Rules*, Cambridge: Cambridge University Press.

Brennan, G. and A. Hamlin (2000), *Democratic Devices and Desires*, Cambridge: Cambridge University Press.

Brennan, G. and A. Hamlin (2008), 'Revisionist public choice theory', *New Political Economy*, **13** (1), 77–88.

Brennan G. and L. Lomasky (1993), *Democracy and Decision*, Cambridge: Cambridge University Press.

Brennan, G. and P. Pettit (2004), *The Economy of Esteem*, Oxford: Oxford University Press.

Brennan, G. and N. Southwood (2007), 'Feasibility in action and attitude', in T. Rønnow-Rasmussen, B. Petersson, J. Josefsson and D. Egonsson (eds), *Homage à Wlodeck: Philosophical Papers Dedicated to Wlodeck Rabinowicz*, www.fil.lu.se/homageawlodeck.

Broome, J. (1991), *Weighing Goods*, Oxford: Blackwell.

Buchanan, J.M. and G. Tullock (1962), *The Calculus of Consent*, Ann Arbor, MI: University of Michigan Press.

Christiano, T. (1996), *The Rule of the Many: Fundamental Issues in Democratic Theory*, Boulder, CO: Westview Press.

Christiano, T. (2004), 'Is normative rational choice theory self-defeating?', *Ethics*, **115**, 122–41.

Cohen, G.A. (2003), 'Facts and principles', *Philosophy and Public Affairs*, **31** (3), 211–45.

Copeland, C. and D. Laband (2002), 'Expressiveness and voting', *Public Choice*, **110**, 351–63.

Forbes, H.D. (2004), 'Positive political theory', in G.F. Gaus and C. Kukathas (eds), *Handbook of Political Theory*, London: Sage, pp. 57–72.

Hamlin, A. (2006), 'Political dispositions and dispositional politics', in G. Eusepi and A.P. Hamlin (eds), *Beyond Conventional Economics: The Limits of Rational Behaviour in Political Decision-Making*, Cheltenham, UK and Northampton, MA, USA: Edward Elgar, pp. 3–16.

Hardin, R. (1999), *Liberalism, Constitutionalism and Democracy*, Oxford: Oxford University Press.

Lewis, D. (1969), *Convention: A Philosophical Study*, Cambridge, MA: Harvard University Press.

Mason, A. (2004), 'Just constraints', *British Journal of Political Science*, **34**, 251–68.

Rae, D.W. (1969), 'Decision rules and individual values in constitutional choice', *American Political Science Review*, **63**, 40–56.

Schuessler, A.A. (2000), *A Logic of Expressive Choice*, Princeton, NJ: Princeton University Press.

Smith, A. (1981 [1776]), *An Inquiry Into the Nature and Causes of the Wealth of Nations*, ed. R.H. Campbell and A.S. Skinner, Indianapolis, IN: Liberty Fund.

Taylor, M.J. (1969), 'Proof of a theorem on majority rule', *Behavioural Science*, **14**, 228–31.

Tyran, J.R. (2004), 'Voting when money and morals conflict: an experimental test of expressive voting', *Journal of Public Economics*, **88**, 1645–64.

PART III

Political market processes and liberal ethics: tax
fairness vs tax morale

8. The deregulation of the political process: towards an international market for good politics

Reiner Eichenberger[1] and Michael Funk

INTRODUCTION

Elections are deemed to mediate the provision of public goods along the citizens' preferences. However, it is obvious that politicians often renege on their campaign promises and tend to be captured by powerful special interests; furthermore, they are temped to create political business cycles. In order to increase the government's incentives to cater for the citizens' preferences, public choice scholars typically propose to adjust political institutions. Many authors focus on federalism and hence, on strengthening the citizens' exit option. Other scholars concentrate on increasing the impact of the citizens' voice in the democratic process, for example, by institutionalizing direct democracy. But while high migration costs prevent federalism from achieving full efficiency (for example Epple and Zelenitz, 1981), direct democracy cannot eradicate the asymmetric influence of special interests, although there are strong improvements over representative democracy (Frey, 1994; Eichenberger, 1999a), especially when direct democracy is combined with an extended role of elected auditors (Eichenberger and Schelker, 2007).

In this chapter, therefore, a new proposal for reform of the political process is presented, which targets both the executive as well as the legislative branches. The concept aims directly at the political process, which is regulated by three kinds of restrictions:

- Protectionist rules: almost everywhere, only nationals are allowed to run for political office. Moreover, the candidates often have to live in their constituency.
- Production process regulations: usually only individuals can run for office. Parties and firms are not allowed to do so, but have to nominate individual candidates. Moreover, parties must be non-profit organizations, and their internal structure is heavily regulated.

- Price regulations: all explicit prices of political services, that is, the salaries of politicians and state subsidies for political parties, are fixed by law.

In this chapter it is argued that such regulations hamper political competition, weaken the politicians' incentives and ultimately enable special interests to seize their rents. Consequently, it is proposed to abolish them. From such a deregulation of politics the citizens benefit in a similar way as consumers benefit from the deregulation of the consumer-goods markets. It strengthens the influence of the weakly organized social groups, and it enhances efficiency in politics. This proposal brings the market back into politics. We acknowledge that public goods often cannot be provided by markets. But we argue that government politicians should be controlled by the incentives of a competitive market.

The deregulation of politics, as proposed in this chapter, differs fundamentally from other politico-economic reform proposals.[2] It proposes new rules for the 'game of politics' which strengthen the policy suppliers' incentives to cater for the citizens' preferences. However, it does not give any recommendation on politicy content. Thus, the suggestion is not more market and less government. Indeed the deregulation of politics goes a decisive step ahead of federalism and direct democracy: by opening political constituencies for external policy suppliers, it adds the mobility of politicians to the mobility of citizens and firms. Moreover, the strict emphasis on the supply side complements the demand focus of direct democracy.

The remainder of this chapter is organized as follows. The next section explores why politics so often deviates from the citizens' preferences. It emphasizes the role of incomplete information as well as of incomplete contracts. The third section analyzes the impact of the above-mentioned regulations on politics and outlines the consequences of political deregulation. We then consider arguments which are potentially raised against the concept here proposed. The final section concludes.

POLITICS FAR FROM CITIZENS' PREFERENCES

Four aspects shape the design of today's politics: (1) politicians cater for their own interests which often diverge from the citizens' interest; (2) social groups differ with respect to their organizational potential; (3) campaign promises are not binding; and (4) the citizens' information on the platforms and achievements of parties and politicians, as well as the politicians' information on the preferences of the citizens, is far from perfect. These four defects of today's politics result in two main effects.

Politicians and Parties Deviate Systematically from Citizens' Preferences

Today's democratic elections do not effectively prevent politicians from deviating from the citizens' preferences. If citizens are dissatisfied with the selfish policy of the government, they will not automatically vote for the opposition party. They know that the politicians of the opposition parties would face the same constraints as today's government as soon as they were elected into government. Thus, citizens do not necessarily expect today's opposition to govern differently than the present government (for example Funk and Eichenberger, 2007). Therefore, governments have some discretionary power to pursue selfish policies which result in larger budgets, less efficient government services, higher deficits, higher debts and more regulations than the citizens prefer.

Politicians furthermore prefer short-term policies because they have a relatively short time horizon. They face in each election a high probability of dropping out without the perspective of gaining an equivalent job. Therefore, the institutional design forces upon politicians a low value of continuation, which mitigates incentives to build up long-term reputational capital (Funk, 2008). Yet, politicians and parties do not have any interest in improving political accountability. Rather, they try to diminish political competition by harmonizing and centralizing policies, and by erecting entry barriers for new parties, as well as by designing laws on party finance which favor the established parties.

The Influence of Social Groups is Asymmetric

Well-organized social groups have a stronger influence on politics than weakly organized groups for at least three reasons (for example Olson, 1965; Lohmann, 1998). Firstly, well-organized groups can supply politicians with more tangible resources, for example campaign contributions and lucrative positions in associations and firms.

Secondly, they can supply politicians with more information on their members' preferences, and they can provide their members with better information on the performance of politicians and parties. A politician's incentives to cater for the demands of a specific individual are the higher the more he or she knows about the individual's preferences and the better the individual is informed about the politicians' behavior (for example Eichenberger and Serna, 1996). A politician can target his or her policies more effectively at those groups about which he or she is well informed, and can be confident that the well-informed groups attribute the respective benefits to him or her. Thus, politicians tend to use the resources they control to benefit the well-organized interest groups rather than weakly organized groups such as consumers and taxpayers.

Thirdly, well-organized groups are in a better position to make politicians comply with their campaign promises. They can better evaluate whether, why and to what extent politicians comply with their promises, and they have better means to sanction politicians who fail to perform. Therefore, promises to well-organized groups are more credible and more effective than promises to weakly organized groups. Hence, politicians target serious promises mainly at well-organized groups, while they tend to appease weakly organized groups with fine words, aiming to induce expressive voting behavior (Brennan and Lomasky, 1993).

No wonder today's politics mainly serves the interests of well-organized groups while the interests of weakly organized groups such as consumers and taxpayers are systematically neglected. The resulting policies mainly serve to protect and create privileges and rents. Thus, they are short-sighted, status quo-oriented and distribution-focused, and do not center on allocative efficiency.

REGULATION DECREASES AND DEREGULATION INCREASES WELFARE

The Supremacy of Political Competition

Political economics has convincingly established that political competition improves the citizens' welfare (for example Besley et al., 2007). The asymmetries in favor of the established suppliers of politics, well-organized interest groups and short-sighted policies can be undermined by strengthening political competition. The concept of deregulating the political process intensifies competition among the policy suppliers by allowing for a new type of competition between and within countries.

The deregulation of the political process has quite similar effects as the deregulation of markets in general. The decision and information problem of the voters is closely related to that of consumers of goods and services. In the goods market, too, producers are selfish, competition is restricted, advertising is not fully credible and the consumers' and producers' information is far from perfect. But it is generally accepted that deregulation intensifies competition and forces producers to cater more closely for the preferences of the consumers. The globalization of markets via abolition of protectionist measures increases the consumers' menu of choice and weakens producer cartels. Enlarging markets strengthens the incentives of the producers to develop brand names with a credible international reputation, and it makes producers more independent of local pressure groups. In the following, these arguments are transferred to politics.

The Limitation of Political Competition

In today's democracies, political competition is constrained by three kinds of regulations, which prevent democratic institutions benefiting from the healing forces of market competition.

Almost anywhere, only nationals are allowed to run for political office. Moreover, politicians often have to live in their constituency during their term and even when campaigning. These provisions have a strong protectionist impact: the voters are only allowed to demand political services from national or local suppliers. Political competition is weakened and the leeway of national and local policy suppliers is increased. They may even form outright policy cartels or collude in other ways, as foreign suppliers are not allowed to step into the market (on policy cartels see Grossmann and West, 1994).

Moreover, in most countries, only individuals can run for office. While a party determines a list of candidates, it is always an individual who is elected. This procedure makes it even more difficult for the citizens (that is, the principals) to control the politicians (the agents) because they often have less information on the individual candidates than on the parties as a whole. In fact, parties cannot fully tie their members of parliament and government to the party program. While they can exclude from the party representatives who do not stick to the party program, they usually cannot recall them from office. However, collective reputation will only work if the respective group can punish and ultimately exclude a non-cooperative individual. If it cannot do so this in fact has the adverse effect of locking its members into low performance (Tirole, 1996). Moreover, the exclusive focus on individual candidates reduces the flexibility of the supply side: that is, job rotation and job-sharing among part-time politicians as well as functional specialization become almost impossible.

Finally, the explicit compensations of politicians are determined by law. Candidates cannot supply better services for higher prices. Because explicit compensation is usually much below the salary a qualified candidate could earn in the private sector, explicit payments have to be matched by implicit compensations. Such compensations are traditionally provided by interest groups. This is one of the main channels through which the special interests compete for influence. But the various groups' potentials to implicitly compensate politicians differ strongly. Thus, the constraints on explicit transfers increase not only the implicit transfers, but also the strong influence of well-organized groups.

The abundant regulations weaken political competition and restrain new suppliers. Today, politics is nowhere a contestable market. Foreign and non-local as well as profit-seeking suppliers are excluded, either directly by law or indirectly by the above-mentioned regulations. The capital owners of a firm can only realize profits when the revenue can easily be transferred within the firm. But only explicit revenue is easily transferable. Implicit payments are much more difficult to transfer. Usually, their value is specific to individuals, subject to asymmetric information and sometimes even at the limit of legality. Moreover, profit-seeking suppliers should be able flexibly to substitute underperforming employees, which will be impossible if individuals are elected but not firms.

Close regulations also impede market entry of new suppliers. Political entrepreneurs who detect new demands of the citizens quicker than others cannot easily found new parties and supply their program on a broad base, because they cannot effectively bind the prospective representatives to their platform. Rather, they have to select candidates who cater intrinsically for the same aims and who are believed by the voters to be credibly committed to these aims. This, however, is time-consuming, costly and often impossible.

The Deregulation Program

The various legal restraints weaken the positive forces of democratic competition, mitigate political accountability, and prevent successful policy suppliers from transferring their reputation to other constituencies. Therefore, it is here proposed to abolish these regulations.

Firstly, outside political suppliers should be allowed to run for office. Today's rules of origin and residential requirements should be abolished and foreigners and non-residents allowed to run for all offices. The effect of deregulation is quite similar to the economic effects of free trade. It increases the number of potential candidates and, thus, the competitive pressure, which also makes domestic producers more efficient. But there is also another more interesting incentive effect: in a closed political system the quality and performance of the opposition candidate defines the re-election benchmark and therefore the performance of the incumbent. In contrast, in an open market each actor has larger opportunities and thus more effective incentives. For instance, in today's politics the most able policy suppliers have few incentives because they get re-elected anyway. In an open market, however, the most able suppliers have the strongest incentives because they have a high probability of being elected in the most attractive constituencies (Funk, 2008). Moreover, there is also a fruitful reputation effect: honesty and success in one constituency raise credibility and, thus, the chances of being elected in other constituencies. In such an open market for politics it is profitable for a supplier to build up an international reputation for being a high-quality and credible policy producer.

Secondly, parties and firms should be allowed to directly run for political office, without nominating specific individuals (but, of course, individuals would still be allowed to run). If such a firm is elected, it can delegate the task depending on the mandate; that is, it can also substitute new delegates for hitherto active ones and, thus, bring in specialists for the problems to be solved. This deregulation forces domestic and foreign policy suppliers to stick more closely to their promises. Therefore, the credibility of campaign promises is increased. The market is opened for internationally active policy suppliers whose success depends on the professional competence of the organization as a whole rather than on the individual celebrity of their exponents. Some of the control problems of the political process are then shifted to the collective accountability mechanism of the firms, which have better means to control and discipline their members. Thus, internationally reputed private organizations can directly step into politics, such as well-known consulting firms or human rights watch and environmentalist organizations (see also Fisman and Werker, 2007).

Thirdly, explicit revenues of politicians should be set by market mechanisms. The competition among jurisdictions for able politicians would most probably lead to increasing explicit compensations for politicians. However, differences in salaries between jurisdictions provide the politicians with forceful incentives to perform. Increasing explicit revenues would crowd out implicit revenues and, thus, decrease the asymmetry among interest groups. The influence of the weakly organized groups increases. Moreover, the market is opened for profit-seeking firms which are more dependent on explicit income than traditional policy suppliers. The explicit revenues of politicians can be increased to cover their full opportunity cost. Another, even more attractive, option is to design a market for determining the appropriate compensations. For instance, they could be determined in a process related to submissions for public orders. The suppliers could publicize their compensation demand before the election. If they are elected, they get the posted compensation. As another possibility, every citizen could be given a budget which they can allocate with a new type of a secondary vote to the politicians and parties they prefer. This strengthens the candidates' incentives to submit reasonable compensation demands.

Multiple Advantages

The proposed reform substantially changes the political landscape. Successful politicians would start an international (or at least 'interjurisdictional') career, which allows them to transfer their reputation to more attractive constituencies. At the other end constituencies would actively look for suitable candidates, which they might try to poach by means of a higher salary. In addition to the traditional suppliers of politics, internationally active policy firms could run for office. If they were elected, they could delegate domestic and foreign professionals into parliaments and governments. Such firms would have stronger incentives to stick to their campaign promises because they would be more frequently engaged in election contests. Because their performance in one country influences their chances in another one, they depend much more strongly on their reputation than traditional suppliers. Moreover, the voters can easier judge internationally active suppliers, because they can access a much larger sample of observations than for only domestically operating parties.

International policy suppliers have much stronger incentives to stick to promises, which are against their own interest as political actors. This increases the chance of welfare-enhancing constitutional reforms which strengthen the influence of the citizens but are not in the interest of the political establishment, such as federalism (Frey and Eichenberger, 1996) or direct democracy (see Frey and Stutzer, 2000; Kirchgässner et al., 1999; Eichenberger, 1999a). Today, political parties most often do not follow up their promises to strengthen these institutions, because such reforms are against their interests as soon as they are part of the majority. In contrast, in an international market, parties have incentives to become political turnaround managers who have a reputation for implementing institutional reforms that benefit the citizens but weaken the politicians' influence.

Increasing explicit revenues of politicians crowds out implicit revenues. This is a consequence of various mechanisms. Firstly, explicit compensations are paid by the state. The influence of the citizens increases, because they can decide on the allocation of compensations with their vote. Secondly, the suppliers have to build up an international reputation of not relying on implicit compensations. Thirdly, higher explicit compensations strengthen the incentives of new firms to enter the market, which increases the competitive pressure. Profit-seeking policy suppliers depend more heavily on explicit compensations than traditional parties. Fourthly, high explicit compensation has an effect similar to efficiency wages. When explicit compensation increases, losing one's job becomes more expensive. Thus, politicians try to stay in government; that is they are willing to adapt their policy to suit the citizens' preferences. It is well known that higher salaries of bureaucrats crowd out corruption (see, for example, World Bank, 1997).

Consequently, the differences between well- and weakly organized groups become less important. Thus, policy aims increasingly at the citizens' preferences and caters less for specific interests. At the same time, market entry of new suppliers becomes more likely. Therefore, suppliers have to react quicker to new problems and unsatisfied demands. As the differences between the various suppliers are larger in an international market, producers find it increasingly difficult to form cartels. Finally, the deregulation of the political process leads to a new type of harmonization of politics. Citizens who wish to see closer international policy coordination can vote for suppliers who are active in various countries. This new type of endogenous policy coordination strongly contrasts with other types of global governance.

Opportunities Abound

Deregulation enhances the efficiency of all political systems, be they presidential, parliamentarian, proportional or majoritarian. The deregulation is even more beneficial when a country's present institutions perform badly. Thus, deregulation offers especially promising perspectives to countries which suffer from underdevelopment and internal conflicts.

In most developing countries, elections take place occasionally or even regularly (for example Barro, 1997). During the election campaign, all the candidates usually condemn inefficiency, pervasive corruption and misuse of power. However, when a candidate is elected, the constraints change dramatically. The incentives of a president, a minister or a parliamentarian not to be corrupted are small. Frequently, the rules and the result of the forthcoming elections can be influenced (for example, by gerrymandering, reforms of the electoral system or by outright fraud). Such strategies do not cost much in terms of votes, because the citizens know that such behavior is not specific to today's government and most opposition candidates would behave similarly. But as soon as a country deregulates its market for politics, the situation changes fundamentally. Then, reputed foreign policy suppliers (individuals and firms) can run for office, which also increases the incentive for the domestic politicians to stick to their promises.

Political deregulation is also especially fruitful within federalist and strongly decentralized countries. Today, politicians at subnational levels usually have to live in the jurisdictions where they hold political office. This restrains political competition. After deregulation, politicians could run for office in various jurisdictions at the same time, and they could have several parallel mandates. This would not only strengthen political competition, but also solve a serious problem of highly decentralized political systems. While today's small-scale jurisdictions often have difficulties in finding qualified (part-time) politicians among their citizens, political deregulation (even if it applies to the subnational level only) allows the local jurisdictions to engage non-residential politicians. Such politicians could cumulate political positions in different jurisdictions. Thus, a career in local politics would become an attractive job opportunity even for highly qualified individuals. Moreover, politicians could benefit from the economies of scale and scope inherent in doing related jobs for several jurisdictions.

ALLEGED PROBLEMS

The idea of deregulating the political process meets stiff opposition by politicians. In the following, some of their standard arguments are discussed.

Assertion 1: 'The Citizens would not Elect Foreign and Non-Local Politicians'

This argument is typically brought forth without reference to empirical observations. However, there is evidence that citizens are willing to delegate power to foreign politicians as soon as this offers promising opportunities. After all, an increasing number of countries import large parts of their legislation, especially from multilateral organizations. An example is provided by the sheer number of countries whose population wishes to join the European Union, which inevitably involves delegation of governmental power to foreign politicians. Also, countries which unilaterally peg their currency to another currency give away some of their decision power to foreign policy-makers. Actually, it would be surprising if individuals never voted for foreign politicians, since they consume foreign products, marry foreigners, work in foreign-owned firms or under foreign managers, and have foreign nurses to take care of their children. Indeed, in the German state of Baden Württemberg where non-residents can run for the office of Mayor, almost 80 per cent of the elected mayors were initially outsiders. Finally, it has to be emphasized that the citizens' preferences for domestic politicians do not justify rules of origin for politicians. If the citizens strongly prefer domestic politicians, international policy suppliers are either not successful, or they have to adapt. They would mainly delegate local candidates, exactly as international consulting firms engage local consultants in order to satisfy their clients' respective demands.

Assertion 2: 'Deregulation is Expensive'

It is argued that increasing explicit compensation for politicians increases the costs of the political process and makes the influence of money even more prevalent. However, explicit revenues partly substitute for implicit revenues. Moreover, there is no evidence that explicit compensation crowds out intrinsic motivations more strongly than implicit compensation (see Frey, 1997). Finally, the cost of policy reforms should be evaluated against their beneficial effects. Obviously, the explicit compensation of the politicians is most often irrelevant when compared to the benefits of good politics. Finally, it has to be noted that the cost of politics can easily be reduced by decreasing the size of the parliament. This measure would hardly have noticeable drawbacks. Thus, few observers would argue that the US Senate with its 100 members or the second chamber of Switzerland (the Ständerat) with 46 members do a worse job than the Italian parliament with 630 representatives or the German Bundestag with 672 members.

Assertion 3: 'Deregulation Hampers the Poor'

Sometimes the concept of deregulating politics is criticized, for being noxious for poor countries, because international policy suppliers would concentrate on rich countries. However, the opposite tends to happen. The open market for politics induces suppliers of politics to become active in those countries where they are needed most urgently. The deregulation of explicit compensation allows them to appropriate part of the value added that they create. This stops the brain drain from, and even leads to an inflow of political human capital into, political hotspots. Therefore, there is no danger of a race to the bottom with respect to the quality of politicians. It pays for politicians to behave like turnaround managers, who enter firms with the largest unexploited opportunities. Still another incentive to supply political services in poor, troubled countries is the reputation which can be gained by doing a good job in such countries.

Assertion 4: 'The Proposal is Utopian'

Historically, in most countries foreigners were allowed to play a much more active role than they did in the twentieth century. It was often by marriage and succession that foreign aristocrats became kings and princes. Sometimes, they even were elected as kings. For instance, in 1573 the Polish aristocracy elected the then 23-year-old Henry III, the brother of King Charles IX of France, as King of Poland. But Henry returned to France in 1574 after his brother's death and became King of France himself. Therefore, the Poles had to look for another king. In 1575, they elected Stephan IV Bathory, the Prince of Transylvania, as their new king. He stayed in office until 1586 and is known to be one of the most successful Polish kings. Another example is provided by the French Marshal Jean-Baptiste Bernadotte who was elected King of Sweden in 1810. Up to the nineteenth century, foreigners on the throne were no exception, as is illustrated, for example, by the first kings of Greece, Rumania and Bulgaria who were all born in Germany. But high-ranking ministers were also imported. A well-known example is Klemens Wenzel Metternich, the powerful Austrian minister, who was not only born in Germany but who also began his political career in Germany. Finally, our proposal is closely related to the *podestà* in the enormously prosperous Italian city states of the twelfth and thirteenth centuries. In this governmental system non-local and foreign political entrepreneurs were elected as leaders of city-states for a predetermined period of time, most commonly six months or one year. Because of the strict term limits – and quite unintended – a market for *podestà* was launched with several hundred participants and high gains for success, but also severe losses from failure (see Funk and Eichenberger, 2006).

The role of foreigners as political decision-makers is not confined to history. Today, international organizations have some features in common with our proposal. Other examples are provided by non-governmental organizations, which play an increasingly important role, not only at the international, but also at the national level, even though they are often dominated by foreigners. In business firms and in academia, foreigners play an even more important role. It is commonplace that chief executives and professors are foreigners or, at least, come from outside. Actually, nominations of external candidates are often seen as preferable to internal nominations.

The opposition to the deregulation of politics is related to the opposition to the deregulation of sports markets some years ago. In football and hockey, for example, the player unions defended quotas and other restraints with the argument that the fans wanted to see domestic players. However, recent experience shows the opposite. With an increasing proportion of foreigners, the quality of the game as well as the enthusiasm of the fans has been raised dramatically. Actually, today even in national teams it is often a foreigner who is the most important man – the coach.

SUMMARY AND CONCLUSIONS

Economic growth and development have been boosted by deregulation. In contrast to the economy, politics has been protected from the efficiency-enhancing forces of markets, competition and free trade. Thus, political reforms should unleash those forces by deregulating the political process. Deregulation means to mitigate those forces which hinder political competition: rules of origin for politicians, regulation of the production process and prescriptions on the compensation of politicians.

This program changes politics fundamentally by strengthening the incentives of both local and non-local policy suppliers. Moreover, international policy entrepreneurs could run for office and delegate domestic and foreign specialists to parliament and to government. Such international policy suppliers would have much stronger incentives to stick to their promises than today's politicians and parties, because they depend on their international reputation. While the increasing explicit compensation for holding political office crowds out implicit revenues, the asymmetries among well- and weakly organized groups decrease. Thus, politics caters increasingly for the preferences of the citizens by promoting efficiency and individual freedom. Finally, the globalization of politics would lead to a new form of policy coordination. As soon as some policy suppliers gain influence in many countries, politics becomes coordinated almost automatically.

The concept proposed here differs fundamentally from most other proposals for policy reform. It is strictly process-oriented. It does not propose any specific policy, but it proposes new rules that strengthen political competition and, thus, the incentives of policy suppliers to cater for the preferences of the citizens.

The arguments brought forward against the concept of deregulating politics are not convincing, and nor is the idea utopian. However, it is evident that many members of the political establishment, who make a good living in today's protected political environment, are not enthusiastic about the idea.

Two questions remain to be clarified. Firstly, are additional institutional prerequisites necessary in order to prevent the abuse of power by international policy suppliers? It is noteworthy that international policy suppliers have strong incentives to propose effective institutional mechanisms that constrain them from abusing their own powers, because this enhances their credibility. Nevertheless, there is no damage when multilateral organizations develop a best-practice standard for competition regulation which specifies the market rules and bans the development of monopolies.

Secondly, the questions of how and where the deregulation of politics could be put into effect should be tackled. The deregulation is welfare-increasing in every country. It is the more fruitful, the smaller a country and the worse the country's political situation. Additionally, incentives increase with the size of the market; that is, every additional country deregulating its political system increases welfare in the other countries. However, deregulation is especially promising for countries with a federalist structure and for countries which intend to strengthen federalism. The deregulation of politics within such countries already promises important welfare gains. Finally, the deregulation of politics has better chances when it follows a deregulation of the economic sector. In the European Union, for instance, the deregulation of politics with its 'free movements of politicians' seems only to be the logical complement to the four well-known economic freedoms.

NOTES

1. Center for Public Finance, University of Fribourg, Switzerland.
2. The idea was first developed in Eichenberger (1999b).

REFERENCES

Barro, Robert J. (1997), *Determinants of Economic Growth: A Cross-Country Empirical Study*, Cambridge, MA: MIT Press.
Besley, Timothy, Torsten Persson and Daniel Sturm (2007), 'Political competition and economic performance: theory and evidence from the United States', mimeo.
Brennan, Geoffrey and Loren E. Lomasky (1993), *Democracy and Decision: The Pure Theory of Electoral Preference*, Cambridge: Cambridge University Press.
Eichenberger, Reiner (1999a), 'Mit direkter Demokratie zu besserer Wirtschafts- und Finanzpolitik: Theorie und Empirie', in Hans H. von Arnim (ed.), *Adaequate Institu-*

tionen: Voraussetzung für 'gute' und bürgernahe Politik? Berlin: Duncker & Humblot, pp. 259–88.

Eichenberger, Reiner (1999b), 'Dereguliert, liberalisiert und globalisiert die Politik! Ein politisch-ökonomischer Reformvorschlag', *Studia Philosophica*, **58**, 99–121.

Eichenberger, Reiner and Mark Schelker (2007), 'Independent and competing agencies: an effective way to control government', *Public Choice*, **130** (1–2), 79–98.

Eichenberger, Reiner and Angel Serna (1996), 'Random errors, dirty information, and politics', *Public Choice*, **86** (1–2), 137–56.

Epple, Dennis and Allan Zelenitz (1981), 'The implications of competition among jurisdictions: does Tiebout need politics?', *Journal of Political Economy*, **89** (6), 1197–217.

Fisman, Ray and Eric Werker (2007), 'Local company politics: a proposal', *Capitalism and Society*, **2** (1), 1–7.

Frey, Bruno S. (1994), 'Direct democracy: politico-economic lessons from Swiss experience', *American Economic Review*, **84** (2), 338–42.

Frey, Bruno S. (1997), *Markt und Motivation: Wie ökonomische Anreize die (Arbeits-) Moral verdrängen*, München: Vahlen.

Frey, Bruno S. and Reiner Eichenberger (1996), 'To harmonize or to compete – that's not the question', *Journal of Public Economics*, **60** (3), 335–49.

Frey, Bruno S. and Alois Stutzer (2000), 'Maximizing happiness?' *German Economic Review*, **1** (2), 145–67.

Funk, Michael (2008), 'Political market design', mimeo.

Funk, Michael and Reiner Eichenberger (2006), 'Strangers in politics: the market for good politicians in medieval Italy and its lessons for modern democracy', mimeo.

Funk, Michael and Reiner Eichenberger (2007), 'It's the challenger, stupid! Elections and the theory of rank-order tournaments', CREMA Working Paper 2007–20.

Grossmann, Philip J. and Edwin G. West (1994), 'Federalism and the growth of government revisited', *Public Choice*, **79** (1–2), 19–32.

Kirchgässner, Gebhard, Lars P. Feld and Marcel R. Savioz (1999), *Modern, erfolgreich, entwicklungs- und exportfähig: Die direkte Demokratie der Schweiz*, Basel: Helbing und Lichtenhahn.

Lohmann, Susanne (1998), 'The information rationale for the power of special interests', *American Political Science Review*, **92** (4), 809–27.

Olson, Mancur (1965), *The Problem of Collective Action: Public Goods and the Theory of Groups*, Cambridge, MA: Harvard University Press.

Tirole, J. (1996), 'A theory of collective reputation (with applications to the persistence of corruption and to firm quality)', *Review of Economic Studies*, **63**, 1–22.

World Bank (1997), *World Development Report 1997: The State in a Changing World*, Washington, DC: World Bank.

9. Do we really know much about tax non-compliance?

Lars P. Feld

INTRODUCTION

Social norms have been a central theme in economics for many years. Indeed, the norms that guide individual behavior in the market place (and beyond) belonged to the main concerns of Adam Smith when he analyzed the role of morale for the functioning of societies in his *Theory of Moral Sentiments* (1759), long before he published his *Wealth of Nations* (1776 [1976]). Since Hayek (1960), economists also know that norms of reciprocity provide for a crucial precondition of market exchange even in large groups. According to Buchanan (2005, Chapter 2, p. 15 et seq.) such a Kantian norm generally forms the basis of modern market economies: 'The Kantian norm dictates constraints on behavior in accordance with fairness criteria, defined in terms of respect for the other person in some basic ethical sense' (p. 15), 'I can scarcely imagine an interaction setting in which persons refrain from cheating, stealing and keeping promises only because of some fear of punishment' (p. 16).[1] Without a basic individual willingness to reciprocate in market exchange, far less contracts between private parties will be concluded as the enforcement of each claim to the contracts in society becomes extremely expensive. Societies with properly working social norms thus obtain an economic advantage as compared to societies in which contract partners cannot rely as heavily on social norms.

Only recently has this importance of social norms in studying compliance with the law been rediscovered in law and economics (Ellickson, 1991). In addition to the direct deterrence effects of legal sanctions, other ways of how lawmaking may influence behavior have been suggested (Sunstein, 1996; Cooter, 1998). For example, Posner (1998, 2000a, 2000b) argues that deterrence signals social norms to citizens in order to educate them as to what they should do. Smith and Mackie (2000, p. 377) note: 'Norms must be brought to mind before they can guide behavior. They can be activated by deliberate reminders or by subtle cues, such as observations of other people's behavior.' From that perspective, social norms may reinforce the effects of deterrence on compliance, but may also be the outcome of reciprocity and other continuing experiences with pro-social behavior. Social norms are thus endogenous and not simply exogenously given as the result of socialization during childhood.

Similar considerations have led many researchers of tax compliance to think about the impact of tax morale as a particular aspect of social norms, and how it is determined. Feld and Frey (2007) speak of a psychological tax contract between the state and its citizens, under which an exchange takes place between public goods and services provided by the state, and tax payments undertaken by citizens. This psychological tax contract goes beyond pure monetary exchanges and also involves aspects of loyalty and affection. Citizens are willing to comply with the psychological tax contract and pay their taxes accordingly if the state and the other citizens as contract partners also stick to the contractual content. With respect to the other citizens this means that taxpayers pay taxes honestly if they expect others to be honest as well. With respect to the state this means that it can shape the psychological tax contract by: (1) providing public goods and services in exchange for tax payments which taxpayers evaluate positively; (2) relying on procedural fairness in decisions about public policies, in particular about income redistribution; and (3) treating citizens as contract partners instead of subordinates in a hierarchical relationship. Regarding deterrence, the theoretical idea of a psychological tax contract allows for underlining a potential adverse influence of deterrence measures: deterrence may crowd out individuals' tax morale as an intrinsic motivation to pay taxes according to the psychological tax contract (Frey, 1997).

While there is some experimental evidence (Feld and Tyran, 2002; Tyran and Feld, 2006) and field evidence for Switzerland (Feld and Frey, 2002a, 2002b; Frey and Feld, 2002) supporting the claim that deterrence shapes tax morale, much less evidence exists on this relation in other countries. In this chapter, the role of deterrence and social norms for tax compliance is elaborated for the German case. Germany is interesting in several respects. First, the federal government has followed a strict deterrence policy since the beginning of the new millennium in order to fight tax evasion and the shadow economy (Feld and Larsen, 2008; Feld et al., 2007). Second, reunification in 1990 united two parts of Germany with formerly quite different political, legal and social constitutions, but similar cultural traditions. Torgler (2003) highlights the differences in tax morale between East and West Germany, but he does not have a closer look at the role of deterrence. I draw on different types of evidence to gain some insights as to the influence of deterrence (and thus the success of recent policies), but also to consider its interaction with social norms.

The remainder of the chapter is organized as follows. First, I discuss the theoretical background underlying the analysis. Second, the data restrictions posed in the context of tax compliance for the German case are considered. I then summarize the evidence on deterrence, social norms and tax compliance. Finally, some remarks on policies fighting tax non-compliance conclude this chapter.

THE THEORETICAL BACKGROUND

There are different forms of tax non-compliance which can usually be attributed to different groups in society. Tax evasion by wealthy people not declaring their capital incomes received in foreign tax havens may nurture particular prejudices of what is involved, but is far from providing a comprehensive picture. Tax non-compliance also comprises the taxes evaded when individuals work in the shadow economy; or tax avoidance by multinational firms becoming illegal when a (financial) court reaches a final verdict on particular tax saving schemes; or the sophisticated trading schemes which allow for evading commodity taxes; or donations by family members to their supposed heirs to evade inheritance taxes; and so on. Tax compliance is moreover related to the broader concept of tax morale, which also includes the attitudes of honest taxpayers who have never under-reported their true incomes, and potential tax non-compliance of their dishonest fellow citizens.

Given these different facets of tax non-compliance, a useful starting point for a theoretical discussion of non-compliance behavior is the paper by Allingham and Sandmo (1972) on income tax evasion. While the shadow economy and tax evasion are not congruent, activities in the shadow economy in most cases imply the evasion of direct or indirect taxes, such that the factors affecting tax evasion will also affect the shadow economy. Allingham and Sandmo argue that the decision to comply with the tax laws depends on the expected costs and benefits of non-compliance. The benefits of tax non-compliance result from the expected marginal income change and thus from the individual marginal tax rate and the true individual income. In the case of the shadow economy, the individual marginal tax rate is obtained by calculating the overall marginal tax burden from indirect and direct taxes including social security contributions. The individual income generated in the shadow economy is usually categorized as labor income, but – less probably – also as capital income. The expected costs of non compliance derive from the countermeasures imposed by the state. Tax non-compliance could be detected and punished, such that the expected costs depend on the state's auditing activities raising the probability of detection and the fines individuals face when they are caught. As individual morality also plays a role in compliance, additional costs could pertain beyond pure punishment by the tax administration in the form of psychic costs like shame or regret, but also additional pecuniary costs if, for example, reputation loss results.

Kanniainen et al. (2004) incorporate many of these earlier insights in their model of the shadow economy by also considering labor supply decisions. They obtain a direct positive effect of taxes on the size of the shadow economy; that is, tax increases unambiguously increase the shadow economy, while the effect of public goods financed by those taxes on the shadow economy depends upon the ability of those with activities in the shadow economy to access public goods. In Allingham and Sandmo (1972) and the subsequent literature on tax evasion, in contrast, the effects of marginal income taxes (and true individual income) depend on the underlying risk preferences of individuals and the shape of the income tax schedule such that tax increases could even have negative effects on tax evasion. Public-good effects are however not considered. Moreover, morality is also included in the analysis of Kanniainen et al. (2004). But the costs for individual non-compliers resulting from moral norms appear to be mainly captured by state punishment, although self-esteem also plays a role.

A shortcoming common to both papers consists in the neglected endogeneity of tax morale and good governance. Based on the insights of Feld and Frey (2007), it could be argued that tax compliance is the result of a complicated interaction between tax morale and deterrence measures. While it must be clear to taxpayers what the rules of the game are, and as deterrence measures serve as signals for the tax morale a society wants to elicit (Posner, 2000a, 2000b), deterrence could also crowd out the intrinsic motivation to pay taxes. Moreover, tax morale is not only increased if taxpayers perceive the public goods received in exchange for their tax payments to be worth it. It also increases if political decisions on public activities are perceived to follow fair procedures or if the treatment of taxpayers by the tax authorities is perceived to be friendly and fair. Tax morale is thus not exogenously given, but is influenced by deterrence, the quality of state institutions and the constitutional differences among states.

This leaves us with a rich set of variables that might influence tax non-compliance. On the one hand, marginal tax rates and income determine the potential benefits of (income) tax non-compliance. Their signs are, however, indeterminate depending on risk preferences and the shape of the income tax schedule. On the other hand, fines and audits provide for the costs of tax non-compliance. Their signs are also indeterminate as they first serve their traditional deterrence purposes but, second, potentially crowd out tax morale as the intrinsic motivation to pay taxes. Finally, tax morale has a positive influence on tax compliance. It is shaped by many factors ranging from exogenously given religious and social norms to government action supporting fiscal exchange under procedural fairness. Empirical results could thus help to find responses as to what should be expected with respect to the determinants of tax non-compliance.

DATA ON TAX NON-COMPLIANCE

Unfortunately, reliable data on tax non-compliance are more difficult to obtain than data in other areas of economic research. The quest for empirical enlightenment is thus particularly burdensome in that area. Each alternative measurement approach faces its own problems which might similarly lead to biased estimates. If economic research does not want to abstain totally from measuring the unmeasurable, there is only the choice between several imperfect approaches.

There are indirect and direct methods of measurement. The first indirect method is called the income gap approach. It uses the basic definition in national accounts that the income measure should be the same as the expenditure measure of the domestic product. If there are statistical discrepancies, they might occur because the quality of the data is insufficient. However, it is highly implausible that these statistical discrepancies increase substantially over time. Thus, tax evasion explains why people in an economy buy more products and services than they officially have money for, given their earned income according to income tax declarations. In Europe, Larsen (2002) uses this method for Denmark, and Gorodnichenko et al. (forthcoming) for Russia. Pommerehne and Weck-Hannemann (1996) and Feld and Frey (2002b) apply it to measure Swiss tax evasion.

The second indirect measurement method is based on monetary approaches. On the one hand, the transactions approach, starting from the Fisher equation of the quantity theory of money, relates total nominal gross national product (GNP) to total transactions. The GNP of the shadow economy is obtained by subtracting official GNP from total nominal GNP, assuming a base year in which the ratio of total transactions to total nominal GNP was normal, that is, no shadow economy existed (Feige, 1989). On the other hand, the currency demand approach assumes that transactions in the shadow economy are more often made in cash than transactions in the official economy in order to leave no accounting traces (Schneider, 2007; Kirchgässner, 1983). The size of the shadow economy is then inferred by simulating currency demand with and without tax variables.

The third indirect method is the electricity consumption method (Schneider and Enste, 2000). It assumes that electricity serves as a good indicator of overall economic activity also assuming an electricity-to-gross domestic product (GDP) elasticity of close to one. Then, a calculation can be made of how large the actual total GDP of a country is. The difference from official GDP provides an estimate of the shadow economy.

The fourth indirect method is the hidden variable approach (Frey and Weck, 1984). Macroeconomic indicators, usually the labor participation rate, real GDP growth, currency demand and working hours, are used as indicator variables for the shadow economy and linked to explanatory variables such as tax rates or the regulatory burden using LISREL techniques (structural causal modelling techniques, or the DYMIMIC approach; see Schneider and Enste, 2000). With the hidden variable approach, only a relative assessment of the size of the shadow economy is possible such that analyses using this method often relate their estimates to the currency demand approach (Pickhardt and Sardà Pons,

2006). In contrast to the income gap method, the latter three approaches capture activities in the shadow economy, but not overall tax evasion as they are not able to account for undeclared income from capital.

There are three main direct methods. The first focuses on black activities, as a part of the shadow economy, by using surveys in which individuals are directly asked whether they have carried out black activities, either for cash payments or payments in kind (Feld and Larsen, 2005). The second direct method, applied by the US Internal Revenue Service (IRS), is based on actual tax auditing and other compliance methods (Engel and Hines, 1999). In 1963 the IRS started to conduct periodic tax audits (Taxpayer Compliance Measurement Program – TCMP) measuring understatement of income, overstatement of deductions and exemptions, and so on, for a random sample of individual income taxpayers. The data are used to calculate tax evasion for the whole population. The IRS also applies an income gap method for non-filers by calculating the discrepancy between the declared income and actual income of randomly audited individuals (Andreoni et al., 1998). The third direct method aims at measuring tax morale instead of tax evasion in surveys. For instance, the World Values Survey elicits tax morale for a representative sample of individuals by asking whether cheating on tax can be justified (Torgler, 2007).

Any of these indirect and direct methods has disadvantages. The income gap method has to cope with the unreliability of statistical errors. The monetary methods may overestimate the rationality of the money market. In addition, many transactions in the shadow economy take place without cash payments. As indirect methods minimize strategic problems that emerge if individuals are directly confronted with questions about tax honesty, it could be argued that the indirect methods provide for an upper boundary of tax evasion or the shadow economy. The survey approach is sensitive to the formulation of questions, and participants in the survey may behave strategically and simply not tell the truth. Even in face-to-face interviews, which promote the greatest degree of participation in the survey, a respondent may simply lie. Moreover, household surveys include black activities by professional firms at most incompletely. The survey method may thus measure a lower limit of black activities in the economy. The tax auditing method is prone to sample selection bias, because the selection for audit is based on the properties of the tax returns submitted to the tax office and thus not independent of the probability of evading taxes. Those taxpayers identified as tax cheaters could be only the tip of the iceberg because it is highly improbable that tax authorities would detect all tax cheaters even if they wanted to (Erard and Feinstein, forthcoming). The survey of individual tax morale measures hypothetical tax morale and not real tax compliance. Nevertheless all methods taken together to some extent measure the phenomenon and provide insights as to its determinants.

THE EVIDENCE ON DETERRENCE, SOCIAL NORMS AND TAX COMPLIANCE IN GERMANY

In the case of Germany, several of these methods have been applied, but only the hidden variable approach, surveys of tax morale and of undeclared work (black activities) have been used to analyze tax non-compliance in recent times. Each one of these methods offers interesting results on the impact of social norms and deterrence.

Evidence from the Hidden Variable Approach

Schneider (2007) provides the most extensive and consistent data on tax non-compliance in Germany. For each year since 1970, he reports the size of the shadow economy in Germany based on a combination of the hidden variable approach (using DYMIMIC techniques) and the currency demand approach. Figure 9.1 reproduces his estimates of the size of the German shadow economy together with concurring results provided by Pickhardt and Sardà Pons (2006). Both time series reveal an increasing trend in the German shadow economy until the new millennium.

Schneider's estimates show three periods. A first subperiod from 1970 to 1980 is characterized by a steep increase of the shadow economy in Germany with a significantly higher slope of the curve than afterwards. During this time, the social welfare state was extended, effective marginal income tax rates (including social security contributions) increased and labor market regulation was significantly tightened. A second subperiod from 1980 to 2003 indicates growth rates of the shadow economy lower than before, but still remarkably positive. While the tax burden was somewhat lightened, a real and significant relief of individual incomes was not achieved. Similarly, the tight labor market regulation was only negligibly lifted. This overall assessment of the economic situation in Germany was not affected by reunification according to Schneider's estimates, while reunification increased the shadow economy further according to Pickhardt and Sardà Pons (2006). The third subperiod as of 2003 onwards reveals a turning point in the series with a decline of the shadow economy for the first time since 1970. These years followed the first income tax reform in Germany with a real reduction of the tax burden. Labor market regulation remained tight, but active labor market policies and unemployment benefits were considerably reformed. According to Pickhardt and Sardà Pons, the decline in the shadow economy began in 1999.

This description of the data and the general economic situation suggests mainly an influence of tax rates, social security and labor market regulation on the size of the shadow economy. Indeed, Schneider (2007) provides evidence that these are its three main determinants ('causal factors'). The impact of

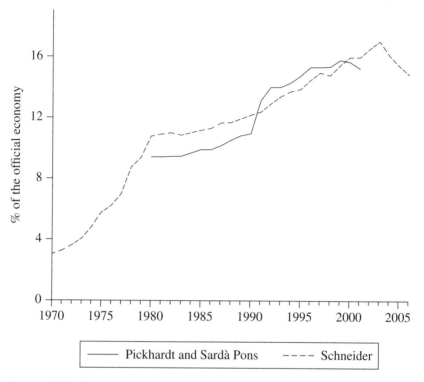

Source: Feld et al. (2007).

Figure 9.1   The size of the German shadow economy, 1970–2006

deterrence has however not been discussed until recently. Feld et al. (2007) were the first to study the impact of deterrence on the German shadow economy, using time series data between 1974 and 2001. Their data on deterrence indicate that the sum of penalties and prison sentences in Germany increased between 1974 and 2001, but that audit capabilities of tax authorities, in particular regarding small firms and self-employed taxpayers, declined in the same time period.

In a time series analysis, the authors investigate whether deterrence and the shadow economy determine each other. According to their results, deterrence does not have any consistent effect on the German shadow economy. According to Granger causality tests, the direction of causation (in the sense of precedence) is also ambiguous, leaving room for an impact of the shadow economy on deterrence instead of deterrence on the shadow economy. While there is some evidence of a negative effect of a higher tax morale on the shadow economy for

Organisation for Economic Co-operation and Development (OECD) countries, its influence on the German shadow economy has not been analyzed yet. Körner et al. (2006) find such a significant positive effect of tax morale in the OECD. Although their study is focused on Germany, they do not establish any empirical evidence on deterrence, tax morale and the shadow economy for Germany specifically.

Evidence from the Surveys on Tax Morale

While there are many recent empirical studies analyzing tax morale (see in particular Torgler, 2007, and for Germany, Torgler, 2003), there is not much evidence on its interaction with deterrence. Torgler (2005) is the only study explicitly testing on this relation, using data for Switzerland without finding any robust effect. Regarding deterrence and tax morale, Germany is interesting because reunification between its western and eastern parts induced the adoption of the German criminal tax code by the new *Länder*. They thus shifted from a dictatorial regime with high penalties for tax offences, but remarkable room for black market activities and undeclared work (that is, for the shadow economy), to a system with the rule of law and clearly defined incentives to comply with the tax code. An old system of deterrence for tax non-compliance was replaced by another which was well known in advance.

As Figure 9.2 shows, East Germany started with significantly higher tax morale levels than West Germany in 1990 which may also reflect, as Feld et al. (2008) suggest, that East Germans offered a lot of trust which the West German state had to prove being worthy of afterwards. Indeed, the higher East German

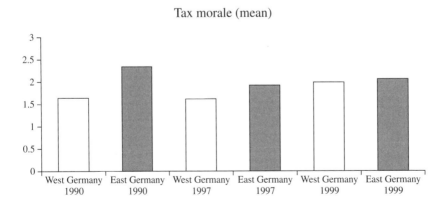

Source: Feld et al. (2008).

Figure 9.2   Tax morale (WVS) over time in Germany

tax morale slowly converged to the lower West German levels in subsequent years (Figure 9.2), a development which cannot be explained by other variables according to the multivariate regression models of Feld et al. (2008). It should be noted, however, that this convergence process did not only result from a reduction in East German tax morale, but also from a significantly higher tax morale in West Germany in 1999 as compared with 1990.

Given that the German federal government started intensifying its fight against tax non-compliance with a public campaign at the end of the 1990s, the increase of tax morale in West Germany is remarkable. More interestingly, the decline of East German tax morale took place despite the efforts of the federal government to increase its deterrence levels, for example by higher penalties and prison sentences. In addition unification may have been seen as a shock for West German tax morale. In order to find out whether this is the case, Feld et al. (2008) use tax morale data from the 1981 World Values Survey and compare them with those from 1990. They report that tax morale in West Germany was significantly lower in 1990 than in 1981. West Germans simply capitalized to a certain extent the expected costs of unification, and they anticipated a loosening of the positive exchange relationship between the state and its West German citizens.

Overall, the analysis of tax morale in Germany after unification hints at the complicated interaction between deterrence and social norms in the context of a psychological tax contract. The evidence is unfortunately not sufficiently conclusive to support the predictions of the psychological tax contract, although does not provide support for the pure deterrence model of tax compliance.

Evidence from the Surveys on Undeclared Work

In a sequence of studies, Feld and Larsen (2005, 2006, 2008, forthcoming) analyze the impact of deterrence and social norms on tax non-compliance using survey data on undeclared work for representative samples of German citizens in each year since 2004. The survey is oriented at the contingent valuation method used to elicit non-use values in environmental economics (see Kopp et al., 1997 for an earlier reference). It is divided into three parts, of which the first part contains questions on household services in general, the second part is focused on undeclared work and the third part concludes with socio-demographic questions. In the second part, respondents are asked directly about their undeclared work. Based on the survey data, Feld and Larsen (2005) calculate that undeclared work in Germany amounted to 3.1 percent of GDP in 2004. This is much less than the 16.1 percent of GDP Schneider obtains on the basis of the DYMIMIC cum currency demand approach for the German shadow economy in the same year. Feld and Larsen (2006) attribute these differences to the facts that only households, but not firms, are included in the survey; that the shadow economy comprises additional illegal behavior apart from undeclared work; and that respondents to the survey may not completely tell the truth despite the careful interview techniques employed.

Still, the most important advantage of direct methods such as survey data must be attributed to the possibility to ask questions on perceived deterrence and on social norms, and thus evaluate their differential impact. Regarding these variables, the results of the logistic regressions conducted by Feld and Larsen (2005) are summarized in Table 9.1. It turns out that subjectively perceived deterrence is largely insignificant and does not affect the probability of carrying out black activities, while social norms have a highly significant impact on

Table 9.1 *Summary of logistic regressions of the probability of participating in black activities (18–74-year-olds, Germany, 2004)*

	Men 2004		Women 2004	
	With full deterrence	With social norms	With full deterrence	With social norms
Age	***	***	***	***
Marital status	***	***	***	***
Children under 6	*	*	ns	ns
Occupation	ns	ns	**	**
Education	***	***	ns	ns
Income	*	*	ns	ns
Length of unemployment (months)	ns	ns	***	***
Region	*	*	ns	ns
Owner-occupier / tenant	ns	ns	ns	ns
Perceived risk of discovery	ns	ns	*	ns
Perceived penalty	ns	ns	ns	ns
Social norms	–	*	–	***

Notes:
The dependent variable has the value 1 if the respondent has carried out black activities within the last 12 months, and the value 0 otherwise.
***: The variable is significant at the 1% level.
 **: The variable is significant at the 5% level.
  *: The variable is significant at the 10% level.
 ns: The variable is not significant.
Joint significance of several variables has been tested by likelihood ratio tests. The sample has been drawn at the household level, and a weight has been applied to make the sample representative as to sex and age distribution and other characteristics of the total population.

Source: Feld and Larsen (2005), Table 10.2, p. 87.

women's black activities as well as a marginally significant effect on men's black activities. According to the most recent results reported in Feld and Larsen (2008, forthcoming), the perceived risk of being detected negatively affects undeclared work of women significantly in 2004–05 and 2006–07, while it has the same effect on men's undeclared work only in 2004–05. Perceived sanctions do not turn out to be significant in any of the years studied. Social norms do, however, have a consistent and significant effect on undeclared work: the higher the tax morale, the lower the probability that individuals work in the shadow economy. Deterrence is therefore not totally unimportant for tax non-compliance in the sense of undeclared work, but reveals a clearly less robust effect than tax morale.

Without stretching these results too far, as much further analysis is necessary, they are in line with those obtained by Feld et al. (2007), mentioned before. They are also supported by the further analyses conducted on tax morale and deterrence for Germany (Feld et al., 2008). Also, experimental evidence supports this view (Tyran and Feld, 2006). Finally, the results are in line with Buchanan's (2005, Chapter 2, p. 16) assessment mentioned at the beginning of this chapter: 'I can scarcely imagine an interaction setting in which persons refrain from cheating, stealing and keeping promises only because of some fear of punishment.'

CONCLUDING REMARKS

In this chapter, I have argued that, from a theoretical perspective, the most important unresolved issue in the analysis of tax non-compliance is on the impact of deterrence. On the one hand, and fully in line with the traditional view of the economic theory of crime and punishment, deterrence provides incentives to behave honestly. On the other hand, people comply with the (tax) law because they follow social norms. These social norms are not exogenously given, for example as the result of education and socialization during child-hood, but are endogenous. They could be influenced by the way the state shapes its relationships with its citizens. The social norm of honestly paying taxes, that is, tax morale, is first influenced by deterrence. Sanctions in the criminal tax code signal how taxpayers are expected to behave, but deterrence could also crowd out tax morale if it is perceived to be unfair or intrusive. Second, fiscal exchange according to a psychological tax contract matters for tax compliance. The psychological tax contract has elements of gain (or distributive justice), of participation (or procedural justice) and of respect (or interactional justice).

Experimental evidence and field evidence for Switzerland on tax compliance support the theoretical underpinnings of the psychological tax contract. The evidence reported for Germany, though much less direct than the Swiss evidence, is also in line with this broader perspective on tax compliance. It turns out that deterrence has only an inconclusive effect on the shadow economy and on undeclared work, while developments of German tax morale are even less compatible with changes in deterrence. Tax morale, in turn, appears to have a much more robust and consistent moderating impact on undeclared work than deterrence. Given the recent increase in the intensity with which German authorities fight tax non-compliance, these results provide some cautionary advice as to the success of the most recent campaign.

Focusing on the theoretically most interesting question, that is the impact of deterrence on non-compliance behaviour, different routes for future research remain open. First, extended time series on the shadow economy in different countries could be studied if deterrence has sufficiently fluctuated across time. Second, further improved survey evidence could be used as it allows the inclusion of questions on perceived deterrence and social norms. Regarding the results reported in this chapter, additional robustness analyses and replication are necessary. While the previous literature has focused on the usefulness of different approaches to measure non-compliance from a statistical or econometric perspective, it will be useful to ask which approach allows for an investigation of the deterrence hypothesis. This is particularly important as deterrence measures appear to be the policy of choice in most OECD countries. Without any proper empirical evidence on the impact of deterrence on non-compliance, let alone any proper evaluation of recent deterrence policies, governments contend that this is the only way to fight undeclared work, tax evasion and the shadow economy. Policy-makers seldom acknowledge that deterrence might have its drawbacks on the functioning of a civic society. These drawbacks could be severe. Hence, my emphasis on studying the effect of deterrence.

NOTE

1. For recent analyses of reciprocity norms in modern (experimental) game theory see Sugden (1984), Fehr and Gächter (2000) or Falk and Fischbacher (2006).

REFERENCES

Allingham, M.G. and A. Sandmo (1972), 'Income tax evasion: a theoretical analysis', *Journal of Public Economics*, **1**, 323–38.
Andreoni, J., B. Erard and J. Feinstein (1998), 'Tax compliance', *Journal of Economic Literature*, **36**, 818–60.
Buchanan, J.M. (2005), *Why I, Too, Am Not Conservative: The Normative Vision of*

Classical Liberalism, Cheltenham, UK and Northampton, MA, USA: Edward Elgar.

Cooter, R.D. (1998), 'Expressive law and economics', *Journal of Legal Studies*, **27**, 585–608.

Ellickson, R.C. (1991), *Order without Law: How Neighbors Settle Disputes*, Cambridge, MA: Harvard University Press.

Engel, E. and J.R. Hines (1999), 'Understanding tax evasion dynamics', NBER Working Paper No. 6903, Cambridge, MA: NBER.

Erard, B. and J. Feinstein (forthcoming), 'Econometric models for multi-stage audit process: an application to the IRS National Research Program', in J. Alm, J. Martinez-Vazquez and B. Torgler (eds), *Tax Compliance and Tax Evasion*, London: Routledge.

Falk, A. and U. Fischbacher (2006), 'A theory of reciprocity', *Games and Economic Behavior*, **54**, 293–315.

Fehr, E. and S. Gächter (2000), 'Fairness and retaliation – the economics of reciprocity', *Journal of Economic Perspectives*, **14** (3), 159–81.

Feige, E.L. (1989), *The Underground Economies: Tax Evasion and Information Distortion*, Cambridge: Cambridge University Press.

Feld, L.P. and B.S. Frey (2002a), 'Trust breeds trust: how taxpayers are treated', *Economics of Governance*, **3**, 87–99.

Feld, L.P. and B.S. Frey (2002b), 'The tax authority and the taxpayer: an exploratory analysis', unpublished manuscript, University of Zurich.

Feld, L.P. and B.S. Frey (2007), 'Tax compliance as the result of a psychological tax contract: the role of incentives and responsive regulation', *Law and Policy*, **29**, 102–20.

Feld, L.P. and C. Larsen (2005), 'Black activities in Germany in 2001 and in 2004: a comparison based on survey data', Study No. 12, The Rockwool Foundation Research Unit, Copenhagen.

Feld, L.P. and C. Larsen (2006), 'Strafen, Kontrollen und Schwarzarbeit: Einige Anmerkungen auf Basis von Befragungsdaten für Deutschland', in D. Enste and F. Schneider (eds), *Jahrbuch Schattenwirtschaft 2006/2007*, Berlin: Lit Verlag, pp. 81–107, 211–13.

Feld, L.P. and C. Larsen (2008), '*Semper aliquid haeret?* Undeclared work, deterrence and social norms in Germany', mimeo, University of Heidelberg.

Feld, L.P. and C. Larsen (forthcoming), *Undeclared Work in Germany 2001–2007: Impact of Deterrence, Tax Policy, and Social Norms: An Analysis Based on Survey Data*, Berlin et al.: Springer.

Feld, L.P. and J.-R. Tyran (2002), 'Tax evasion and voting: an experimental analysis', *Kyklos*, **55**, 197–222.

Feld, L.P., A. Schmidt and F. Schneider (2007), 'Tax evasion, black activities and deterrence in Germany: an institutional and empirical perspective', mimeo, University of Heidelberg.

Feld, L.P., B. Torgler and Bin Dong (2008), 'Coming closer? Tax morale, deterrence and social learning after German unification', CREMA Working Paper No. 2008–09, Basel.

Frey, B.S. (1997), 'A constitution for knaves crowds out civic virtues', *Economic Journal*, **107**, 1043–53.

Frey, B.S. and L.P. Feld (2002), 'Deterrence and morale in taxation: an empirical analysis', CESifo Working Paper No. 760, August.

Frey, B.S. and H. Weck (1984), 'The hidden economy as an "unobserved" variable', *European Economic Review*, **26**, 33–53.

Gorodnichenko, Y., J. Martinez-Vazquez and K. Sabirianova Peter (forthcoming), 'Myth and reality of flat tax reform: tax evasion and real side response of Russian households', in J. Alm, J. Martinez-Vazquez and B. Torgler (eds), *Tax Compliance and Tax Evasion*, London: Routledge.

Hayek, F.A. von (1960), *The Constitution of Liberty*, Chicago, IL: University of Chicago Press.

Kanniainen, V., J. Pääkönen and F. Schneider (2004), 'Fiscal and ethical determinants of shadow economy: theory and evidence', mimeo, Linz: Johannes-Kepler University.

Kirchgässner, G. (1983), 'Size and development of the West German shadow economy, 1955–1980', *Journal of Institutional and Theoretical Economics*, **139**, 197–214.

Kopp, R.J., W.W. Pommerehne and N. Schwarz (1997), *Determining the Value of Non-Marketed Goods: Economic, Psychological, and Policy Relevant Aspects of Contingent Valuation Methods*, Boston, Dordrecht, London: Kluwer.

Körner, M., H. Strotmann, L.P. Feld and F. Schneider (2006), *Steuermoral – Das Spannungsfeld von Freiwilligkeit der Steuerhinterzahlung und Regelverstoß durch Steuerhinterziehung*, Tübingen: IAW Forschungsbericht Nr. 64.

Larsen, C. (2002), 'Underdeklaration af personlig indkomst måt ved sammenligning af dansk skatte- og nationalregnskabsstatistik' (Unreported personal income estimated by examining discrepancies between Danish national accounts and tax statistics), mimeo, Institute of Economics, University of Copenhagen.

Pickhardt, M. and J. Sardà Pons (2006), 'Size and scope of the underground economy in Germany', *Applied Economics*, **38**, 1707–13.

Pommerehne, W.W. and H. Weck-Hannemann (1996), 'Tax rates, tax administration and income tax evasion in Switzerland', *Public Choice*, **88**, 161–70.

Posner, E.A. (1998), 'Symbols, signals, and social norms in politics and the law', *Journal of Legal Studies*, **27**, 765–89.

Posner, E.A. (2000a), *Law and Social Norms*, Cambridge, MA: Harvard University Press.

Posner, E.A. (2000b), 'Law and social norms: the case of tax compliance', *Virginia Law Review*, **86**, 1781–1820.

Schneider, F. (2007), 'Shadow economies and corruption all over the world: what do we really know?', Economics Discussion Papers 2007–9, March, www.economicsejournal.org/economics/discussionpapers.

Schneider, F. and D. Enste (2000), 'Shadow economies: size, causes, consequences', *Journal of Economic Literature*, **38**, 77–114.

Smith, A. (1759), *The Theory of Moral Sentiments*, New York: Prometheus Books.

Smith, A. (1776), *An Inquiry into the Nature and Causes of the Wealth of Nations*, reprinted (1976), Chicago, IL: Chicago University Press.

Smith, E.R. and D.M. Mackie (2000), *Social Psychology*, 2nd edn, Philadelphia, PA: Psychology Press.

Sugden, R. (1984), 'Reciprocity: the supply of public goods through voluntary contributions', *Economic Journal*, **94**, 772–87.

Sunstein, C.R. (1996), 'On the expressive function of law', *University of Pennsylvania Law Review*, **144**, 2021–31.

Torgler, B. (2003), 'Does culture matter? Tax morale in an East–West comparison', *FinanzArchiv*, **59**, 504–28.

Torgler, B. (2005), 'Tax morale and direct democracy', *European Journal of Political Economy*, **21**, 525–31.

Torgler, B. (2007), *Tax Compliance and Morale: A Theoretical and Empirical Analysis*, Cheltenham, UK and Northampton, MA, USA: Edward Elgar.

Tyran, J.-R. and L.P. Feld (2006), 'Achieving compliance when legal sanctions are non-deterrent', *Scandinavian Journal of Economics*, **108**, 135–56.

10. Searching for fairness in taxation: lessons from the Italian school of public finance

Luisa Giuriato[1]

> The safeguard of the essential goes to the benefit also of the general welfare; on the contrary, if what lies at the foundations is betrayed, it takes revenge on everything, welfare included.
>
> (Romano Guardini, *Ethics*)

INTRODUCTION

The taxpayer's decision to comply with his fiscal duties or to evade taxes[2] is taken within a complex set-up, which includes the expected utility maximization calculus, elements of coercion and an individual's attitude towards the fisc, that is, his intrinsic motivation to pay taxes, the so-called tax morale. Tax morale is often employed as a residuum variable to explain tax compliance when the formal models predict instead that, given the probability of being caught, the size of the fines and the measure of risk aversion, the optimal choice of a rational taxpayer would be to declare no income.[3] As Feld and Frey (2002) argue, tax morale is a sort of black box, related to the meta-preferences of the taxpayer. It is shaped by a host of factors (Torgler, 2007), including social and demographic variables, formal and informal institutions, trust, civic virtues, national pride and the perception of fairness or unfairness in the relationship with the government.

Investigating tax morale, I focus on the individual's perception of the tax system and on what the taxpayer considers his or her fair share in the tax burden and in the services offered by the state (Pommerehne, 1985). Along the same lines, Spicer and Lundstedt (1976) and Bordignon (1993, 1994) deem that the rational calculus of the net benefits of tax evasion is preceded by the more or less conscious evaluation of equity in the tax system and by the definition of a preferred level of tax evasion. In turn, the preferred level of tax evasion depends on the gap between the taxpayer's actual fiscal balance with the government and their general impression concerning what should be their own and others' fair terms of trade with the government.

Institutional factors and political participation rights influence this gap and, in particular, mutual trust between the taxpayers and the fisc helps to narrow it. For example, in democracies equipped with popular initiatives and referenda, the citizens are more involved in political decisions and can influence the rules of the tax game more readily: as a consequence, they are engaged in a sort of psychological trust contract with the tax authority, they are more prone to believe that the taxes they pay represent their fair share, and this increases their tax compliance (Pommerehne and Weck-Hannemann, 1996; Feld and Kirchgässner, 2000). Feld and Frey (2002) add that direct democracies seem to be associated to a less suspicious and more respectful treatment of the taxpayer, which also positively affects tax compliance.

In representative democracies, on the contrary, citizens have fewer chances of expressing their discontent with the tax policy, they have a more dubious perception of the link between tax payment and the provision of public goods, and are less prone to a relationship of trust with the tax authority. Data on Italy are eloquent on the profound mutual distrust that exists between taxpayers and the fisc: 18.6 percent of the interviewees in the ISAE (2006) survey believe taxes are an unjust abuse, 51.2 percent view them as an inescapable duty and only 24.1 percent as a contribution to a collective effort. The absence of a psychological contract between the citizens and the tax authority, and thus the dominance of a rational attitude towards tax compliance, combined with low probabilities of detection and punishment, could then explain tax evasion and Italy's shadow economy, which are higher than the European average: the shadow economy in Italy amounts to 24.9 percent of gross domestic product (GDP), compared to 15.9 percent in Germany and Norway and approximately 12 percent in France, the UK and the Netherlands (Schneider, 2005).

Remedies for low levels of tax compliance would then be either to coerce people to pay taxes by increasing the probability of detection and the size of the fines, that is, by changing the variables that affect the rational choice between paying and evading taxes, or to create positive incentives and a moral climate fostering tax compliance. This chapter focuses on the second perspective, examining how a trust contract between the taxpayers and the fisc can be established in representative democracies, and how just taxation can contribute to this purpose. In the analysis I draw suggestions from the contributions of the Italian school of public finance which, due to the influence of A. De Viti de Marco and L. Einaudi, elaborated at length on the individual's terms of trade with the government. According to the Italian public finance tradition, which was critical of both the benefit and the ability-to-pay approaches to tax-sharing, the exchange relationship between the individual and the state cannot be specified as a strict *quid pro quo*,[4] rather it requires reference to the interest of the individual in the state's activities. A. Smith's original principle of interest was thus resumed, first by F. Ferrara and then by A. De Viti de

Marco and L. Einaudi, and it was embedded in the Italian public finance thought.

The principle of interest found its most interesting and extreme applications during the post-war constitutional phase and the subsequent tax reform (1945–51). E. Vanoni and L.V. Berliri developed it to identify solutions to the issue of fairness in taxation. Berliri's contribution is probably the last attempt to design scientifically a pure, fair tax to finance non-redistributive expenditure, while Vanoni employed an extended definition of interest to rebuild the relation between taxpayers and the fisc in a context of redistribution. Berliri and Vanoni's contributions are essentially normative and provide little in the way of operational propositions: the generality of their construction is, however, compensated by their suggestions for re-examining fiscal relationships.

The analysis is structured as follows. The next section exemplifies the issue of fairness in fiscal relationships by accounting for tax morale and tax evasion in Italy. The third section introduces the definition of the preferred level of tax evasion and the fourth section discusses justice in taxation, presenting the controversial issues which it raises. The fifth section focuses on the contributions of the Italian school of public finance. The following two sections are respectively dedicated to Berliri's and Vanoni's analyses of fairness and tax compliance. The last section contains the conclusions.

FAIRNESS IN THE RELATIONSHIP WITH GOVERNMENT: THE PERCEPTIONS OF THE ITALIAN TAXPAYERS

The surveys by Tagliacozzo (1984) and ISAE (2006)[5] on the perception of taxes in Italy show the dominance of a negative approach among taxpayers (Table 10.1). In 2006, 51.2 percent of the interviewees considered taxes as an inescapable duty and 18.6 percent as an unjust abuse, a violence exercised by a superior authority. Twenty years earlier, in 1984, the ratios were respectively 32.5 and 26.3 percent. The degree of negativity seems to have diminished over time. However, the number of people who believe that taxes are a contribution to a collective effort has also diminished, from 41.2 percent in 1984 to 24.1 percent in 2006.

Tax perception seems to be related to income, age, education and geographical area. Taxes are considered positively by the highest income classes, while the perception of taxes as an abuse increases among low-income groups. Higher education levels and lower age cohorts are associated to the highest shares of people giving taxes a positive value. In the Southern regions and among industrial workers we find the highest share of interviewees who perceive taxes as an unjust abuse.

When considering the perceived fiscal balance (Table 10.1), only an insignificant number of respondents believe they receive more from the state than

Table 10.1   The perception of taxes and fiscal balances in Italy (1984 and 2006, %)

	Tagliacozzo (1984)	ISAE (2006)
Perception of taxes		
Contribution to a collective effort	41.2	24.1
Necessity	32.5	51.2
Abuse	26.3	18.6
No answer	–	6.1
Total	100	100
Perceived fiscal balance		
Positive	4.9	3.2
Negative	72.2	65.9
Parity	22.9	22
No answer	–	8.9
Total	100	100

Note: A positive balance means benefits from public expenditure in excess of taxes; a negative balance stands for taxes in excess of benefits.

Source: Tagliacozzo (1984) and ISAE (2006).

they contribute: 4.9 percent in 1984 and 3.2 percent in 2006. The vast majority perceive a negative balance, which is surprising, given the country's long history of high deficits and debts.[6] In both surveys, only 22 percent of the interviewees believe the fiscal balance to be even.

The perceived fiscal balance is related to the role assigned to taxes (Figure 10.1): a positive or zero fiscal residuum is associated with a positive perception of taxes, while 81 percent of those who view taxes as an abuse also believe they have a negative fiscal balance with the public administration. People with a perceived negative balance are principally concentrated in the Southern regions and in the 30–65 age cohort, they are mainly industrial workers or self-employed and they have lower education levels.

Income distribution shows a slightly positive relation with the perceived fiscal balance (Figure 10.2): individuals in the last quintile tend to have a positive (5.6 percent) or null fiscal residuum (26.5 percent), although the majority believe they contribute far more than they receive. Individuals in the first quintile are less satisfied with their perceived fiscal balance: 2.2 percent believe they have a positive balance, 15.6 percent that they are even and 71.6 percent that they have a negative residuum. For all income brackets, the majority of taxpayers believe they contribute far more than they receive; tax evasion could be then

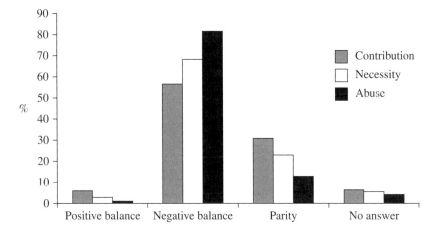

Note: A positive balance means benefits in excess of taxes; a negative balance means taxes in excess of benefits.

Source: Elaborations on ISAE (2006).

Figure 10.1 Perceived fiscal balances and the role of taxation (2006, %)

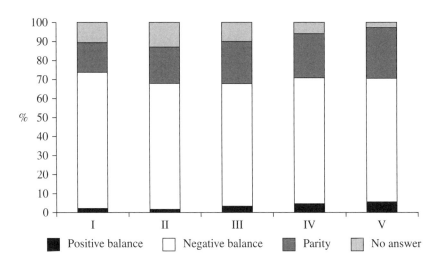

Note: The population is distributed according to quintiles of income. For each quintile, data on the fiscal balance are expressed as a percentage.

Source: Elaborations on ISAE (2006).

Figure 10.2 Perceived fiscal balances and income distribution (2006, %)

interpreted as a means to reduce unjust fiscal imbalances generated by the state's inability to efficiently provide for public goods and for redistribution: the fiscal system itself would then be an endogenous cause of tax evasion.

This hypothesis seems to be only partially confirmed by the results of a Bank of Italy survey on the reasons for tax evasion (Cannari and D'Alessio, 2007):

Table 10.2   The perceived reasons for tax evasion (2004, %)

How much do you agree with the following statements?	Not at all (%)	Little (%)	So and so (%)	Enough (%)	Very much (%)
Some evade taxation because of the state's inefficient use of fiscal revenues	10.92	15.20	28.77	28.35	16.76
Some evade taxation to survive market competition	12.67	14.19	31.68	30.23	11.23
Some evade taxation because the tax system is too complicated	26.22	20.71	27.61	18.74	6.72
People are more eager to pay taxes if they know that everybody complies with their fiscal duties	2.68	5.53	15.24	35.22	41.33
Some evade taxation because tax rates are too high	10.24	13.88	29.37	31.36	15.15
Some evade taxation because it implies only minor risks	7.11	11.40	27.70	33.55	20.24

Source: Cannari and D'Alessio (2007).

45 percent of the sample agreed sufficiently or very much with the statement that tax evasion is motivated by the state's inefficient use of resources (Table 10.2), while 20 years earlier Tagliacozzo (1984) reported that the same statement received the approval of 82 percent of the interviewed people. The main reason for tax evasion is currently the lack of reciprocity among all the citizens with respect to tax compliance (76.55 percent of the sample are sufficiently or very much convinced of this): 20 years earlier the same hypothesis received the approval of 43 percent of the sample (Tagliacozzo, 1984). This means that tax evasion arises not only from a failure in the relationship between the citizens and the state, but also from a failure in the relationships among citizens, as already predicted by some experimental studies (Spicer and Becker, 1980). The rational approach to tax evasion is also supported, as 53.8 percent of the sample motivate tax evasion with the probability of being detected being sufficiently low.

The widespread perceptions that taxes are not a contribution to a collective action, but a necessity or an abuse, and that the overall balance with the fisc is negative, convey the impression that something fundamental is missing in the relationship between citizens and the state and in their relationship with each other. Taxpayers, feeling they are not the object of fair fiscal treatment, are not involved in any sort of trust contract with the state and with other taxpayers, and tend to assume a purely rational attitude towards tax payment. As a consequence, when the probability of being caught and the size of the penalties are sufficiently low, they rationally evade. Are deterrence policies the only response or can we envisage other incentive mechanisms to improve the interaction between citizens and government?

THE ETHICAL ASSESSMENT OF TAX EVASION: A FAIRNESS PERSPECTIVE

As the surveys on taxes and tax compliance in Italy suggest, the choice between tax evasion and compliance stems from the rational assessment of the parameters that influence the gamble (likelihood of detection, amount of penalties, probability of future tax amnesties) but also from an ethical assessment that founds the intrinsic motivation to pay or evade taxes. Some studies (Friedland et al., 1978; Baldry, 1987; Bordignon, 1994) suggest that the ethical assessment of tax evasion is a prior mechanism to the rational decision to evade: the decision-making process in tax evasion would thus be a two-stage mechanism, where 'the ethical evaluation of the evasion behaviour fosters the choice to evade even before assessing the expected benefits or losses of evasion' (Bordignon, 1994, p. 206).

The ethical assessment of tax evasion depends on many factors, including the social view of tax evasion (Cowell, 1990), the interdependence existing among the taxpayers' behaviours (Spicer and Lundstedt, 1976; Spicer and Becker,

1980; Benjamini and Maital, 1985; Gordon, 1989) and the perception of fairness in the terms of trade with the government. As a matter of fact, individuals perceive their relationship with the government not only in terms of coercion but also in terms of an exchange relationship, where the taxpayer exchanges purchasing power in the market in return for government goods and services (Bordignon, 1994; Spicer and Lundstedt, 1976).

The exchange relationship between individuals and the government should not be considered just a *quid pro quo*, since individuals evaluate public services not only according to the subjective benefits accruing to them, but also according to the 'satisfaction of their desire that public services benefit other individuals or serve a common higher purpose' (Lindahl, 1928 [1958], p. 217). The full and correct evaluation of this exchange at the individual level is a complicated process and a function of many factors. Therefore:

> it can be argued that many taxpayers are not able to assess the exact value of what they pay for or of what they receive from the government in return. However, it seems reasonable to suggest that taxpayers have general impressions and attitudes concerning their own and others' terms of trade with the government. (Spicer and Lundstedt, 1976, p. 296)

The perceived fairness in the terms of trade with the government determines the ethical assessment of taxation and the desired level of tax evasion. In Bordignon (1994), an individual i's desired level of tax evasion (Z_i) depends on the difference between the taxes he pays (tI_i) and what he deems would be his fair share (q_i^F) in the financing of the goods and services provided by the government:[7]

$$Z_i = tI_i - q_i^F \tag{10.1}$$

When Z_i is positive, the individual tries to restore fairer terms of trade with the government: tax evasion would then be 'a means by which taxpayers attempt to restore equity' (Spicer and Becker, 1980, p. 173).[8]

In this framework, we can add the expenditure side of the individual's balance with the government: G_i are the goods and services which actually go to the benefit of individual i and G_i^F is his desired share in the public expenditure. The individual's terms of trade with the government are evaluated not for what they are, but rather considering what other taxpayers do, especially those belonging to the individual's reference groups (Spicer and Lundstedt, 1976). The difference (W_i) between individual i's actual balance with the government (S_i) and the balance he deems fair (S_i^F) is expressed in equation (10.2):

$$W_i = (tI_i - G_i) - (q_i^F - G_i^F) = S_i - S_i^F \tag{10.2}$$

Combining actual and desired balances can result in a positive, negative or zero value of W_i, the perceived equity in the relationship with the government. A negative value for W_i means a perception of unfairness in the terms of trade and could motivate a taxpayer's search to restore greater equity by means of tax evasion.

Variable S_i^F expresses the individual's assessment of his fair share in the public expenditure and financing and it is obviously affected by the dominant public opinion, by psychological factors and by the social climate. When the taxpayer identifies himself with his nation-state (Torgler, 2007) or simply trusts the state due to cultural, ideological or political reasons, and when the government treats the taxpayer with respect and equity, the value of S_i^F is likely to approximate the actual balance, S_i, then the taxpayer, quite naturally, perceives fairness in his terms of trade with the government ($W_i = 0$).

The psychological contract between the citizens and the state that Feld and Frey (2002) (but also Frey, 1997; Pommerehne and Weck-Hannemann, 1996) associate with direct democracies, is an example of this perceived fairness in the taxpayers' fiscal relationship with the government:

> The existence and survival of this tax contract requires a certain behaviour on the part of the two parties concerned. In particular, tax authorities must acknowledge and support the contract with the taxpayers by acting in a respectful way towards them, but also by preventing honest taxpayers from being exploited in the process. (Feld and Frey, 2002, p. 89)

The breach of this contract would jeopardize the citizens' engagement with the government and their tax morale, and it would entail the assumption of a purely rational attitude towards tax compliance and evasion.

A psychological contract with the tax administration is not a prerogative of direct democracies only, as similar trust relationships can also be found in representative democracies. Cosciani (1948) accounts for the mutual trust, and even esteem and cordial relationships, that ran between the British taxpayer and the tax administration in the 1940s, even in presence of high (and sometimes confiscatory) effective tax rates. W. Churchill could even declare: 'no body of Taxpayers meets their obligation with greater readiness than the British Taxpayers' (quoted in Cosciani, 1948, p. 506).[9]

When the terms of trade with the government are perceived as unfair ($W_i <$ 0), public intervention should aim at restoring respect, impartiality and confidence (and thus making S_i more acceptable), and at increasing fairness in the distribution of taxes and expenditures. Fair taxation reduces the gap between the actual distribution of benefits and burdens, S_i, and the individual's assessment of his fair share, S_i^F, and thus wins resistances to tax compliance. The perception of a fair distribution of burdens and benefits nourishes the taxpayer's assent to the taxation mechanism, as 'we have a fundamental natural duty … to comply with just institutions' (Rawls, 1971, p. 115). Tax-sharing principles must be felt as 'just, otherwise the ethical and social forces of friction and resistance to taxation become so strong that no device or public power are sufficient to win them' (Berliri, 1945, p. 4): thus, justice gives tax laws their strength, while penalties would only add to their moral sanction. Penalties without justice would highlight the unfairness of the law and would contribute to justify tax evasion and tolerance of, or collusion with, the transgressors.

The theory of public finance has long elaborated on the principles of just taxation, which were established on a variety of normative foundations. The benefit principle reflects the fairness of the *quid pro quo*; the equal sacrifice principle provides equal treatment of taxpayers in terms of loss of utility; the ability to pay principle postulates equity in correlating tax liability and the indicators of the taxpayer's financial capacity; Smith's interest principle, from which the benefit principle originated,[10] declines fairness in terms of stakes in the state's activities.[11]

These pages inquire into the possibility of founding the ethical assessment of taxation and of the fair terms of trade with government on the principle of interest. The principle of interest was originally conceived for non-redistributive finance and was stated in these terms by A. Smith: 'The expense of government to the individuals of a great nation, is like the expense of management to the joint tenants of a great estate, which are all obliged to contribute in proportion to their respective interests in the estate' (Smith, 1776 [1993], p. 451). Our focus is justified by the role that the principle of interest played in the contributions of the Italian public finance scholars during the post-war constitutional phase and the 1951 tax reform. In particular, on the principle of interest L.V. Berliri (1945) designed a 'pure fair tax' to share the financing of both divisible and indivisible non-redistributive expenditure. Vanoni (1934 [1961]; 1932 [1961]), who was also Minister of Finance, employed an extended definition of interest as the cornerstone to rebuild the ethical relationship between the taxpayers and the fisc in the context of redistribution. The presentation of the contributions by Vanoni and Berliri is preceded by a quick review of the just taxation debate and of the position of the Italian school of public finance on the sharing of the burden of taxation.

ISSUES OF JUSTICE IN TAXATION

As Wicksell argued: 'in the case of tax justice, the sole, but all the more formidable difficulty lies in the discovery of the basic principles' (Wicksell, 1896 [1958], p. 73). Around these basic principles revolved the long and controversial debate on justice in taxation. The first basic issue concerns the meaning of justice in taxation. The dominant view in public economics is that justice consists in a fair distribution of the tax burden and in the adoption of a standard for evaluating differences in the tax treatment of different peoples: related concepts are those of vertical and horizontal equity. This approach to justice in taxation was criticized by Wicksell (1896, [1958]) and more recently, from different perspectives, by Murphy and Nagel (2002)[12] and Kaplov and Shavell (2002).[13] They argue that, if we assume that the problem of fair taxation cannot be conceived as a pure fiscal problem, but as part of a more comprehensive problem of justice, then the different treatment of people in similar situations will depend on the overall theory of justice.

Besides, principles of justice need to be defined so as to display their rationale and avoid tautological statements, which are indeed very common in public policy issues. A good example is provided by Lindahl: 'The meaning of the demand for justice in taxation is that it should be regulated according to the moral rights of the citizens' (Lindahl, 1919 [1958]). Hume's (1751 [1957]) comments on circular statements[14] are perfectly applicable here. Against the reference to these 'highest principles' in public finance, Myrdal (1929 [1953]) also exercised his criticism: 'Highest principles are important because they give the resulting interpretations the appearance of scientific objectivity. The tendency is always to keep them sufficiently general to be beyond dispute … For anybody who does not already associate them with a definite creed, [these requirements] are completely empty' (Myrdal, 1929 [1953], p. 159).

When discussing just taxation, both sides of the fiscal account, taxes and public expenditure, must be taken into consideration. This is the Wicksell (1896 [1958]) – Buchanan (1949 [1960]) problem. Even in the case that we reject the ethical premise that there exists a *quid pro quo* relationship between the individual and the government in favor of other basic principles, there should be a way of taking into account the expenditure side of the fiscal account: 'this is obviously a theoretical difficulty which must be resolved if there is to be any science of public finance in the true sense of this term' (Wicksell, 1896 [1958], p. 77). Buchanan adds that even 'untested explicit hypotheses concerning benefit accrual are preferable to omission altogether' (Buchanan, 1949 [1960], p. 16). Omission would imply either that the theory is incomplete, as it provides no justification for the existence of public expenditure,[15] or that the implicit assumption is made that individual benefits are roughly equivalent, and thus expenditure can be disregarded altogether.[16] More recently, Murphy and Nagel (2002) recalled that: 'theories of vertical equity are frequently myopic, in that they attempt to treat justice in taxation as a separate and self-contained political issue … For what counts as justice in taxation cannot be determined without considering how government allocates its resources' (Murphy and Nagel, 2002, p. 14).

Finally, justice in taxation must be evaluated against a benchmark, which is generally the pre-tax distribution. Therefore, an answer, or at least some consideration, should be given to the problem of fairness in the pre-tax distribution of income and property, as the issue is preliminary to the solution of the just distribution of taxation:

> Apparently justice in taxation presupposes tacitly a just view of the problem of income and property, from whichever point of view the problem is judged ... The attempt to base a just tax system upon an unjust property system is an attempt to take a fair share out of an unfair whole. (Wicksell, quoted in Myrdal, 1929 [1953], p. 178)

However, the existence of a pre-tax world, that can be used as a baseline to assess the fairness of the distribution of tax burdens, can be questioned. As taxes themselves contribute to the creation of property rights, we are compelled to evaluate the justice of the whole system, taxes included: 'Tax justice must be part of an overall theory of social justice and of the legitimate aims of government' (Murphy and Nagel, 2002, p. 38).

However, this is not the perspective of those who believe in the existence of pure fiscal principles. Lindahl was conscious that the solution to the pure fiscal problem depended on the hypothesis that property distribution could be considered just. This proviso made him say that: 'the doctrine of just taxation is entirely hypothetical' (Lindahl, 1919 [1958]). However, he did not deny its enforceability:

> Pure fiscal principles are, unlike socio-political principles, always relevant and independent of the ethical evaluation of the distribution of property. Even if distribution is unjust, the relation between taxation and a just distribution is not without significance. The solution of this problem is therefore the most important – and the most difficult – task of the practical theory of public finance. (Lindahl, 1919 [1958])

DEFINING THE TERMS OF TRADE WITH GOVERNMENT: THE ITALIAN SCHOOL OF PUBLIC FINANCE

The Italian school of public finance was particularly critical of both the benefit and the capacity approaches to justice in taxation. The first was deemed scarcely useful as it could not be applied to indivisible services – except in the case where the public activity produces differentiated specific benefits, and in this case the appropriate financing is by means of public prices (Einaudi, 1916). The ability-to-pay principle was considered a *petitio principii* by Einaudi, without operational content. Also the sacrifice principles were criticized (Barone, 1937 [1970]; Einaudi, 1929), both because they required interpersonal utility comparisons, which depended on the precise form of the individual utility functions, and because they omitted the benefits drawn from public expenditure. However, the Italian public finance scholars did not attempt to develop alternative principles and often adopted political criteria of evaluation, in line with the German approach:[17]

> The principle of tax sharing is a political problem, which is scientifically indeterminate. Its solution depends on historically changing presuppositions, which are influenced by the overall economic and political conditions and by the moral sentiments and forces within a social community. (Borgatta, 1929, p. 384–5)

An attempt to interpret taxation outside the strict logic of benefit was made first by Francesco Ferrara and then by Antonio De Viti de Marco and by Luigi Einaudi, reflecting on the role of the state in the economic system. In De Viti's democratic state, all citizens who pay taxes also consume public services: both sides of the fiscal account matter. The state's role as an organizational factor justifies taxation (tax-prices) as the contribution to the production of public goods and services. Each unit of real income is born with a tax claim against it, because its production cost includes the costs for the provision of public services. In the case of indivisible public goods, when demand is only presumptive, De Viti was aware that it is not possible to assess tax-prices on the basis of marginal utility: 'it is not necessary to compare the tax that every single citizen pays and the share of public services that he consumes: it is sufficient to compare the individual evaluation of the tax and the individual evaluation of the general public service' (De Viti de Marco, 1934). In De Viti's cooperative state, the best proxy for evaluating the demand for public goods is produced income, while the proportional income tax is the best proxy for the tax-price.

Einaudi too defines taxes as the price for the services provided by the state, even if he denies that the sacrifice of the taxpayer should be equal to his or her benefits. The reason for taxation lies in the services provided by the state, as 'capital and labour would be useless without the protection and support provided by the State. Therefore the State has the right to claim a share of the product that can be normally obtained' (Einaudi, 1940). Neither De Viti nor Einaudi went further into the investigation of the difficulties of the exchange principle applied to public finances. Distributive concerns were put aside with respect to those of efficiency and certainty of taxation: for Einaudi, the state of a country's public finances is to be judged more by the quality of its expenditure than by the distribution of its tax burden (Steve, 2002).

The issue of justice in taxation was resumed at the end of World War II when the Constituent Assembly animatedly debated the foundations of the new social contract, which included the principles of tax-sharing. Two of the most interesting contributions came from the liberal jurist Berliri and from the Catholic economist Vanoni. They were both members of the Economic Commission of the Constituent Assembly. Vanoni was also member of the Christian Democratic party and Minister of Finance from 1947 to 1954: he promoted the first tax reform in 1951. They both thought that justice in taxation was an essential part of the new constitutional order, a prerequisite for the efficiency of the tax system and for higher tax compliance and morale.

In post-war Italy, tax evasion was widespread for certain types of income: the total amount of wages paid by the Public Administration was 20 times the declared taxable income of all real estates and 13 times the declared taxable income of all farmers. Tax evasion could partly be explained by serious transgressions of the principles of vertical and horizontal equity. As Berliri (1945) reports: a private employee who received 300 000 lire income was required to pay 20 000 lire taxes (6.7 percent), while an independent professional paid 117 000 lire taxes out of the same income (39 percent).

Berliri and Vanoni shared scepticism concerning the traditional principles of tax-sharing. Berliri defined the ability-to-pay principle an 'agnostic theory', whose success is due to the fact that it can be interpreted either according to the benefit principle ('those who have more should pay more, because having more they benefit more from the collective organization') or according to the principle of sacrifice ('those who have more should pay more, because having more they can pay with less sacrifice'). Vanoni deemed the principles of tax-sharing as formal concepts that are filled with content by the dominant political thinking; he was also aware of the complex formation of the financial decisions, which are the result of the influence exerted by individuals and groups on the collective will, of rational and irrational elements which are far from the pure utilitarian calculus (Forte, 1956). Although both Berliri and Vanoni shared De Viti's belief in the individuals' interest in the state's activities, they developed the concept of interest in two different directions. Berliri tried to solve the technical difficulty of constructing a just tax, that is, of imputing shares of the aggregate common benefit from non-redistributive public expenditure to specific individuals according to criteria that taxpayers would deem fair. Vanoni elaborated on the ethical premise of the principle of interest to establish a mutual trust contract between the taxpayer and the tax authority.

THE PRINCIPLE OF INTEREST AND THE SOLUTION OF THE 'PURE FISCAL PROBLEM'

Berliri (1945) approached tax morale and just taxation by isolating a pure fiscal problem à la Lindahl. He thus distinguished between pure fiscal and extra-fiscal aims of taxation, that is, between the financing of non-redistributive and redistributive expenditure. According to him, the problem of just taxation can be correctly defined only with respect to non-redistributive expenditure and it is the problem of 'making the contribution ratios fit with the sharing ratios in the public expenditure for indivisible services among all those who are interested in the existence and activity of the State' (Berliri, 1945, p. 43). The just tax is thus: 'the individual tax share corresponding to the just expenditure share for a given group of public services, when the sharing out is an end in itself, with no further aim but the financing of the collective expenditure' (Berliri, 1945, p. 16). Redistributive taxation entails reductions or increases in the individual just share to pursue political aims; as such, redistributive taxation is neither just nor unjust.[18]

Berliri tries to close the gap between S_i and S_i^F by employing Einaudi's concept of justice, *giustizia grossa*, the simple and rough justice of the man in the street, who considers and compares his own situation to that of the other taxpayers.[19] In this sense, justice is not perfect by definition, it is a fact, a general and insistent yearning of the *Homo economicus* who feels and suffers injustice above all. Therefore, even if a perfectly just tax does not exist, it is always possible to find sharing criteria that fulfill 'justice as a limit concept, as a trend that almost always is obtained by approximation' (Berliri, 1945, p. 25).

With this approximate concept of justice, Berliri faces the logical impossibility of sharing the undifferentiated utility of indivisible public goods and services. His originality lies in the appeal to the juridical category of interest. He thus reduces the problem of justice to a practical problem, a comparison of interests, similar to those that the civil law deals with: 'whenever it is impossible to identify both the cost of the individual consumption and the real individual advantage, the sharing out of the expenditure for services, made in the interest of a community of subjects, must be related to the individual share of interest in the execution of the expenditure' (Berliri, 1945, p. 46). As a matter of fact, jurisprudence does not give up sharing the indivisible when it has to deal with expenditure for the collective services of a condominium, for the status of the family as an indivisible community or for the defense of a product by an industrial trust. Similarly, just taxation is the relative share of the individual's interest in the execution of public services.

According to Berliri, interest is not a proxy for the benefits nor for the willingness to finance public goods, nor for Lindahl's prices. As such, it does not require preference revelation, as Lindahl prices do, and it precedes the execution of the expenditure. It is linked to the representation of the possible effects of the service (while benefits pertain to real effects), and it is objectively evaluated according to a parameter: income, wealth and/or consumption (while benefits are only subjectively evaluated). The objective evaluation requires an equity assessment, like jurisprudence does, and the reference to common economic and social values. Individual preferences in the social welfare function would thus be replaced by a sort of jurisprudential social welfare function, where the individual welfare depends on income, wealth and consumption in a way that is objectively defined by the jurisprudential equity assessment of the legislator.[20]

The individual interest in public activity is then specified as interest in one of the three main functions performed by public expenditure: improving the production conditions of the economy, improving wealth preservation or improving conditions for individual consumption enjoyment. The state is here De Viti's cooperator in production and the guardian of consumption. Income, wealth and consumption are objective indicators, proxies for the individual interest in each separate function, and they are the bases for three parallel and additional contributions. Along the line of De Viti and Einaudi, Berliri suggests that taxation of income and wealth should be proportional, as the indivisible benefits associated to the productive and conservative functions of public expenditure objectively – that is proportionally – affect each single particle of income and wealth.[21] The allocation of public expenditure with respect to its three different functions, and thus the distribution of the total financing among the three taxes, becomes a technical and political evaluation problem, which is to be solved with the approximate degree of justice that the common social and economic conscience deems adequate.

By adopting the concept of interest and by making the evaluation objective and prior to the provision of services, Berliri overcomes the logical impossibility of imputing shares of the aggregate common benefit from public services to specific individuals: he avoids measuring individual benefits, entrusting to a practical principle of fairness the sharing of the indivisible expenditure. In the relationship between the taxpayer and the government, the *quid* based on the subjective evaluation of the individual benefit is replaced by a *quid* based on the general interest in the existence of the state and in the functions it performs. The relationship between individuals and the state is no longer one of strict exchange, as the individual's interest can be larger than the strict subjective benefit accruing to him or her. In conclusion, when a jurisprudential concept of interest and a rough but shared concept of justice are employed, the actual and the perceived fair terms of trade with government, S_i and S_i^F, naturally tend to coincide and set to zero the desired level of tax evasion.

However, Berliri does not provide for operational propositions: his approach is essentially more a logically consistent restatement of the question than an operational contribution to its solution. His conclusions reach Einaudi's results, but starting from a different and original theoretical position. Besides, focusing only on the pure fiscal problem, Berliri ignores some central issues of just taxation: for example, Wicksell's problem of the formation of the collective judgement in a democratic state, where justice (that is, the correspondence between the value and countervalue at an individual level) should require unanimous decision-making. Berliri also sidesteps the problem of who is going to evaluate interests: the law-maker, either the democratic parliament or the benevolent despot; or a collective agent? The judge's evaluation of private interests is in fact very far from the formation of a collective evaluation in a democratic state. Besides, the appeal to the *giustizia grossa* and to common social and economic values is similar to Wicksell's recourse to the 'modern concepts of law and equity' to evaluate the justice of the pre-tax distribution of property (Wicksell, 1896 [1958], p. 109) and to Lindahl's moral rights of the citizens: without further specification, these run the risk of becoming circular statements. Finally, as the judge who decides on the sharing of indivisible expenditure does not take into account justice in the distribution of positions, income and wealth to the parties before evaluation, so also Berliri deliberately ignores the problem of the pre-tax distribution of property.

THE PRINCIPLE OF INTEREST AND THE ETHICAL FOUNDATIONS OF TAXATION

Berliri's attempt to forge a just tax system may apply to liberal systems where the role of the state is limited, while it meets formidable difficulties in contemporary states also performing redistributive functions. The limits of Berliri's approach were clear to Vanoni, who however continued to elaborate on the principle of interest, while attempting to found the ethical bases of taxation on a trust contract between citizens and the state.

Vanoni roots his analysis in the consideration that an exchange between the individual and the state is conceptually impossible, as public activities satisfy general and not reciprocal needs: the former require the cooperation and association of individuals, the latter require an exchange. However, although Vanoni rejects a strict *quid pro quo* relationship, he highlights 'a healthy part in the exchange theory', which corresponds to the indication of an equivalence between the total amount of taxes and the total amount of services provided by the state.[22] This equivalence links the general interest of the state[23] to the interest of the individuals: they sum up to the one and same interest that the state exists and that it satisfies its legitimate aims.

The duty to pay taxes does not arise from 'external causes, such as the subjection to the State's sovereignty or coercion, but from the need for the public body to exist' (Vanoni, 1934 [1961], p. 38). Public activity, which aims at the satisfaction of general wants, is the ratio of the state's power to tax, that is, its economic and juridical justification.[24] Citizenship per se implies the enjoyment of benefits from public activity and therefore the duty to pay taxes. There is no need of a quantitative and immediate correspondence between the individual benefit and the tax, as the relationship between the state and the individual is not one of exchange, but one of interest.

The financial activity is redistributive by its very nature: 'considering the unlikelihood that the sacrifice caused by taxes and the utility arising from expenditure are equal for the same individual, we can say that public finance transfers wealth from one subject to another, from one class to another' (Vanoni, 1943 [1976], p. 117). Proportional taxation is no longer justified, once we assume that the state's aim is broader than providing each individual with services adequate to his income (Vanoni, 1932 [1961], p. 58). Thus the duty to pay taxes persists even if the public activity does not meet its objectives or if it meets them only partially: the duty is abrogated only when the ratio of the taxes does not exist, that is, when no public activity is performed or when its aims are not legitimate and cannot be defined as public aims.[25]

Vanoni adds an ethical element to the De Viti–Einaudi approach: not only does the state play a fundamental role in social and economic life, but also Vanoni claims that the duty to contribute is of an ethical nature. Taxes therefore are: 'the expression of the moral and civil duty, that concerns each of us, to contribute to the good of society' (Vanoni, 1950, p. 14). The principle of interest thus becomes the ethical premise of taxation:

> The State performs its activities in order to reach its goals, which are of general interest. Their attainment implies that all those who belong to that community, and who therefore have an interest in the State's activity, have a moral, rather than a juridical obligation to concur to financing the expenditure. On the bases of the current political, economic and ethical principles, the legislator will discipline the tax sharing. However, the individual's duty to pay the taxes and the State's right to impose them were established as soon as the State began to perform its public functions. (Vanoni, 1932 [1961], p. 107)

The problem of justice in taxation is not only a fiscal problem, but also an ethical and political issue concerning the terms of the social contract that had to be signed in the new Italian democratic state. Vanoni worked to translate his ethical foundation of taxation both into the 1948 Constitution and the 1951 Tax Reform. In the Report for the Constituent Assembly, he suggested that the Constitution should explicitly affirm the citizens' duty to contribute to public expenditure and the right of the public administration to taxation: the aim was 'to declare that the democratic State is everybody's business and that everybody has the duty to contribute to the common effort by means of his own personal sacrifice' (Vanoni, 1946 [1961], p. 480). On the other hand, the state must provide for a fair treatment of the taxpayer: 'There is no possible defence of freedom and democratic institutions, when one of the pillars of the State's organizations fails, i.e. the just sharing of the public burdens among all citizens' (Vanoni, 1948, p. 20).

In 1951 the Tax Reform introduced the general duty to present the annual tax return. Vanoni aimed at overcoming the hostile relationship between the tax authority and the citizens by means of an ethical-political objective: fighting tax evasion by reconstructing a trust contract in which the perception of 'hateful taxation was substituted by taxation as the citizen's contribution to society and to the general interest' (Steve, 1958, p. 11). Tax evasion was the symptom of widespread attitudes denying the general interest and the duty to contribute to it, and it was nourished by an erroneous conception of taxation. The 'moral commitment of the citizen to the tax system' (Berliri, 1945) was lacking and Vanoni believed that no technical device could replace it.[26] The duty to present the annual tax return was the cornerstone of the new contract between the citizens and the tax authority, an agreement of mutual trust: the citizen committed to make a truthful statement, and the tax authority to abide by principles of fairness. In this sense, Vanoni was trying to elicit positive reciprocity between the honest taxpayers and the fisc, believing that a correct and trustful behavior on behalf of the state would increase tax compliance. As in Smith (1992), the cycles of antagonism between the tax authority and the taxpayers had to be broken by a positive concession from the government.

Vanoni's approach to fairness in taxation can be termed as more consequentialist, more realistic but also less ambitious than Berliri's (Forte, 1956, p. 69): Vanoni does not search for a just tax, rather he elaborates on his own view of justice, which was influenced by the Catholic social doctrine and by the lively debate among Catholic intellectuals in the 1940s.[27] Under their influence, Vanoni further qualified the concept of interest in public activity as interest in the common good. The common good is defined as 'the utility of all members of the society and especially of those who cannot contribute with their sacrifice to the financing of the public expenditure, as their weakness makes them the first natural beneficiaries of the public action' (Vanoni, 1945 [1976], pp. 149–50). Thus, Vanoni introduces a difference principle, similar to other formulations introduced by contemporary political doctrines (Laski, 1931), which is reminiscent of Rawls's approach. A theory of justice, based on the common good and including a variant of the difference principle, De Viti's revised principle of interest and the relationship of positive reciprocity between the honest taxpayers and the tax authority would thus be the cornerstones of the new trust contract between citizens and government in a representative democracy. Within this context, recognizing the ethical foundations of taxation, the taxpayer would, quite naturally, perceive fairness in his terms of trade with the government and renounce tax evasion.

CONCLUSIONS

Inquiring into the reasons for tax morale and tax evasion, I have recalled the existence of a two-stage mechanism in the decision-making process for tax evasion (Bordignon, 1994; Spicer and Lundstedt, 1976): the ethical evaluation of the evasion behavior concurs with the decision to evade before the assessment of the expected benefits and losses from evasion itself. The ethical assessment of tax evasion depends on many factors, including the perception of fairness in the terms of trade with the government. Individuals perceive their relationship with the government not only in terms of coercion but also in terms of an exchange relationship, where the taxpayer exchanges purchasing power in the market in return for government goods and services. Perceived fairness or unfairness in the terms of trade with the government contributes to the ethical assessment of taxation and to the taxpayer's search to restore greater equity by means of tax evasion.

As a result, the fight against tax evasion requires other, different instruments of tax policy rather than more traditional analyses. In particular, the government can restore a psychological contract between the citizens and the state and increase mutual trust between the taxpayers and the tax authority. This is maybe easier in direct democracies (Feld and Frey, 2002; Pommerehne and Weck-Hannemann, 1996), but it can be established even in representative democracies, as Vanoni tried to do in the Italian post-war constitutional phase and through the 1951 Tax Reform.

Vanoni dealt with the ethical grounds of taxation, assuming an interest relationship between citizens and the state, encompassing all productive and redistributive functions performed by the modern state: the interest that the state exists and that it satisfies its legitimate aims is then the ratio of taxation. On this concept of taxation Vanoni tried to rebuild a new trust contract between the Italian taxpayers and the fisc, founded on the taxpayers' duty to present the annual tax return and on the government's commitment to abide by principles of fairness concerning both tax and expenditure.

In the same period, Berliri provided an alternative theoretical solution to reduce the perception of inequity in the taxpayers' terms of trade: he attempted to establish a perfect just tax to approximate the taxpayers' general impressions and attitudes concerning their own and others' terms of trade with the government. His originality lies in using an exchange framework without resorting to the hedonistic calculus of benefits and sacrifices: the interest in the functions performed by the state is the object of a rough but objective evaluation, that does not require the specification of utility functions and preference revelation and that precedes the provision of services. Berliri and Vanoni's contributions are essentially normative and provide little in the way of operational propositions. The generality of their construction is, however, compensated by the suggestions they provide for reviewing the fiscal relationship between the state and its citizens. Their lesson is centered on the extension of the principle of interest. As public activities satisfy general needs and not reciprocal ones, the relationship between citizens and the democratic state should be perceived not just as a strict *quid pro quo*, but as an interest relationship. Interest is not a subjective benefit, but an objective expectation of the advantages accruing from the activities performed by the public administration. This interest relationship is the ratio of taxation, the source of its ethical premises. Once they are given this ethical connotation, taxes are neither a necessary sacrifice nor an abuse by a superior, but the contribution to a collective action chosen by means of freely voted financial laws. As Vanoni stated, the duty to pay taxes does not arise from subjection to the state's sovereignty or from coercion, but from the need that the public body itself exists. Tax evasion denies the existence of the public body and of the general interest and is nourished by an erroneous conception of taxation; therefore, the fight against tax evasion requires the recovery of the sense of this interest relationship with the state and of the correct foundations of taxation.

As a consequence, both normative appeals and administrative measures may be adopted in this perspective. Administrative measures should be taken not only as a means of repression, but also with the aim of consolidating a relationship of positive reciprocity and mutual trust between the citizens, who comply with their fiscal duties, and the fisc, that abides by principles of fairness. Moral suasion in taxation seems to be less effective: evidence on it is weak and contradictory (Torgler, 2007; Blumenthal et al., 2001). Probably, to be effective on tax compliance, normative appeals should 'take the form of educational programmes aimed both at existing taxpayers and children as potential taxpayers' (Spicer and Lundstedt, 1976, p. 302); they should be implemented regularly and by means of a wide range of communication channels.

In the perspective of increasing fairness to increase tax compliance, the two sides of the fiscal account should be taken into consideration. The omission of the spending side implicitly corresponds to the assumption of Einaudi's *imposta grandine* (hailstorm taxation), which can be useful only in partial equilibrium analysis. The difficulties of treating the expenditure side can be approached by evaluating the objective interests touched by the different expenditure programs, as in Berliri. These interests are prior to the execution of the programs: a consistent framework of the fiscal account should thus be completed in advance before voting on taxes and expenditure. Thus, estimates of the citizens' balances with the Public Administration (such as those performed by Musgrave et al., 1974 and De Vincenti and Pollastri, 2004) are valuable tools to evaluate the *ex ante* impact of public policies, while keeping in mind that the state's scope is broader than providing each individual with the services that correspond to the taxes he or she pays.

Some critical aspects are present in the analysis. First, I assumed that the perception of equity in terms of trade with government contributes to the level of tax compliance. However, it still needs to be ascertained that the causal flows are really from perceived inequity to higher tax evasion and not the other way round: from tax evasion to perceived inequity as a means of rationalizing an illegal behavior. Furthermore, I focused only on the concept of equity or inequity in the fiscal relationship, while tax morale is influenced also by many other factors: the social and cultural climate, the natural tendency to free-ride in the presence of public goods, the interdependence existing among the taxpayers' behaviour. In particular, the issue of reciprocity and the importance of reference group behavior in the choice to evade should be further developed.

The contributions by Vanoni and Berliri add support to the argument that the fight against tax evasion would require a range of instruments in terms of tax policy in addition to the traditional coercive ones. In the light of the current serious problems of tax compliance, particularly in Italy, the cycles of antagonism between the tax administration and the taxpayers must be broken by the offer of mutual trust contracts from the government and by consolidating a correct concept of taxation, as 'the expression of the moral and civil duty, that concerns each of us, to contribute to the good of society' (Vanoni, 1950, p. 14). This perspective should be seriously considered by policy-makers because 'establishing conditions of fairness in the relationship among taxpayers and between taxpayers and the government, may be a more effective instrument [against tax evasion] than the simple increase of coercive policies' (Bordignon, 1994, p. 235).

NOTES

1. Department of Public Economics, Sapienza University of Rome, Italy. The chapter is dedicated to the former Italian Minister of Finance, Tommaso Padoa-Schioppa, who in 2007 stated that 'taxes are beautiful, the most civil way to contribute all together to essential public goods'. The chapter was presented at the ECSPC-CIDEI Conference 'Objective Values, no Values and Subjective Values: The Ethical Bases of Market and the State', 15–16 December 2006, Sapienza University of Rome. The author is especially indebted to Antonio Pedone for having raised the subject and for his helpful suggestions; to Geoffrey Brennan, Alessandra Cepparulo and Umberto Galmarini, for their advice and their attentive reading of a previous version. The author gratefully acknowledges the helpful comments made by Giuseppe Eusepi, Bruno Frey and conference participants. The usual disclaimer applies. Italian texts are translated by the author.
2. For surveys on tax evasion, see Andreoni et al. (1998), Slemrod (1992), Pyle (1990), Cowell (1990).
3. See Alm et al. (1992), Graetz and Wilde (1985), Graetz et al. (1986), Lewis (1982), Pyle (1990), Roth et al. (1989), Skinner and Slemrod (1985), Slemrod (1992).
4. This expression of J.S. Mill was translated as 'Leistung und Gegenleistung' by Wicksell, and as 'value and countervalue' by J. Buchanan.
5. In Tagliacozzo (1984) the survey was made of a random sample of 1000 individuals, drawn from the Bank of Italy survey on incomes and savings (32 600 individuals). ISAE (2006) employs a survey on 8000 individuals by means of a random two-stage sampling.
6. An attempt to estimate the distribution of fiscal burdens and benefits can be found in Musgrave et al. (1974): they calculate the net benefits and burdens for the US 1968 incomes and indicate the break-even point for the combined federal, state and local levels at about $8500, a level that divides the population nearly equally between gainers and losers, 'a result which is not uninteresting from the point of view of voting theory. The mythical median vote, it appears, strikes again' (p. 300). A recent attempt to estimate objectively the fiscal balances for Italy is provided in De Vincenti and Pollastri (2004). The authors try to measure the revenue side, the spending side and the overall balance of the citizens' budgets with the Public Administration, in order to evaluate the redistributive impact of public policies. In 2001, Italian families were considered to have positive balances with the Public Administration, amounting to 3.3 per cent of gross domestic product (GDP), a result in striking contrast with the general perception.

7. In Bordignon (1993, 1994), fairness is drawn from Kantian principles of justice.

8. Spicer and Lundstedt (1976) underline how the results of the empirical studies do not allow us to infer unambiguously the causal relationship between inequity and tax evasion. Perceptions of inequity could actually increase tax evasion or could simply be a means employed by the taxpayers to rationalize their own illegal behaviour.

9. Cosciani (1948) ascribed the exceptional level of tax compliance in the UK to a mixture of elements, which contributed to both a trust relationship with the tax authority and to effective coercion: a high civic sense and honesty, fairness in the relationship with the tax administration, high and effective penalties for tax evasion, and an efficient organization of the tax administration.

10. The principle of interest was deeply criticized by J.S. Mill for the difficulty of specifying its content and of evaluating interests in practice: 'Government must be regarded so pre-eminently as a concern of all, that to determine who are the most interested in it is of no real importance' (Mill, 1848 [1961], p. 2). Interest was promptly interpreted as the benefit accruing to the individuals from public expenditure and was restated in marginalistic terms (Sax, Mazzola, Pantaleoni, Wicksell and Lindahl), both in positive and in normative analysis. It found a formidable obstacle, however, in the indivisibility of public goods. However, as Buchanan comments, 'the rejection of the benefit theory of taxation should rest not upon the difficulty of individual isolation of specific benefits but upon the unacceptability of the ethical ideal of the individual *quid pro quo*' (Buchanan, 1949 [1960], p. 14). The ability-to-pay principle seemed easier to apply, especially as it focuses on the taxation side only, eliminating the difficult estimate of the benefits accruing to individuals from indivisible public goods and services.

11. Smith combined two principles of tax sharing: the ability-to-pay principle and the interest principle. Myrdal argues that the term 'ability to pay' had been used by Smith just as 'a persuasive slogan without much content' and that Smith held true the principle of interest: 'For Smith the principle of ability had no other function than to lend greater plausibility to his conclusion of proportionality which is derived from the principle of interest. Other classical economists [Ricardo, McCulloch] took much the same view. They used the principle of ability only as a disguise for the principle of interest in order to strengthen the authority of their particular interpretation of that principle' (Myrdal, 1929 [1953], p. 164).

12. Murphy and Nagel (2002) argue that property rights are a legal convention, defined also by the tax system. Therefore there is no pre-tax world against which fairness in the distribution of tax burdens can be assessed, unless in a purely libertarian world. Thus: 'justice or injustice in taxation can only mean justice or injustice in the system of property rights and entitlements that results from a particular tax regime' (Murphy and Nagel, 2002, p. 8).

13. Kaplov and Shavell's (2002) definition of fairness principles (but also of justice, rights and related concepts) implies that at least some weight is given to factors that are independent from the individuals' well-being. They argue that utilitarianism should be the sole principle to decide on fiscal and public policy issues.

14. 'No, say you, the morality consists in the relation of actions to the rule of right ... What then is this rule of right? In what does it consist? How is it determined? By reason, you say, which examines the moral relations of actions. So that moral relations are determined by the comparison of actions to a rule. And that rule is determined by considering the moral relations of objects. Is not this fine reasoning?' (Hume, 1751 [1957], p. 159).

15. After the rejection of the benefit principle, fiscal analysis has proceeded as if all taxes were net subtraction from social income, never to be returned (Buchanan, 1949 [1960]). On the contrary the real bargaining between government and parliament is made on the basis of an approximate measure of the utility of public expenditure: 'otherwise, the deliberations of the tax-approving assemblies about whether or not this or that public expenditure is to be accepted or rejected, would be completely without purpose' (Wicksell, 1896 [1958], p. 77).

16. Buchanan (1949 [1960]) observes that De Viti de Marco was among the first to recognize the role of the equal-benefits assumption.

17. In 1920 von Tyszka began his discussion of the principles of taxation by saying that the idea of equity changes continually and develops with cultural, economic and social conditions. 'It is relative and historical ... The concrete meaning of this abstract concept has changed from

age to age … We cannot simply accept what earlier times have considered to be equitable, but we must ask: which system of taxation is compatible with our present idea of equity, in our present political, economic and social conditions, in short in our civilization?' (quoted in Myrdal, 1929 [1953], p. 159).

18. As a matter of fact, Berliri thinks that using taxes with extra-fiscal aims disrupts the trust relationship between the fisc and the citizens. An unacceptable distribution of resources must be corrected by modifying the mechanisms that generate it, not by *ex post* intervention by means of taxation. Better instruments are the public expenditure or the death duties. Murphy and Nagel (2002) underline how the distinction is not just conceptual, but also normative: 'reasons for and against putting resources under government rather than private control are not necessarily reasons for or against redistributing resources among groups or individuals, and vice versa' (Murphy and Nagel, 2002, p. 77).

19. Einaudi's conception of justice rests on innate moral sentiments and intuitions. Literature has devoted increasing attention to the biological as well as social origins of our innate sense of justice: see Wilson (1993) and Singer (1981).

20. The author thanks Umberto Galmarini for raising this point.

21. The arguments of Berliri and De Viti present here a logical mistake, as they are based on the very truth that they are trying to explain: that the state provides public services to the individuals in proportion to their respective income. The point was first raised by Vanoni (1932 [1961]).

22. This equivalence was stated also by De Viti (1934) and Einaudi (1916).

23. The general interest, according to Vanoni, is not the sum of the individual interests of the members of the society, it is the result of the individual interests as modified by their coexistence within one single society.

24. On this point Vanoni elaborates on Griziotti's first intuition of the importance of the concept of *causa* for a precise definition of tax.

25. This approach corrected the juridical approach to taxation and opposed the hateful character of taxation that had dominated the juridical doctrine. Tax laws are not exceptional laws that limit the individual's rights and that require restrictive criteria of interpretation: 'financial activity, far from being a limit to the individual's rights and personality, is its necessary precondition: without it, the State would not exist, and without the State, rights would not exist' (Vanoni, 1932 [1961], p. 113).

26. 'Each man has a more or less conscious yearning for justice. As a matter of fact, if the train passengers did not believe that paying the ticket is just, the Train Company would manage to collect not even one third of the payments due' (Berliri, 1945, p. 20).

27. Vanoni's concept of justice was expressed in a document which he worked out in 1944–45 together with Pasquale Saraceno and a group of Catholic scholars and intellectuals: the document was named the Camaldoli Code (Istituto Cattolico di Attività Sociale, 1945) and was addressed to the Christian community as a guideline to the problems of rebuilding a new social order at the end of the war.

REFERENCES

Alm, J., B.R. Jackson and W.D. Schulze (1992), 'Why do people pay taxes?' *Journal of Public Economics*, **48** (1), 21–38.

Andreoni, J., B. Erard and J. Feinstein (1998), 'Tax compliance', *Journal of Economic Literature*, **36** (2), 818–60.

Baldry, J.C. (1987), 'Income tax evasion and the tax schedule: some experimental results', *Public Finance*, **42** (2), 357–83.

Barone, E. (1937), *Alcuni studi di economia politica*, reprinted in E. Barone (1970), *Alcuni studi di economia politica*, Padova: CEDAM.

Benjamini, Yael and Shlomo Maital (1985), 'Optimal tax evasion and optimal evasion policy: behavioral aspects', in Wulf Gaertner and Alois Wenig (eds), *The Economics of Shadow Economy*, Berlin: Springer Verlag, pp. 218–26.

Berliri, Luigi V. (1945), *La giusta imposta. Appunti per un sistema giuridico della pubblica contribuzione*, Milan: Giuffrè Editore.

Blumenthal, M., C. Christian and J. Slemrod (2001), 'Do normative appeals affect tax compliance? Evidence from a controlled experiment in Minnesota', *National Tax Journal*, **54** (1), 125–38.

Bordignon, Massimo (1993), 'A fairness approach to income tax evasion', *Journal of Public Economics*, **52** (3), 345–62.

Bordignon, Massimo (1994), *Beni pubblici e scelte private*, Bologna: Il Mulino.

Borgatta, Gino (1929), *Appunti di scienza delle finanze e diritto finanziario*, Milan: Università L. Bocconi.

Buchanan, James M. (1949), *The Pure Theory of Government Finance*, reprinted in J.M. Buchanan (1960), *Fiscal Theory and Political Economy*, Chapel Hill, NC: University of North Carolina Press.

Cannari, Luigi and Giovanni D'Alessio (2007), *Le opinioni degli italiani sull'evasione fiscale*, Rome: Bank of Italy.

Cosciani, C. (1948), 'Perché il contribuente inglese non evade le imposte', *Moneta e Credito*, **1** (4), 506–11.

Cowell, Frank A. (1990), *Cheating the Government: The Economics of Evasion*, Cambridge, MA, USA and London, UK: MIT Press.

De Vincenti, Claudio and Corrado Pollastri (2004), *La partita doppia del welfare – XIV Rapporto CER-SPI*, Rome: Eidesse.

De Viti de Marco, Antonio (1934), *Principi di Economia Finanziaria*, Turin: Einaudi Editore.

Einaudi, Luigi (1916), *Corso di Scienza delle Finanze*, Turin: Giappichelli.

Einaudi, Luigi (1929), *Contributo alla ricerca dell'ottima imposta*, Milan: Università Bocconi Editore.

Einaudi, Luigi (1940), *Miti e paradossi della giustizia tributaria*, Turin: Einaudi Editore.

Feld, L.P. and B.S. Frey (2002), 'Trust breeds trust: how taxpayers are treated', *Economics of Governance*, **3** (2), 87–99.

Feld, L.P. and G. Kirchgässner (2000), 'Direct democracy, political culture and the outcome of economic policy: a report on the Swiss experience', *European Journal of Political Economy*, **16** (2), 287–306.

Forte, F. (1956), 'Il pensiero di Ezio Vanoni sulla teoria e sulla politica dell'imposizione degli scambi', *Rivista di diritto finanziario e scienza delle finanze*, **15** (1), 67–80.

Frey, B.S. (1997), 'A constitution for knaves crowds out civic virtues', *Economic Journal*, **107** (443), 1043–53.

Friedland, N., S. Maital and A. Rutenberg (1978), 'A simulation study of income tax evasion', *Journal of Public Economics*, **10** (1), 107–16.

Gordon, J. (1989), 'Individual morality and reputation costs as deterrents to tax evasion', *European Economic Review*, **33** (4); 797–805.

Graetz, M.J. and L.L. Wilde (1985), 'The economics of tax compliance: facts and fantasy', *National Tax Journal*, **38**, 355–63.

Graetz, M.J., J.F. Reinganum and L.L. Wilde (1986), 'The tax compliance game: toward an interactive theory of law enforcement', *Journal of Law, Economics and Organization*, **2** (1), 1–32.

Guardini, Romano (1962), *Etica: lezioni all'Università di Monaco (1950–1962)*, reprinted in M. Nicoletti and S. Zucal (eds) (2003), *Etica: lezioni all'Università di Monaco (1950–1962)*, Brescia: Morcelliana.

Hume, David (1751), *An Inquiry Concerning the Principles of Morals*, reprinted in C.W. Hendel (ed.) (1957), *An Inquiry Concerning the Principles of Morals*, New York: Liberal Art Press.

ISAE (2006), *Finanza pubblica e redistribuzione*, Rome: ISAE.

Istituto Cattolico di Attività Sociale (1945), *Per la comunità cristiana: principi dell'ordinamento sociale*, Rome: Editrice Studium.

Kaplov, Louis and Steven Shavell (2002), *Fairness versus Welfare*, Cambridge, MA, USA and London, UK: Harvard University Press.

Laski, Harold J. (1931), *Liberty in the Modern State*, London: George Allen & Unwin.

Lewis, Alan (1982), *The Psychology of Taxation*, Oxford: Blackwell.

Lindahl, Erik (1919), *Just Taxation: A Positive Solution*, reprinted in R.A. Musgrave and A.T. Peacock (eds) (1958), *Classics in the Theory of Public Finance*, London: Macmillan.

Lindahl, Erik (1928), *Some Controversial Questions in the Theory of Taxation*, reprinted in R.A. Musgrave and A.T. Peacock (eds) (1958), *Classics in the Theory of Public Finance*, London: Macmillan.

Mill, John Stuart (1848), *Principles of Political Economy*, reprinted in W.J. Ashley (ed.) (1961), *John Stuart Mill. Principles of Political Economy*, New York: A.M. Kelley.

Murphy, Liam and Thomas Nagel (2002), *The Myth of Ownership. Taxes and Justice*, Oxford and New York: Oxford University Press.

Musgrave, R., K.E. Case and H. Leonard (1974), 'The distribution of fiscal burdens and benefits', *Public Finance Quarterly*, **2** (3), 259–311.

Myrdal, Gunnar K. (1929), *The Political Element in the Development of Economic Theory*, reprinted in P. Streeten (ed.) (1953), *G.K. Myrdal. The Political Element in the Development of Economic Theory*, London: Routledge & Kegan Paul.

Pommerehne, W. (1985), 'Was wissen wir eigentlich über Steurhinterziehung?' *Rivista Internazionale di Scienze Economiche e Commerciali*, **32**, 1155–86.

Pommerehne, W. and H. Weck-Hannemann (1996), 'Tax rates, tax administration and income tax evasion in Switzerland', *Public Choice*, **88** (1–2), 161–70.

Pyle, D.J. (1990), 'The economics of taxpayer compliance', *Journal of Economic Surveys*, **5**, 163–98.

Rawls, John (1971), *A Theory of Justice*, Oxford: Oxford University Press.

Roth, Jeffrey A., John T. Scholz and Ann D. Witte (eds) (1989), *Taxpayer Compliance: an Agenda for Research*, Philadelphia, PA: University of Pennsylvania Press.

Schneider, F. (2005), 'Shadow economies around the world: what do we really know?' *European Journal of Political Economy*, **21**, 598–642.

Singer, Peter (1981), *The Expanding Circle: Ethics and Sociobiology*, New York: Farrar, Strau & Giroux.

Skinner, J. and J. Slemrod (1985), 'An economic perspective on tax evasion', *National Tax Journal*, **38** (3), 345–63.

Slemrod, Joel (ed.) (1992), *Why People Pay Taxes: Tax Compliance and Enforcement*, Ann Arbor, MI: University of Michigan Press.

Smith, Adam (1776), *An Inquiry into the Nature and Causes of the Wealth of Nations*, reprinted in K. Sutherland (ed.) (1993), *Works and Correspondence of Adam Smith*, Vol. I, Oxford: Oxford University Press.

Smith, Kent W. (1992), 'Reciprocity and fairness: positive incentives for tax compliance', in Joel Slemrod (ed.), *Why People Pay Taxes: Tax Compliance and Enforcement*, Ann Arbor, MI: University of Michigan Press, pp. 223–58.

Spicer, Michael W. and Lee A. Becker (1980), 'Fiscal inequity and tax evasion: an experimental approach', *National Tax Journal*, **33** (2), 171–5.

Spicer, Michael W. and S.B. Lundstedt (1976), 'Understanding tax evasion', *Public Finance*, **31** (2), 295–305.

Steve, Sergio (1958), *Commemorazione di Ezio Vanoni*, Venice: Istituto Universitario di Economia e Commercio e di Lingue e Letterature Straniere.

Steve, Sergio (2002), 'Gli studi di finanza pubblica: qualche aspetto della tradizione italiana', *Economia Pubblica*, **32** (5), 5–11.

Tagliacozzo, Amedeo (1984), *Per una sociologia dell'evasione fiscale*, Rome: Carucci Editore.

Torgler, Benno (2007), *Tax Compliance and Tax Morale: A Theoretical and Empirical Analysis*, Cheltenham, UK and Northampton, MA, USA: Edward Elgar.

Vanoni, Ezio (1932), *Natura ed interpretazione delle leggi tributarie*, reprinted in F. Forte and C. Longobardi (eds) (1961), *Ezio Vanoni. Opere giuridiche*, Vol. I, Milan: Edizioni Giuffré.

Vanoni, Ezio (1934), *Elementi di diritto tributario*, reprinted in F. Forte and C. Longobardi (eds) (1961), *Ezio Vanoni. Opere giuridiche*, Vol. II, Milan: Edizioni Giuffré.

Vanoni, Ezio (1943), *La finanza e la giustizia sociale*, reprinted in A. Tramontana (ed.) (1976), *Ezio Vanoni. Scritti di finanza pubblica e di politica economica*, Padova: Cedam.

Vanoni, Ezio (1945), *La persona umana nella economia pubblica*, reprinted in A. Tramontana (ed.) (1976), *Ezio Vanoni. Scritti di finanza pubblica e di politica economica*, Padova: Cedam.

Vanoni, Ezio (1946), *Diritto all'imposta e formazione delle leggi finanziarie. Rapporto della Commissione economica presentato all'Assemblea Costituente*, reprinted in F. Forte and C. Longobardi (eds) (1961), *Ezio Vanoni. Opere giuridiche*, Vol. II, Milan: Edizioni Giuffré.

Vanoni, Ezio (1948), *Discorsi pronunciati alla Camera dei Deputati ed al Senato della Repubblica in sede di discussione del bilancio: ottobre 1948*, Rome: Istituto Poligrafico dello Stato.

Vanoni, Ezio (1950), *La perequazione tributaria*, Rome: Tipografia del Senato.

Wicksell, Knut (1896), *A New Principle of Just Taxation*, reprinted in R.A. Musgrave and A.T. Peacock (eds) (1958), *Classics in the Theory of Public Finance*, London: Macmillan.

Wilson, James Q. (1993), *The Moral Sense*, New York: Free Press.

11. Cooperation, reciprocity and self-esteem: a theoretical approach

Marcello Basili and Maurizio Franzini

INTRODUCTION

Cooperation among genetically unrelated agents is widely observed in behavioral experiments and in everyday life, even when repeated interaction is absent. In most cases economic theory does not contemplate it. Basically, cooperation among strangers is ruled out by the usual assumptions of self-interested behavior. Only repeated interaction may reconcile traditional self-interest with cooperation. We lack an explanation of how cooperation can develop among strangers, in a setting potentially open to free-riding and opportunism. Recently, several experiments have expanded our knowledge of important features of cooperative behavior under different circumstances. On the basis of that knowledge, an interesting hypothesis has been proposed: most agents are strong reciprocators, that is, they are ready to punish those who behave opportunistically, even when this is costly to them (Bowles and Gintis, 2004; Gintis et al., 2003; Gintis, 2004). Compared to other possible explanations of cooperation, strong reciprocity seems to enjoy the positive feature, at least from an economist's point of view, of demanding a rather weak relaxation of the assumption that agents are self-interested.

The analytical foundations of strong reciprocity are, however, still unclear. In particular, it has not been demonstrated whether such behavior can be derived from a rational process of maximization. The main goal of this chapter is to offer a possible explanation of strong reciprocity or, more generally, cooperative behavior as the end result of rational decision-making based on utility maximization.

In our interpretation, a rational foundation for a more cooperative-prone behavior can be provided by the twin assumptions that agents include self-esteem in their utility function, and that the amount of self-esteem depends on how they behave in social situations. The latter reflects an idea of moral system that is different and not based on reputation effects only. In considering moral values as an important component of individual decision-making, we follow Sen's criticism of the traditional conception of rationality. However, we try to take a step forward by explicitly considering moral values within a maximization process. Such a model regards cooperation and reciprocity as a possible, not necessary, outcome. This is precisely what experiments and experience suggest we need: not a theory that invariably predicts cooperation but a more general framework that allows for cooperation as a possible outcome.

Moreover the explanation we offer fits well with the observed attempts to induce cooperation through a sort of gift-giving – as in the famous essay by Akerlof (1982) – and also with the apparent existence of limits to cooperative behavior.

The chapter is organized as follows. First we introduce and evaluate the strong reciprocity hypothesis. Next we present our basic model of interaction between utility maximization and moral values, based upon the notion of self-esteem; we also illustrate how such utility function can lead either to cooperative or to more traditional behavior. We then analyze more precisely in a principal–agent setting the notion of reciprocity and how it relates to self-esteem. Next, the relationship between self-esteem and fairness is investigated, while in the following two sections self-esteem is considered in a moral hazard and an adverse selection setting, to see how it influences the best contract. Concluding remarks end the chapter.

STRONG RECIPROCITY: EXPERIMENTAL EVIDENCE AND THEORETICAL FOUNDATIONS

Many empirical studies document that individuals cooperate in situations in which, according to economic theory, cooperation would not be a rational behavior (Fehr et al., 1997; Fehr and Gächter, 2000). In particular, there is a large body of evidence about the existence of cooperation in situations involving public goods, common pool resource, ultimatum games and principal–agent interactions (Yamagishi, 1986; Ostrom et al., 1992; Fehr and Gächter, 2002).

In their attempt to understand such behavior better, and to give it rational foundations, Bowles and Gintis, among others, take a clear stand in favor of strong reciprocity. In their own words: 'cooperation is maintained because many humans have a predisposition to punish those who violate group-beneficial norms, even when this reduces their fitness relative to other group members' (Bowles and Gintis, 2004). The resulting human behavior is called 'strong reciprocity' and is defined as a sort of altruistic behavior that, among others, may confer 'group benefits by promoting cooperation, while imposing upon the reciprocator the cost of punishing shirkers' (Bowles and Gintis, 2004).

The distinguishing behavior of strong reciprocators is that they punish a defector, when they detect one, even though such behavior is costly to them.

Strong reciprocators are considered altruistic people, insofar as they bear privately the cost of action that is beneficial to the community. Therefore, individuals – at least some of them and at least in some situations – seem to have a preference for punishing others. How can this be reconciled with rationality?

Gintis (2004) convincingly argues that it is not possible to offer a theoretical explanation of observed cooperation that fulfills some reasonable conditions,[1] while retaining the assumption that agents are strictly self-interested. Indeed, the latter is to be relaxed.

Since we are faced with acts of volition carrying implied costs, reconciling strong reciprocity with rationality is not a trivial task. How and why is punishing others evaluated by the agents? Are there limits to the costs one is willing to bear in order to punish others? And if so, which are they? We lack a general model for the rational foundations of strong reciprocity or the cooperation-prone behavior that makes it possible to answer specifically these and other questions. More generally, we do not know how to modify traditional utility functions in order for such behavior to become a possible, but not necessary, result.

To this end, it might be a good idea to start from Sen's more recent criticism of the traditional rational model of choice, which is structured in three steps (Sen, 2002, p. 34). The first is related to a notion of self-centered welfare, whereby 'a person's welfare depends only on her own consumptions and other features of the richness of her life'. The second criticism concerns what Sen calls 'self-welfare goal', that is, the assumption that welfare maximization is the individual's only goal. The last criticism points to self-goal choices, whereby a person's choices are exclusively geared to the pursuit of his or her own goals.

Sen clearly aims at enriching the traditional model by weakening, in particular, the assumption that people pursue a too narrowly defined welfare. But, of the three criticisms he levels against conventional wisdom, the less convincing is precisely the last one, essentially because we are left practically without an operating theory of choice. If people, as Sen argues, are maximizers but also care about things different from their own welfare, how do they solve their maximization problem?

Sen does not say much on this. The solution we propose is largely in line with Sen's approach but departs from it in the assumption that people do maximize their utility function as enriched with an endogenously determined moral variable. More specifically, individuals are endowed with a moral system which transforms their actions into self-esteem. The latter, as determined by such a system, enters their utility function and helps to define their choice within a utility-maximizing process. Therefore, self-esteem brings utility but its amount is determined also by a moral system that lies outside the preference system sustaining the utility function.

In our definition, a moral individual has a high propensity to destroy self-esteem when his or her actions are not consistent with his or her moral values. This will be reflected in his or her final utility, given that self-esteem is positively related to utility. Therefore, the individual's actions, insofar as they destroy his or her own self-esteem through the moral value mechanism, are not determined by a too-restricted notion of self-welfare. In this respect, we share Sen's approach. However, the inclusion of self-esteem in the utility function (which could very well be defined as a goal-function) allows us to treat the choice problem as a typical maximization problem and give a formal solution to it.

SELF-ESTEEM, MORAL VALUES AND UTILITY MAXIMIZATION

To explain reciprocity independently of repetition of the game, we assume that individuals may produce through their behavior self-esteem, which in turn is amenable to cooperation and reciprocity. Self-esteem is created according to different mechanisms in dissimilar situations. We refer to a principal–agent framework which is broad enough to encompass many interesting cases. In such a framework, the agent's self-esteem depends on the effort made (or, more generally, on limiting opportunism) in relation to the compensation obtained by the principal.

It is common knowledge that the *Homo sapiens* species is highly gregarious, and there is a huge literature about affiliation among people without family relations. Psychologists, in particular, identify at least four different motivations that prompt human beings to affiliate: 'to receive social attention, to obtain emotional support, because they find other people stimulating, and for social comparison' (Leary et al., 2003). Motivations are internal and external. Internal or intrinsic motivation is supported by innate psychological needs and there is proof of the strong links between intrinsic motivation and competence as well as satisfaction of the need for both autonomy and relatedness. It is worth bearing in mind 'that people will be intrinsically motivated only for activities that hold intrinsic interest for them, activities that have the appeal of novelty, challenge, or aesthetic value' (Ryan and Deci, 2000, p. 71). On the contrary, external or extrinsic motivation refers to performance of an activity in order to attain some separable outcome and 'the extrinsically motivated behaviors are performed to satisfy an external demand or contingency' (Ryan and Deci, 2000, p. 71). As a result of the interaction between intrinsic and extrinsic motivation:

> people can be motivated because they value an activity or because there is strong external coercion. They can be urged into action by an abiding interest or by a bribe. They can behave from a sense of personal commitment to excel or from fear of being

surveilled. These contrasts between cases of having internal motivation versus being externally pressured are surely familiar to everyone. (Ryan and Deci, 2000, p. 72)

Referring to this psychological literature,[2] self-esteem takes into account both extrinsic and intrinsic motivations. It depends positively on the effort and negatively on the compensation, but only for the part of the effort that can be considered a gift, that is, the part in excess of the price paid for the effort. As the gift gets larger, the agent will suffer a loss of self-esteem if he or she refrain from making a greater effort. Thanks to self-esteem, the behavior of the agent can be seen, therefore, as the product of two antagonist forces: altruism (the utility of reciprocating a gift) and self-interest (the disutility of greater efforts).

In a principal–agent framework it is appropriate to assume that self-esteem demands greater efforts as compensation increases: the agent knows that the principal seeks greater efforts and is willing to offer a gift to that effect. In other settings the appropriate assumptions for self-esteem may be different. For example, in some cases self-esteem may increase by reducing the effort when compensation increases, because the recipient wants to show that his or her effort was a function of intrinsic motivation, not money. This conception of self-esteem may reinforce – or even supplant – the reputation effects that are considered as the root cause of money crowding out intrinsic motivation for cooperative behavior. Reputation in such models depends on others believing that we behave out of intrinsic motivation and not for money (Benabou and Tirole, 2006a, 2006b). However in a principal–agent framework – and maybe not only in it – it seems more appropriate to assume that agents take the exchange ethics as a reference point in establishing what is fair. If I get more money from my principal I owe him or her a greater effort. If I fail to provide this effort I look at myself as a person deserving less esteem. The reputation-for-intrinsic-motivation framework may apply in different situations and is not so general.[3]

In order to understand how self-esteem works in a general setting, let us assume that our agent gets money (m) in exchange for his or her effort (e). Were it not for self-esteem, his or her indirect utility function would be of the following type, $U = U(m, e)$, and usual assumptions on derivatives are: $U_m > 0$; $U_{mm} < 0$; $U_e < 0$; $U_{ee} < 0$; $U_{e,m} < 0$.

We can assume that e cannot be perfectly monitored, so that the agent is free to choose e, given m. There is no reason for e to increase when m changes and, in particular, for e to be lower than the minimum possible value it can take. We now let self-esteem (E) into the picture:

$$E = E(m, e) \text{ with } E_m < 0; E_e > 0$$

In other words: an agent will increase (decrease) his or her self-esteem when, given m, he or she provides a higher (lower) effort or when, given e, he or she gets a lower (higher) compensation. The agent, through his or her behavior, produces or destroys self-esteem according to the above function. On the other hand, the agent enjoys utility from self-esteem, which therefore enters his or her utility function. The E-function represents the agent's moral system, the utility function his or her goal function, borrowing from Sen's terminology. Therefore the agent faces the following constrained maximization problem:[4]

$$Max\ U = U(m, E, e)$$
$$\text{Subject to } E = E(m, e) \qquad (11.1)$$

Consistent with what we said before, we assume that m is given for the agent and that his or her control variable is only e. Therefore, after substituting the constraint in the goal function, we get the first-order condition:

$$U_e + U_E E_e = 0 \qquad (11.2)$$

The optimum effort, e^*, is the value of e which solves:

$$U_e = -U_E E_e \qquad (11.3)$$

The meaning of this condition is clear: a maximizing individual will take his or her own moral values into account when making a choice. The chosen e must be such that it balances the disutility of any additional effort with the utility of additional E induced by e itself. It can also be formulated as a condition of equality between the marginal rate of substitution between e and E (how the individual is ready to trade off lower efforts for higher self-esteem), on the one hand, and the marginal productivity of e on E, on the other:

$$\frac{U_e}{U_E} = -E_e \qquad (11.4)$$

In order for the level of effort satisfying this equation to be a maximum, the second-order conditions are to be satisfied.[5] This imposes some restrictions on the admissible set of utility functions. Assume that $U(e, E(e, m), m)$ is of class C^2 so that mixed derivatives coincide, in particular $U_{eE} = U_{Ee}$; to guarantee that e^* is a point of maximum it is required that:

$$U_{ee} + U_{eE} E_e + U_{Ee} E_e + U_{EE} E_e^2 + U_E E_{ee} < 0 \quad \text{that is,}$$
$$U_{ee} + 2U_{eE} E_e + U_{EE} E_e^2 + U_E E_{ee} < 0 \qquad (11.5)$$

Assume U is linear in E, that is, $U(e, E(e, m), m) = \Theta(e, m)E(e, m) + \Gamma(e, m)$, then $U_{EE} = 0$. Also, recall that, $U_{ee} < 0$, $U_e = \Theta_e E + \Gamma_e < 0$, $E_e > 0$, and $E_e = -\dfrac{U_e}{U_E}$ at e^*, therefore $U_E = \Theta > 0$ at e^*; the second order condition at e^* becomes:

$$U_{ee} + 2U_{eE}E_e + U_E E_{ee} < 0 \tag{11.6}$$

with

$$U_{ee} + 2U_{eE}E_e + U_E E_{ee} = \frac{-2U_{eE}U_e + U_{EE}^2 E_{ee}}{U_E} = \frac{-2\Theta_e(\Theta_e E + \Gamma_e) + \Theta^2 E_{ee}}{\Theta}$$

Certainly, $U_{ee} + 2U_{eE}E_e + U_E E_{ee} < 0$ at e^* when $2U_{eE}E_e + U_E E_{ee} < 0$, or $2U_{eE}E_e < U_E E_{ee}$, since $U_{ee} < 0$.

If these conditions are fulfilled, equation (11.4) shows that the choice is the result of both moral and pleasure mechanisms. Moral values dominate the self-esteem-producing mechanism while pleasure or welfare mechanisms set the rate at which the two goals can be substituted for each other. It is important to stress that the moral mechanism endogenizes self-esteem, enabling us to understand that a moral individual is not only someone who gets pleasure from self-esteem but also – especially – someone who behaves cooperatively in order to enhance his or her goal-function. Individuals differ from one another from a moral point of view, because they attach a different marginal utility to self-esteem or because they transform bad behavior into a greater or smaller amount of lost self-esteem. Our model takes both aspects into account. In particular, it shows that the optimum effort level will be higher for any m when there are self-esteem effects. These self-esteem effects set an endogenous lower limit at e.

To be really general as well as consistent with the experimental results of principal–agent situations, the proposed interpretation should be able to include cooperation among the possible outcomes. Cooperation should not be the only possible outcome. This is desirable also from the point of view of the degree of generality of the theory.

In fact, in a much-quoted experiment Fehr et al. (1997) divided subjects into two sets, employers and employees, and considered their interaction in a principal–agent framework. Firstly, they found that many employers offered generous wages and were reciprocated in terms of higher efforts from the employees, which resulted in a greater payoff for both. Secondly, they noticed that there existed, however, a significant difference between the level of effort agreed and the level of effort applied. They observed that this was not the behavior of a small group of fraudulent individuals, because only 26 percent, that is, a small minority, of individuals honored their stated commitment.

Nonetheless, this evidence 'is compatible with the notion that the employers are purely self-interested, since their beneficent behavior vis-à-vis their employees was effective in increasing employer profits' (Gintis et al., 2003, p. 157). Allowing for the possibility that employers reward and punish employees, Fehr et al. (1997) observe an increase by up to 40 percent of the pledged payoff of all subjects.[6] The comment by Gintis et al. (2003) is that:

> the subjects who assume the role of employee conform to internalized standards of reciprocity, even when they know there are no material repercussions from behaving in a self-interested manner. Moreover, subjects who assume the role of employer expect this behavior and are rewarded for acting accordingly. Finally, employers draw upon the internalized norm of rewarding good and punishing bad behavior when they are permitted to punish and employees expect this behavior and adjust their own effort levels accordingly. (Gintis et al., 2003, p. 157)

The above situation can be represented in a principal–agent framework where it is in the principal's interest to induce reciprocal behavior by the agent, and the agent may choose to cooperate – even independently of any material punishment – because he or she is a social being, feels part of a community (altruism) and, at least up to a certain extent, will lose self-esteem if he or she does not cooperate. However – and this is an important point in a rationality-based approach – such a mechanism will not work in every case and regardless of an accurate consideration of the relevant costs and benefits. The loss of self-esteem implied by lack of cooperation is not always high enough to ensure unlimited cooperation. In fact, as recalled above, experiments give support to the idea that there are limits to cooperative behavior.

Our attempt is to show, within a unique theoretical framework, that altruistic individuals do not necessarily choose cooperative behavior. Indeed, it is remarked that 'strong reciprocators are inclined to compromise their morality to some extent' (Gintis et al., 2003). The approach we suggest seems capable of explaining what determines this willingness to compromise: much depends on the characteristics of the agents' moral system and how self-esteem enters their utility functions. The next step is, therefore, to explain the conditions under which reciprocity emerges in our model.

SELF-ESTEEM AND RECIPROCITY

We can now establish whether and how m influences the optimum e, this being the crucial condition for reciprocity effects. To accomplish this comparative static exercise we have to compute the second derivative with respect to m of the equilibrium condition above. To this end, and to simplify our analysis without loss of generality, we assume that the utility function (but not the

E-function) is additive in its three variables (m, E, e). Therefore the problem becomes:

$$Max_{e,E} \; U = f_1(m) - f_2(e) + f_3(E)$$
$$\text{subject to } E = E(m, e)$$

The additivity of the utility function allows us to assume that all mixed second derivatives are zero. This makes the implicit differentiation of the optimum condition easier (11.4), yielding:

$$\left[\left(U_{E,E}E_m + U_{E,E}E_e \frac{de}{dm}\right)E_e\right] + \left[U_E\left(E_{e,m} + E_{e,e}\frac{de}{dm}\right)\right] - U_{e,e}\frac{de}{dm} = 0$$

After some manipulation we get:

$$\frac{de}{dm} = -\frac{[U_{E,E}E_e E_m] + [U_E E_{e,m}]}{[U_{E,E}(E_e)^2] + [U_E E_{e,e}] + [U_{e,e}]} \tag{11.7}$$

To establish whether e will change and in what direction, as m changes, we need to know the signs of all the relevant derivatives. Some are obvious. However, the general conclusion we can draw is that any result can come out and, more interestingly, the same individual may exhibit a different behavior, depending on some crucial conditions. We show both these results by assuming a further simplified version of the utility function, which fulfills second-order conditions and highlights also the specific role that the moral process governing self-esteem plays.

$$U = f_1(m) - f_2(e) + \beta E(e, m) \tag{11.8}$$

In this additive function the marginal utility of self-esteem is constant while the direct marginal disutility of effort is, as usual, increasing (that is, $U_{ee} < 0$). As a consequence, the second derivative of U with respect to effort (taking account of both direct and indirect effects) will be negative. Therefore this function satisfies the required second-order conditions for a maximum.

Since all the mixed second derivatives vanish, equation (11.7) simplifies to:

$$\frac{de}{dm} = -\frac{\beta E_{em}}{\beta E_{ee} + U_{ee}}$$

Hence: $\dfrac{de}{dm} > 0 \Leftrightarrow \dfrac{\beta E_{em}}{\beta E_{ee} + U_{ee}} < 0$, that is

$$[(\beta E_{em} > 0) \wedge (\beta E_{ee} + U_{ee} < 0)] \vee [(\beta E_{em} < 0) \wedge (\beta E_{ee} + U_{ee} > 0)]$$

We have two cases according to the sign of β. With positive self-esteem effects ($\beta > 0$) reciprocity will take place if:

$$[E_{em} > 0] \text{ and } \left[E_{ee} < \frac{-U_{ee}}{\beta} \right] \text{ or } [E_{em} < 0] \text{ and } \left[E_{ee} > \frac{-U_{ee}}{\beta} \right]$$

Given $U_{ee} < 0$ it is also easy to identify a sufficient condition for reciprocity, that is:

$$sign(E_{em}) \neq sign(E_{ee})$$

This very simple condition makes it clear that reciprocity entirely depends on characteristics of the E-function. A sufficient condition for a subject to be a reciprocator is that his or her moral system is characterized by a process of self-esteem creation such that the marginal variation of E with respect to e reacts in the opposite way to a change in m and in e. It is important to stress that the signs of these derivatives may change in accordance with the values of m and e. Therefore, the same agent may hold such moral values as call for reciprocation under some conditions, but not always.

The result undermines the usual assumption that cooperative behavior can be inferred from some fixed features of the agents (their type). We could state, instead, that under very plausible assumptions, the moral attitudes of the agent are not enough to predict his or her behavior under any circumstances. There are no reciprocators, regardless of the other conditions.

FAIRNESS AND SELF-ESTEEM

Self-esteem can help to understand how fairness influences the behavior of a rational agent. In particular, we will demonstrate why, also for an agent endowed with moral values, actual behavior may deviate from what is considered fair behavior. If fairness is, at least to some extent, socially determined we have the possibility to understand how social and individual values may interact. Given m, we can define:

- Maximum effort, e_{max}, as the level of effort that leaves no surplus to the agent.
- Minimum effort, e_{min}, as the level of effort below which the agent cannot go (for example, because of monitoring and effective sanctions).

- Fair effort, $e^°$, as the level of effort that the agent deems fair in relation to the money he or she is paid.

Agents differ as to the determination of $e^°$. Some could identify it with e_{min}, but in general it will be higher than that. We assume that an agent will increase (decrease) his or her self-esteem when he or she provide an effort e greater (lower) than the fair effort, thereby enjoying a lower(higher)-than-fair surplus. A higher-than-fair surplus can be considered a gift (G). Therefore self-esteem and gift are the opposite of each other. A reasonable assumption is that as m grows so does $e^°$ with the result that, at the previous e, E will be reduced while G goes up.

If the agent is offered a given compensation, and is free to choose his or her effort, it is as if he or she were determining his or her gift. Self-esteem effects ensure that G will not be as high as possible. Indeed, self-esteem can be seen as a mechanism setting a ceiling to the acceptable gift by the agent. If the agent's effort falls short of the fairness level, he or she experiences a loss of self-esteem, which might be small or large – and may have a small or large effect upon the agent's utility. The point is to compare this moral loss with the loss of utility implied by a greater effort. Assuming that fairness will always drive behavior is to assume that the loss of utility due to self-esteem is always greater than the loss of utility implied by a greater effort. This is why self-esteem is a more crucial factor than fairness: it allows for the possibility that, despite his or her moral values and his or her sensitivity to fairness, an agent may choose a lower-than-fair effort. Indeed, self-esteem is the moral advantage (or disadvantage) for deviating from fairness.

A simplified formulation of the G is the following:

$$G_i = m - \theta e_i$$

that is, given m there will be a gift (positive or negative) for any effort e_i. The equation implies that the fair effort, that is, the effort level yielding $G = 0$, is:

$$e^° > \frac{m}{\theta}$$

In a principal–agent setting, the principal knows that in order to elicit a certain effort on the part of the agent, he or she has to offer a higher-than-fair m (therefore a gift). The weaker the self-esteem effects, the more m must increase. When a cooperation-prone individual – that is, an individual with positive self-esteem effects – enters a principal–agent relationship playing the role of the agent, the principal may rationally consider the possibility of turning this proneness to his or her own advantage, by devising a contract that transforms it into an effective cooperative behavior. In order to achieve this result, the principal has to bear a cost (much as the gift-type envisaged by Akerlof, 1982), in the expectation that the agent will reciprocate. This may be taken as the cost of an implicit contract based on trust. In this sense, trust, which creates cooperation, is costly and endogenous. It is worth stressing that cooperation-proneness is not the same as effective cooperation. Unlike other approaches, ours draws a clear distinction between propensity to cooperation (that may be understood as a form of altruism) and effective cooperation.

In a previous paper (Basili et al., 2004), we developed a model that made it possible to establish the conditions under which a contract based on trust may yield the principal a higher return than alternative arrangements, like endogenous punishment or auditing. Building on that model we now consider how a cooperation-prone agent may interfere with the choice of the best contract and how it could make the cooperative solution less costly. Our assumption on the utility function of the agent and the relevance of self-esteem has, therefore, an impact on traditional principal–agent models and may alter the relative benefits of different contractual arrangements. However, it is also possible that there is no finite gift that will elicit a certain level of effort or that, despite positive self-esteem effects, it is not worthwhile for the principal to pay the gift required for that effort. Let us see how this works in a simple moral hazard case.

SELF-ESTEEM AND MORAL HAZARD

Let us apply the above analysis to a simple moral hazard case. Typically, in such models the assumption is that the agent can choose between a low and a high effort level. This has an impact upon our analysis because fairness becomes very important. In fact, the agent will never supply the high effort if the principal is not paying compensation that includes a positive gift for the high effort. Therefore the problem is trivial when $G_h < 0$. When, on the contrary, this gift is non-negative the agent will attach the following utilities to the two effort levels:

$$U_h = (m - \theta e_h)$$
$$U_l = (m - \theta e_l) - \alpha E(G_h)$$

The expression for U_h is self-evident: the utility depends on the difference between the utility of compensation and the disutility of effort. On the other hand, U_l includes self-esteem effects. More precisely self-esteem here enters the function as a loss, that is, the loss of self-esteem that the agent experiences when choosing the low effort, even though the principal is offering a positive gift for the higher effort. The higher G_h, the greater the loss of self-esteem associated with the lower effort, which in turn translates into a lower utility through the constant term α.

The high effort will be incentive compatible if:

$$U_h \geq U_l$$
$$(m - \theta e_h) \geq (m - \theta e_l) - \alpha E(G_h), \text{ therefore:}$$
$$E(G_h) \geq \frac{\theta \Delta e}{\alpha}$$

Insofar as E decreases with G_h there seems to be a sufficiently high G_h as to make e_h the best choice for the agent. The marginal cost of differential effort and the marginal utility of self-esteem have a clear effect on the incentive-compatible G_h: the former makes it greater, the latter smaller. It is also obvious that if $\alpha = 0$ (or $E_G = 0$) there will not be self-esteem effects and there is no finite G_h inducing cooperation. We need binding sanctions, as in the traditional shirking models, to obtain this result. Self-esteem effects may make e_h incentive-compatible regardless of any explicit sanction, therefore easing moral hazard problems and making efficiency easier to achieve.

It is to be stressed, however, that this may not happen: indeed, self-esteem effects can be too weak. We can distinguish two cases:

1. self-esteem effects cannot compensate for the higher cost of the effort, however high G_h might be. This happens when there is no finite G_h such that $E(G_h) \geq \dfrac{\theta \Delta e}{\alpha}$;
2. the required G_h may be too high from the principal's point of view.

In conclusion, in a moral hazard situation self-esteem induced by a positive gift may (though not necessarily) give rise – through reciprocity – to a cooperative solution that would be impossible without such effects, however high the gift. Of course, costly sanctions with monitoring, as in the classical shirking model, could achieve the same result. Indeed, self-esteem can substitute for termination of contracts and provide different foundations for efficiency wages.

SELF-ESTEEM IN AN ADVERSE SELECTION MODEL

We will now see the impact of self-esteem in an adverse selection model. Among the various adverse selection models, that which fits our analysis better is the one analyzed in depth by Laffont and Martimort (2002).

Consider a principal–agent model in which the information asymmetry concerns the productivity of the agent, which could be high or low (efficient agent, H, or inefficient agent, L), giving rise to low or high marginal costs, respectively.

Let θ_H be the constant marginal cost of the efficient agent and θ_L the constant marginal cost of the inefficient agent. Since the principal cannot observe θ, he cannot equalize the marginal value of each agent's production, $S'(q)$, to its marginal cost.

If he or she were to offer a contract calling for different compensation levels on the basis of the quantity produced and equal to the respective marginal benefit, the efficient agent could simulate being inefficient (producing less) with a view to pocketing the information rent. The utility that the H-type agent gets from making the high or the low efforts is, respectively, the following:

$$U_{H,H} = m_H - \theta_H q_H$$
$$U_{H,L} = m_L - \theta_H q_L$$

Therefore effort H will be incentive-compatible if:

$$m_H - \theta_H q_H > m_L - \theta_H q_L$$

Considering that:

$$\theta_h = \theta_l + \Delta\theta$$

and that a rational principal will pay the reservation price to the L-type agent:

$$U_L = m_L - \theta_L q_L = 0$$

The incentive-compatibility condition becomes:

$$m_H - \theta_H q_H \geq \Delta\theta q_L$$

$\Delta\theta q_L$ represents the information rent the H-type can reap and is equal to the difference between the two marginal costs at the low production levels. The principal is forced to pay a gift at least equal to that rent. This makes it impossible to write a first-best contract.

Formally, the problem of the principal is that of maximizing profit, or the difference between the value of production and the associated costs. Profit is assumed to be a linear function of the quantity produced q. Let:

- $S(q_H)$ and $S(q_L)$ be the value of production obtained with the efficient and inefficient agents;
- m_H and m_L the compensation of the efficient and inefficient agents, respectively;
- θ_H and θ_L the marginal cost of the efficient and inefficient agents;

- $\Delta\theta q_L$ the value of the information rent;
- v and $(1-v)$ the probability to come across an efficient or inefficient agent, respectively.

Given information asymmetry , the principal's profit maximization problem can be written as follows:

$$\max_{\{q_L, q_H\}} \{v[S(q_H)-m_H]\}+\{(1-v)[S(q_L)-\theta_L q_L]\}$$

such that:

$$m_H - \theta_H q_H \geq m_L - \theta_H q_L$$
$$m_L - \theta_L q_L \geq m_H - \theta_L q_H$$
$$U_H \geq 0$$
$$U_L \geq 0$$

As we know, the incentive constraint implies that $m_H - \theta_H q_H \geq \Delta\theta q_L$, therefore the principal problem becomes:

$$\max_{\{q_L, q_H\}} \{v[S(q_H)-\theta_H q_H - \Delta\theta q_L]\}+\{(1-v)[S(q_L)-\theta_L q_L]\}$$

The solution of this problem calls for the same production as first-best for the efficient agent but a reduction with respect to first-best production for the inefficient agent. Indeed its marginal product will be higher than the agent's marginal cost (implying a lower than optimal q_L):

$$S'(q_L)= \theta_L + \frac{v}{1-v}\Delta\theta$$

This result can be interpreted as follows: in order to induce the *H*-type agent not to choose the contract designed for the less efficient agent (and to pocket the information rent) the principal has to pay the *H*-agent a gift equal to the information rent. This makes it worthwhile for the principal to try to reduce that rent, a goal that he or she can achieve by decreasing q_L. Obviously, there is an optimal level for that reduction.

Let us now introduce self-esteem effects. We will show that they reduce the gift that the principal has to pay below the information rent. This makes it possible to set a higher q_L and therefore to minimize the deviation from first best.

The presence of self-esteem allows for the principal's incentive-compatible condition to be written as follows:

$$U_{H,H} = m_H - \theta_H q_H$$

as in the previous case. But:

$$U_{H,L} = m_L - \theta_H q_L - \alpha_H G_H$$

where, without loss of generality, we assume that: $E_H = -\alpha_H G_H = -\gamma(G_H)G_H$, where $\alpha_H = \gamma(G_H)$ is a positive real valued monotone increasing function, that is, self-esteem can be exchanged with gifts in a way that depends on the characteristic of the agent and the agent's utility function can be written in the following way.

If the H agent chooses the L-type contract, in order to reap the information rent, he or she will suffer a negative self-esteem effect related to the gift received with reference to the h quantity. Therefore the agent will not cheat if:

$$m_H - \theta_H q_H \geq m_L - \theta_H q_L - \alpha_H G_H$$

which, after some manipulation, and remembering that $U_L = 0$, boils down to the following:

$$G_h \geq \Delta\theta q_l - \alpha_H G_H. \text{ Then: } G_H \geq \frac{\Delta\theta q_l}{(1+\alpha_H)}$$

It is clear that the self-esteem effect makes the required G_H lower than the information rent, provided that $\alpha_H > 0$.

The higher α_H the lower the required gift. The latter will always be smaller than the information rent: self-esteem will bring about cooperation even at a monetary cost. The consequences for the principal's optimal solution are immediate. After taking account of the constraints (and in particular of the easing of the incentive-compatible constraints) the function to be maximized becomes:

$$\max_{\{q_L, q_H\}} \left\{ v \left[S(q_H) - \theta_H q_H - \frac{\Delta\theta q_L}{(1+\alpha_H)} \right] + \{(1-v)[S(q_L) - \theta_L q_L]\} \right\}$$

The optimal contract implies that there is:

- no distortion, also in this case, with respect to the first-best solution for the efficient agent;
- a downwards distortion, but smaller than before, with respect to the first-best solution for the less efficient agent, such that:

$$S'(q_L^A) = \theta_L + \frac{v}{1-v} \left[\frac{\Delta\theta}{1+\alpha_H} \right].$$

This proves that self-esteem effects, in this adverse selection model, have an impact on the optimal contract. In particular they imply a smaller gift for inducing cooperation and a slighter deviation from first-best quantities.

CONCLUDING REMARKS

Traditional economic theory is undeniably too pessimistic as to the possibility of cooperation among strangers (Seabright, 2004). Genetic relatedness is not the only condition for cooperation to develop in situations where self-interest would make destructive opportunism the best course of action. A huge bulk of evidence can be invoked to this end. In particular, as Bowles and Gintis have argued, many humans seem to adhere to a strong reciprocity rule of behavior that implies the bearing of a personal cost in order to punish those members of the community who defect from cooperation.

However, the analytical foundation of this type of cooperation-prone behavior, and how it relates to rationality, has not been spelled out yet. In this chapter we have advanced our own explanation, referring to principal–agent situations, relying on the notion of self-esteem and modeling cooperation-prone agents in terms both of a moral function transforming cooperation into self-esteem and of a utility function which includes self-esteem in its argument.

On the basis of this model we have shown that cooperation may be an outcome, depending both on the characteristics of the agent and external conditions. This amounts to making a clear distinction between propensity to cooperation, on the one hand, and effective cooperation, on the other – two often muddled concepts. The model also rules out that cooperation or reciprocation depends just on the type of person.

Interestingly enough, our approach is coherent with Sen's most recent criticism of the standard rational model of choice based on the notion of self-centered welfare, that is, a system in which a person's welfare depends only on his or her own consumption and other features of the richness of his or her life, welfare maximization is the individual's only goal and an individual's choices are exclusively geared to the pursuit of selfish goals (Sen, 2002, p. 34).

However, contrary to Sen, we advocate an operating theory of choice that makes people able to behave as maximizers, particularly with respect to endogenously determined moral variables. More specifically, individuals are endowed with a moral system which transforms their actions into self-esteem. The latter, as determined by such system, enters their utility function and contributes to define their choice within a utility-maximizing process. Therefore, self-esteem brings about utility but its magnitude is determined by a moral system which lies outside the individual's preference system. Eventually, the inclusion of self-esteem in the utility function (which could very well be defined a goal-function) allows us to treat the choice problem as a typical maximization problem and give a formal solution to it.

We have also shown the impact of our hypothesis on the best contract a principal can offer in a moral hazard case and, in a more detailed way, in an adverse selection situation. In particular, we have shown how our model can reduce the inefficiency of asymmetric information and lay the groundwork for a different approach to the best way to elicit cooperation.

NOTES

1. These conditions, as Gintis calls them are: incentive compatibility, dynamic stability, empirical relevance, plausible informational requirements and plausible discount factors.
2. See for example: Ryan and Connell (1989), Ryan et al. (1993), Munir and Jackson (1997), Leary and Baumeister (2000).
3. See Benabou and Tirole (2006b); Ryan et al. (1994, 1997); Baumeister and Leary (1995); Kim et al. (1998).
4. For a utility function that incorporates identity, based on social categories, as a motivation for behavior, see for example Akerlof and Kranton (2000).
5. See also the Appendix for a more detailed case.
6. Employers punish fraudulent employees (68 percent), reward employees that over-fulfill their contracts (70 percent) and reward employees that honor their contracts (Gintis et al., 2003).

REFERENCES

Akerlof, G.A. (1982), 'Labour contracts as partial gift exchange', *Quarterly Journal of Economics*, **97**, 543–69.
Akerlof, G.A. and R.E. Kranton (2000), 'Economics and identity', *Quarterly Journal of Economics*, **115**, 715–53.
Basili, M., C. Duranti and M. Franzini (2004), 'Networks, trust and institutional complementarities', *Rivista di Politica Economica*, **1–2**, 159–80.
Baumeister, R.F. and M.R. Leary (1995), 'The need to belong: desire for interpersonal attachments as a fundamental human motivation', *Psychological Bulletin*, **117**, 497–529.
Benabou, R. and J. Tirole (2006a), 'Belief in a just world and redistributive politics', *Quarterly Journal of Economics*, **121**, 699–746.
Benabou, R. and J. Tirole (2006b), 'Incentives and prosocial behavior', *American Economic Review*, **96**, 1652–78.
Bowles, S. and H. Gintis (2004), 'The evolution of strong reciprocity: cooperation in heterogeneous populations', *Theoretical Population Biology*, **65**, 17–28.
Fehr, E. and S. Gächter (2000), 'Cooperation and punishment', *American Economic Review*, **90**, 980–94.
Fehr, E. and S. Gächter (2002), 'Altruistic punishment in humans', *Nature*, **415**, 137–40.
Fehr, E., S. Gächter and G. Kirchsteiger (1997), 'Reciprocity as a contract enforcement device: experimental evidence', *Econometrica*, **65**, 833–60.

Gintis, H. (2004), 'Modeling cooperation among self-interested agents: a critique', mimeo.

Gintis, H., S. Bowles, R. Boyd and E. Fehr (2003), 'Explaining altruistic behavior in humans', *Evolution and Human Behavior*, **24**, 153–72.

Kim, Y., J.S. Butzel and R.M. Ryan (1998), 'Interdependence and well-being: a function of culture and relatedness needs', paper presented at the International Society for the Study of Personal Relationships, Saratoga Springs, NY, June.

Laffont, Jean-Jacques and David Martimort (2002), *The Theory of Incentives*, Princeton, NJ: Princeton University Press.

Leary, Mark R. and Roy F. Baumeister (2000), 'The nature and function of self-esteem: sociometer theory', in Mark P. Zanna (ed.), *Advances in Experimental Social Psychology*, San Diego, CA: San Diego Academic Press, pp. 1–62.

Leary, M.R., K.C. Herbst and F. Crary (2003), 'Finding pleasure in solitary activities: desire for aloneness or disinterest in social contact?' *Personality and Individual Differences*, **35**, 59–68.

Munir, S.S. and D.W. Jackson (1997), 'Social support, need for support, and anxiety among women graduate students', *Psychological Reports*, **80**, 383–6.

Ostrom, E., J. Walker, and R. Gardner (1992), 'Covenants with and without a sword: self-governance is possible', *American Political Science Review*, **86**, 404–17.

Ryan, R.M. and J.P. Connell (1989), 'Perceived locus of causality and internalization', *Journal of Personality and Social Psychology*, **57**, 749–61.

Ryan, R.M. and E.L. Deci (2000), 'Self-determination theory and facilitation of intrinsic motivation, social development and well-being', *American Psychologist*, **55**, 68–78.

Ryan, R.M., J. Kuhl, and E.L. Deci (1997), 'Nature and autonomy: organizational view of social and neurobiological aspects of self-regulation in behavior and development', *Development and Psychopathology*, **9**, 701–28.

Ryan, R.M., S. Rigby and K. King (1993), 'Two types of religious internalization and their relations to religious orientations and mental health', *Journal of Personality and Social Psychology*, **65**, 586–96.

Ryan, R.M., J. Stiller and J.H. Lynch (1994), 'Representations of relationships to teachers, parents, and friends as predictors of academic motivation and self-esteem', *Journal of Early Adolescence*, **14**, 226–49.

Seabright, Paul (2004), *The Company of Strangers. A Natural History of Economic Life*, Princeton, NJ: Princeton University Press.

Sen, Amartya (2002), *Rationality and Freedom*, Cambridge, MA: Belknap Press.

Yamagishi, T. (1986), 'The provision of a sanctioning system as a public good', *Journal of Personality and Social Psychology*, **51**, 110–16.

APPENDIX

From second-order condition (11.6), at e^* utility is maximized when $2U_{eE}E_e + U_EE_{ee} < 0$, that is:

- if E is linear in e, then $E_{ee} = 0$, hence $2U_{eE}E_e + U_EE_{ee} < 0$ if $\Theta_e < 0$ at any point;
- if Θ is constant, then $2U_{eE}E_e + U_EE_{ee} < 0$ at e^* when $E_{ee} < 0$ there;
- if Θ is not constant, then $2U_{eE}E_e + U_EE_{ee} < 0$ at e^* if $\Theta_e < 0$ and $E_{ee} < 0$ at any point.

In general, however, $U_{ee} + 2U_{eE}E_e + U_EE_{ee} < 0$ at e^* if and only if

$$\frac{-2\Theta_e(\Theta_e E + \Gamma_e) + \Theta^2 E_{ee}}{\Theta} < -(\Theta_{ee}E + \Gamma_{ee}) \text{ at } e^*$$

but this condition gives rise to many more cases involving first- and second-order derivatives.

Index